34.50

This book traces the formation of Australian colonial society and economy within the context of the changing fortunes of British hegemony in the nineteenth-century world economy. But Australia's transition from conservative origins as a penal colony supporting a grazier class oriented to export production, to liberal agrarian capitalism, was not a simple reflex of imperial setting. Domestically, the "agrarian question" – who should control the land and to what end? – was the central political struggle of this period, as urban-commercial forces contested the graziers' monopoly of the landed economy. Resolution in the former's favor led to economic diversification, in turn contributing to the viability of British capitalism as metropolitan protectionism challenged its international supremacy. Nevertheless, embedded in the conflict among settler classes was an international dimension, involving a juxtaposition of laissez-faire and mercantilist phases of British political economy. Colonial graziers, whose origins lay in the older British mercantile system, depended on British policy for their supply of labor and land. In midcentury, as that policy shifted with the liberal currents in both societies, the progressive settler alliance gained power in the newly self-governing colonial states. Land reform resulted, and this, combined with gold wealth and the institutional development and integration of capital markets in London and the colonies, facilitated the subordination of pastoralism to the colonial urban economy. The resulting national "agrocommercial" complex anticipated industrialization in the twentieth century.

Professor McMichael argues that the transition from a patriarchal wool-growing colony to a liberal-nationalist form of capitalist development is best understood through a systematic analysis of the effect of the imperial politicoeconomic relationship on the social and political forces within nineteenth-century Australia. This is, therefore, an original interpretation of the path of development of Australian colonial society prior to Federation in 1901.

AUSTRALIA

INDIAN OCEAN

Darwin

NORTHERN

TERRITORY

QUEENSLAND

GREAT

DIVIDING

TROPIC OF CAPRICORN

WESTERN

AUSTRALIA

SOUTH

AUSTRALIA

Moreton Bay

Brisbane

Port Macquarie

NEW SOUTH

WALES

RANGE

Port Jackson

Sydney

Botany Bay

Perth

Adelaide

VICTORIA

Bendigo

Ballarat ● Melbourne

Port Phillip

SOUTHERN OCEAN

Bass
Strait

TASMANIA

Hobart ● Port Arthur

0 ———————— 500 MILES
0 ———————— 1,000 KM

SETTLERS AND THE AGRARIAN QUESTION
FOUNDATIONS OF CAPITALISM IN COLONIAL AUSTRALIA

PHILIP McMICHAEL
Department of Sociology
University of Georgia, Athens

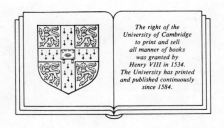

The right of the
University of Cambridge
to print and sell
all manner of books
was granted by
Henry VIII in 1534.
The University has printed
and published continuously
since 1584.

CAMBRIDGE UNIVERSITY PRESS

Cambridge

London   New York   New Rochelle
Melbourne   Sydney

Published by the Press Syndicate of the University of Cambridge
The Pitt Building, Trumpington Street, Cambridge CB2 1RP
32 East 57th Street, New York, NY 10022, USA
10 Stamford Road, Oakleigh, Melbourne 3166, Australia

First published 1984

Printed in the United States of America

Library of Congress Cataloging in Publication Data
McMichael, Philip.
Settlers and the agrarian question
Includes bibliographical references and index.
1. Land tenure – Australia – History – 19th century.
2. Land settlement – Australia – History – 19th century.
3. Squatter settlements – Australia – History – 19th century.
I. Title.
HD1035.M37 1984 306'.32'0994 84-1762
ISBN 0 521 26570 3

To my father, David,
and to the memory of my mother, Catherine

CONTENTS

——

TABLES

PREFACE

Development studies ordinarily take as their unit of analysis the nation-state, even when emphasizing the international context. Although there is a political reality to such analysis, it provides only a partial understanding of the source of change within a particular state. Market relations do not begin and end at geopolitical boundaries, nor do movements of capital and labor. States certainly *secure* these economic exchanges, but they remain part of the broader historical setting that results from the international character of capital and its market. In fact, states exist in a structured interrelation because their European antecedents have, through rivalry, organized an (uneven) world market, and because they make up the political framework of the world market. Thus, what happens within states has bearing on the international setting, and vice versa. Social change cannot be taken for granted as a process internal to states. With this proposition in mind, this book's theme is that the development of colonial Australia was also the process of development of the world-capitalist economy.

I have tackled this theme not by extrapolating *from* the world economy *to* Australia (qua "periphery"). This approach reifies the relationships concerned because it gives the world economy a life of its own. This term needs to be used cautiously, which means ensuring that it is a historical category, not an ideal type. It refers to the *process* of structuring world capitalism, and it derives from the more fundamental analysis of the politics of capitalist development within a world market constituted by interstate relations. Hence, a comprehensive study of social change would examine how the intersections of domestic and international forces are embedded in the sociopolitical dynamic of a particular state. The system of property relations and exchange as well as the administrative structure of that state need to be examined as historical products within the international politicoeconomic setting. From this perspective, we can understand the *world-historical* dimension of social relationships and competing ideologies. And this encourages greater sensitivity to the shifting, and often incongruous, sources of that elusive subject, "class interest."

Accordingly, I have conceptualized Australian settlement as the contradictory process of expansion of the British state and capitalism – contradictory because the process necessarily established uneven political and economic relations. This unevenness was not simply in the metropolitan–colonial relationship, but more fundamentally within colonial society. The resulting tensions (for example, convict versus "free" labor, export staple production versus diversified economy, and estate versus family farming) revealed the juxtaposition of socioeconomic groups with different spatiotemporal horizons. There was a major distinction between (patriarchal) wool growers and (liberal) merchants and farmers that we can represent as epi-sodic; that is, their particular social interests were identified with different phases of world-capitalist development. Wool growers favored the mercantilist relationships of the traditional colonial system, whereas their opponents preferred a liberal-nationalist path of development. The political conflict between these classes in midcentury involved the whole colonial society in what can be called the "agrarian question": How was the land to be productively organized, and therefore what was to be the general social organization of the colonies? The liberals' political victory was aided by the British state, which made a timely concession of self-government to the colonies. Britain affirmed the new balance of social forces, confident that its control of colonial Australia had shifted from formal to market rule. In this context, wool growing itself was reorganized from a mercantile-capitalist to a capital-intensive basis, and a local agrocommercial complex emerged. This transition depended on both a transformation of colonial political structures and Australia's increasingly consequential position as a recipient of British capital as metropolitan rivalry to British global supremacy grew in the second half of the century.

This study is not meant to be exhaustive, but rather illustrative of this way of reinterpreting colonial history as a component part of world history. It is not an economic history of colonial Australia, nor is it a history of colonial society. It is a much more specific attempt to pursue a particular theme of historical sociology. That theme concerns the *remarriage* of theory and history – understanding the *process* of history as a narrative of social action within the structuring forces of the modern world. My own view is that these structuring forces are most usefully conceived of as the political history of capitalism on an international scale. This structuring is not the result of some teleology but is rooted in the variable social divisions and relationships among people that capitalist development produces and that constitute the limits and possibilities of social action.

With this in mind, I selected the period of Australian history from white settlement in 1788 to federation of the independent colonies in 1901, and I focused on the principal southeastern region. This period has no special chronological importance, but it includes the significant agrarian transition in Australia, which echoed similar capitalist transformations of rural economies elsewhere in the metropolitan world. Here, political struggles developed around the increasing penetration of peasant and family farming and/or the challenge to estate farming (including plantations) by the ascendant forces of urban-industrial capitalism. At issue was the social organization of the landed economy and its relation to industrialization. Basically, in metropolitan and settler states these social conflicts marked the consolidation of home markets for industrial capital. They were, of course, complicated by world market considerations. (Settler agriculture, for example, rivaled European agricultural systems, and indeed the structure of the world market altered as primary-producing regions developed.) In turn, the migration of labor from metropolitan to peripheral regions of the world economy increased as the traditional rural economy collapsed. Generally, this represented the transition to the contemporary capitalist world order.

In the study of Australian history, such a focus lends itself to comparisons with other states that addressed the agrarian question in the late nineteenth century. It also allows us to see that the key to industrial capitalist development in this settler colony was the political resolution of the agrarian question to the long-term advantage of urban capital. The absence of such resolution in many Third World states accounts for the absence of an integrated and developed home market. Understanding this requires a world-economic perspective.

The international dimension of the agrarian question concerns not only the trading position of a particular producing region in the world market, but also, and more fundamentally, the way such international relations are expressed *within* the particular state through the balance of class and political forces. Of course, these balances alter as the world capitalist economy develops, so that it is fair to say that there is some correspondence between the structural position of a state within the world economy and the way in which the agrarian question is both posed and resolved (if at all). I have tried to show in this study how this relational matrix worked in Australia.

Setting up such a matrix first requires outlining the trajectory of the nineteenth-century world-capitalist economy. The book begins with a chapter characterizing the British empire (formal and informal). I argue that British hegemony imparted a unique structural dynamic to the nineteenth-century world economy, and that the political and economic consequences of British hegemony shaped Australian colonial development in a particular way.

Following this introductory chapter is Part I, which gives the background of the development of Australian wool growing as a world-market commodity. The two chapters of this section trace the role of the colonial state in establishing a domestic market and capitalist social relations. There was an early divergence between the settlers with local economic horizons and the growers with an interest in appending themselves to the British economy and consolidating themselves as a colonial oligarchy.

Part II is essentially a political economy of the "pastoral age" in colonial Australia during the 1830s and 1840s. Chapter 4 presents an overview of the politics of this form of colonial economy, arguing that whereas colonial wool growing flourished as an increasingly consequential element of British industrialization, colonial pastoralists had to contend politically with Britain's more liberal, or positive, view of its colonial empire. This view opposed colonial oligarchy. Chapters 5, 6, and 7, respectively, examine colonial pastoralism from a different angle within this changing context: as the productive end of an imperial "putting-out" system organized by merchant capital; as an enterprise with consequential effects on the division of labor within the colonial economy; and as a conservative social form organized around the impermanent engrossment of the land through "squatting," dependence on mercantile credit and transported convict labor. Overall, Part II builds a comprehensive view of the social and economic limits to colonial development imposed by the squatting system and the emerging political challenge to the patriarchal pretensions of the large growers within the colonial society.

Part III examines the decline and fall of squatter hegemony in colonial Australia. It begins with the consolidation of opposition to the growers' monopoly of the landed economy. This stemmed from the manifest vulnerability of the staple economy in the wake of the 1840s depression (the subject of Chapter 8). This crisis, and the ensuing attempts of the large growers to reestablish their position, generated a liberal opposition, which was then strengthened considerably by 1850s gold-rush immigrants, who provided a constituency for a populist electoral challenge to the squatting system. The resolution of the agrarian question in land reform legislation is then examined in Chapter 10 in terms of its long-range effects on the social organization of the colonies. This was the (transitional) period of ascendancy of the colonial mercantile bourgeoisie, but it needs to be observed in international perspective because it was also the period of positive colonial state building secured by selling colonial bonds in a reorganized London capital market. The rise of an agrocommercial complex is thus considered in domestic politicoeconomic terms as well as in terms of the development of the international economy. Britain's greater reliance on Dominion markets encouraged a large-scale recomposition of loan capital into social capital in Australia. This process, the integration of the colonial economy, and greater public regulation of the landed economy are all considered as elements of Australian state building.

The conclusion summarizes theoretically, and suggests adapting this kind of sociology of world-economic processes to the comparative historical analysis of societies, with a brief reference to an analogous political conflict over landed relations in the nineteenth-century United States.

In summary, this study is a structural history of colonial development using a combination of primary evidence and analytical reinterpretation of the secondary materials concerned with the varying fortunes of colonial wool growers. They were the pivot of political and economic relations, within the colony and between colony and metropolis, and a focus on their changing patterns of capital accumulation is simultaneously a study of the nexus of world-economic relations surrounding capitalist development in colonial Australia.

In acknowledging those who have assisted and encouraged me with constructive criticism of part or all of this study, I express my gratitude to Giovanni Arrighi, Melanie Beresford, Ken Buckley, Bob Connell, Grant Evans, Shirley Fisher, Richard Garrett, Wally Goldfrank, Terry Irving, Stephen Lehmann, David Levine, Lynn Levine, Martin Murray, Terry O'Shaunessy, John Othic, Peter Phillips, Bob Sherry, David Weiman, and Anna Yeatman. Initial inspiration to undertake this study came from Terence K. Hopkins, who first interested me in the theoretical analysis of development processes and their international context and whose subsequent writing in this area has continued to suggest analytical procedure. Immanuel Wallerstein's writings on the "modern world system" have indeed provided a perspective within which I have endeavored to develop my own analytical view of the political history of capitalism. James F. Petras gave me invaluable and memorable encouragement, feedback, and criticism while I was preparing this study as a dissertation, and he has supported its transformation into a book. Richard Williams has been a permanent sounding board for ideas associated with the project of historical sociology and hence a real intellectual friend. I also received kind assistance in my research from librarians at the Ithaca New York Genealogical Library in the Binghamton Ward Chapel of The Church of Jesus Christ of Latter-day Saints; the Mitchell Library, Sydney; the New South Wales State Archives, Sydney; the LaTrobe Library, Melbourne; and the South Australian State Archives, Adelaide. Additionally, my thanks and appreciation are due to the people who typed this manuscript in its various forms: Pat Terrell, Rosemary Heffernan, Gloria Gaumer, Susan Perkins, Helen DiFeliciantonio, Ellen Dolski, Helene McCann, Sylvia Mapp, and Lori Stapleton. For great encouragement and straightforwardness in the process of revising this manuscript into a book, I thank my editor, Frank Smith. I have also appreciated the supportive advice of production editor Michael Dauman Gnat and the skillful copyediting of Carol Reitz – they have undoubtedly enhanced the presentation of my study. Finally, through all the stages of putting this book together, my wife, Karen Schachere, has been a wonderful friend and companion, ever positive and loving, and so to her I owe my greatest thanks.

1

THE SOCIAL STRUCTURE OF
BRITISH HEGEMONY

INTRODUCTION

This study explores the social forces involved in the making of white-settler Australian society in the nineteenth century. These forces had an international dimension not only because of Australia's colonial relationship with Britain, but also because Australian economy and society were the product of a particular phase of world-capitalist development. Specifically, metropolitan industrial capitalism and its growing world market framed British expansion and socioeconomic possibilities in the colonies. Australian political and economic development, then, stemmed from these larger forces. Australian colonial history cannot be considered a discrete entity or as a study in British imperial relations. It needs a further dimension to locate it in a world-historical context – one that conceptualizes white settlement as an ingredient of the emerging world-capitalist order.

The argument of this chapter is that the changing fortunes of British hegemony governed nineteenth-century *world*-capitalist development. Britain sought to maintain productive superiority in the world market through industrial specialization in an international division of labor. Paradoxically, this worldwide mercantilist frame-

Note: Reference abbreviations used throughout this book:

HRA   Historical Records of Australia
ML   Mitchell Library (Sydney)
NSWSA   New South Wales State Archives (Sydney)
RAHS, J&P   Royal Australian Historical Society, Journal & Proceedings
V&P, NSW   Votes and Proceedings, New South Wales (Legislative Council)

work required the imposition of a free trade regime in the world economy, and this encouraged, rather than suppressed, industrialization in metropolitan states. Not only did they have access to growing peripheral markets,[1] but also free trade made available the productive and military possibilities inherent in British capital-goods exports in midcentury. Such technology laid the material foundations for a mercantilist challenge, as rival states *organized* national economies around this new intensive phase of industrial capital accumulation. This shift expressed the contradictory unity forged by a single hegemonic state within a world market subdivided politically by states.

The focus in this chapter is therefore on the structure of the world market as a historical context for the rise of industrial capitalism. There is no attempt to theorize the process of capitalist development, rather the goal is to characterize the political history of the nineteenth-century world economy, to set a framework for subsequent chapters. There, the concrete processes of capitalist development in Australia are grounded in a discussion of the social relationships established within the colony, some of which derived from the international context.

The global character of British capitalism combined an imperial state structure, strengthened by the post–Napoleonic War settlements, and a consolidated global trading apparatus constructed in the eighteenth century.[2] The political settlements were fundamentally asymmetrical: British imperial power contrasted with the Continental political balance of relatively unorganized states with comparatively localized economies. This facilitated the establishment of British economic (industrial and commercial) superiority in the world through an *extensive* (quantitative) growth of markets for manufactured consumer goods. Britain's Industrial Revolution was essentially the application of the techniques of "textile industrialism" to world market proportions (see Schumpeter 1939, pp. 170, 252). It resulted in the widespread displacement of handicraft production in Europe and the non-European periphery.

---

[1] Kondratieff (1955) has argued that boom years in the world economy are characterized by the incorporation of new primary production regions and technical change in metropolitan industry.

[2] Wallerstein (1980, p. 271), citing Vilar, notes the "globalization of British foreign trade in the eighteenth century" in contrast to the "Americanization" of French trade.

It could be argued that British capitalism was reproducing another colonial system, but this time on a world scale. Hitherto, Western European mercantilist states depended on colonies for supplies, markets, and the social organization of labor for large-scale commodity production to accumulate merchant capital. With the displacement of rival colonial powers in the early nineteenth century, Britain was in a position to fashion a world economy resembling her colonial system and reap the benefits of international commercial supremacy. This was the foundation of the "workshop of the world" ideal. (After the 1840s crisis in textile industrialism, Britain switched to the role of "engineering workshop" with exports of capital goods such as the railway.) Nevertheless, British capitalism broke through the limits of mercantile capital accumulation and promoted the universalist tendencies of industrial capital and its drive to continually revolutionize commerce. In this sense, British capitalism fundamentally transformed the world.

Britain unified the world market in two ways. The first involved the exercise of political and military force – for example, the establishment of the colonial empire, gunboat diplomacy, and the preemption of rivals in spheres of British interest. The second was the substantive exercise of politicoeconomic hegemony, such as the adoption of a free trade regime (whether voluntarily or not) which enhanced British commercial power.[3] The latter, in particular, incorporated economic regions into international exchange through the expanding interstate system. Clearly, some regions were more politically unified than others, but for our purposes it is important to emphasize that the metropolitan thrust of British hegemony was to promote the nationalization of domestic markets. This resulted from the spread of constitutionally administered states. There was, overall, a double movement: the integration of producing regions into the world market (via inputs, outputs, and white settlement in toto) on the one hand and, on the other, the greater political centralization of metropolitan states (in particular) as commercial-industrial capital gained political influence. (Industrialization was a political goal as much as a superior form of capital accumulation based on home-market development.) The latter movement pro-

---

[3] Compare Arrighi (1982). The notion of hegemony comes from the writings of Antonio Gramsci, whereas the application of it to international relations draws on the work of Arrighi as well as Franz Schurmann (1974).

vided the conditions for a national mercantilist challenge to British hegemony as the century ended.

This argument concentrates on the *conditions* of hegemony (and its demise) rather than on its politicocultural consequences. The emphasis is on the politicoeconomic consolidating mechanisms in the world economy as preconditions of British technical superiority. Of course, the actual experience of British hegemony related to the *effects* of these conditions, such as the spread of consumption patterns. and production techniques, which universalized aspects of British material culture. Similarly, transformations in states that adopted forms of government associated with the British parliamentary system represented the spread of British political culture, while colonial elites emulated the British ruling classes, thus reproducing British social behavior. These extensive manifestations of British hegemony, however, cannot be dealt with adequately here.[4]

THE SOCIAL STRUCTURE OF BRITISH HEGEMONY

British hegemony depended on the political organization of markets. Hegemony meant more, then, than superior economic strength and the political capacity to realize this in the world economy.[5] In

---

[4] One impressive analysis in this area is Hobsbawm (1975).
[5] Wallerstein (1980, p. 38) defines "hegemony" as

a situation wherein the products of a given core state are produced so efficiently that they are by and large competitive even in other core states, and therefore the given core state will be the primary beneficiary of a maximally free world market. Obviously, to take advantage of this productive superiority, such a state must be strong enough to prevent or minimize the erection of internal and external political barriers to the free flow of the factors of production.

In addition, in this schema productive superiority brings commercial and financial superiority in its train. The components of hegemony, then, are both economic and political: The one complements the other. This conception is little more than an aggregation of forces on a quantitative plane of relative strength, however. The definition does not do justice to Wallerstein's more qualified analysis of Dutch capacities beyond their phase of "productive superiority," arguing that "the turn to finance is *not* a sign of decline" (p. 57). Nevertheless, Wallerstein (p. 38) argues for the *momentary* character of hegemony: "As soon a state becomes truly hegemonic, it begins to decline: for a state ceases to be hegemonic not because it loses strength (at least not until a long time has elapsed) but because others gain." The danger with this notion of economic competition among core states is that it reduces the concept of hegemony to a zero-sum encounter. It tends to sideline the structural dynamics of the reproduction of the world market – a process of intercapitalist and interstate competition that realigns the world division of labor – and thereby subverts the foundations of hegemony.

addition to market competitiveness, the substantive aspect of hegemony was the imposition of an organizing principle into the world economy as a reproductive device. Britain projected a structure onto world market and interstate relations that was at once unifying and designed to favor the accumulation of British capital (and, therefore, state revenue). Thus, British hegemony in the nineteenth century combined direct imperial power and this substantive dimension. In practice, both aspects were mutually reinforcing; however, distinguishing between them is necessary to determine their origins and their effects on interstate relations. This is particularly important in differentiating Britain's relations with the colonial/non-European regions from those with the states of the North Atlantic region.

Direct British hegemony (*Pax Britannica*) combined Britain's politicomilitary supremacy among European states following the Napoleonic Wars with a worldwide colonial empire. In the postwar period Britain gained dominance among its metropolitan rivals by the preemption of a *Continentally based* imperial state, given the military defeat of Napoleon's "Continental system" (qua land empire). This was formalized in the Continental power balance negotiated in the 1814–15 peace settlement and preserved by British naval supremacy, which gave Britain a virtual monopoly on the global exercise of imperial power (Southgate 1969, p. 155; Gilpin 1975, pp. 81–2; Imlah 1958, pp. 2–3).

Animating the direct elements of British power were the substantive elements responsible for the *reproduction* of British hegemony. Briefly, these were the processes of state formation within the environment of the world economy. Not only did these processes consolidate the liberal aspects of state structures, but also they elevated the accumulation of industrial, and thus commercial, capital to a national (as opposed to simply a private) goal. To the extent that state formation involved the development of home markets by dismantling trade barriers, establishing central banking systems, and importing technology, the British state was able to unify world trading and impose a regime of industrial capitalism in the world market to its advantage, particularly in the third quarter of the nineteenth century. Ultimately the substantive aspects subverted British hegemony, but not until the 1870s crisis revealed the limits of extensive worldwide capital accumulation under British direction.[6] It precipitated political and economic involution in the metropolitan states and their favored spheres of influence.

Direct elements of British hegemony

A major source of British power among the nineteenth-century states was its internationalist, or imperial, character, which distinguished it from other Continental states.[7] The original British state structure was formed through colonization of Scotland, Wales, and Ireland (Lichtheim 1971, p. 34; Wallerstein 1980, p. 123). Further imperial ambitions were necessarily maritime-oriented, promoted by a commercially minded landed elite significantly involved in international commerce (Anderson 1965; Block 1970, p. 140). The uniqueness of the British state stemmed from its parliamentary (and decentralized) character, as opposed to the generally absolutist (and centralized) system on the Continent, where standing armies preserved a feudal and fiscal conservatism (Gilbert 1975, pp. 199, 209, 214). The British navy, an institution of Parliament, served British commercial classes by sustaining commercial and industrial growth through overseas market expansion (Wallerstein 1980, p. 267; Ashton 1972, p. 50).[8]

The Napoleonic Wars gave Britain the opportunity to establish politicomilitary supremacy in Europe. The wars enhanced Britain's military and economic superiority in the world, and the settlements guaranteed European stability while Britain consolidated its com-

[6] Hoffman (1933, pp. 14–16) suggests that, whereas the depression was felt more keenly in Britain ("prosperity having been previously most abundant in England"), the crisis reflected a general glut in the world market of commodities produced by Western European states in competition with those once of predominantly British origin, such as iron goods and textiles.
[7] Lichtheim (1971, p. 39) argues that the eighteenth century saw a conjunction of the two forms of imperialism: the traditional continental form and the emerging modern maritime form, which Britain embodied alone in the post-Napoleonic period.
[8] For an alternative view to Harlow's differentiation of the British Empire, with the post-1776 "swing to the east," see Marshall's (1964) argument that the British Empire assumed global proportions.

mercial empire.[9] Meanwhile, the Continental states were preoccupied with preventing further aggression through the negotiated Continental balance of power and with rebuilding their economies. Accordingly, nineteenth-century British capitalist development had a global orientation, in contrast to the domestic orientation of subsequent capitalist development in rival states.[10]

During the wars, Britain's naval blockade of Europe amounted to a war of attrition against European navies as well as Continental seaborne trade. One result was the destruction of Continental industry that thrived on this trade (including shipbuilding); great seaports such as Amsterdam, Bordeaux, and Marseilles declined, and the maritime regions of the Continent experienced degrees of "deindustrialization" and/or "pastoralization."[11] As a result of these trends and the protectionism associated with wartime dislocation of trade and the commercial assaults of British goods following the wars, the long-term trajectory of Continental economic development was commercial involution, increasingly centered in the Rhine region (bounded by France, Belgium, and Germany) (Crouzet 1964, pp. 578–87; Moraze 1968, p. 174). This situation and the general public insolvency on the Continent account for the flow of British

---

[9] Kiernan (1969, p. 25) writes

So much of Britain's attention was drawn off to the east that from the fall of Napoleon in 1815 to the Anglo-French Entente of 1904 it was more often than not an absentee from European affairs ... If Russia was sometimes held to belong rather to Asia, and Africa was humorously said to begin at the Pyrenees, Britain often appeared to belong to all the other continents more than to Europe: or appeared to itself, with its growing family of white colonies, a continent of its own.

[10] Schurmann (1974, p. 131) notes:

After the French Revolution, France became one of the most national of European capitalisms. The great world market system flowed out of England, not France. The constitutional histories of England and France reveal one major difference – while state power grew bigger, more extensive and more centralized in France, in England the power of the kings constantly diminished in favor of Parliament. Parliament, the body representing the various interests of English society, became the battleground for protracted class struggle, which continues to this day. The bourgeoisie never sought to *seize power* in England, as in France. Thereby preserving its archaic features of strong commitment to local interests along with strong and growing commitment to the most far flung international interests. And, unlike France, England never became a nation.

[11] Tilly's "Discussion" of Crouzet's (1964) paper contests the theory of involution with facts about Continental agricultural and textile exports. The point is, however, that relatively, British and European capitals after the Napoleonic Wars were at odds in their, respective, maritime and Continental commercial capacity and orientation.

capital into Europe between 1815 and 1850. As Hobson (1963, p. 98) has argued: "This was the period of substantial British monopoly in the supply of capital to the world market." English manufacturers also hopped European tariffs and circumvented their own state's embargo on exporting machinery and artisans by setting up branch plants on the Continent (Jenks 1973).[12] Britain's economic relationship to the Continent in this period resembled a colonial pattern of trade; the Continent was Britain's principal market for manufactured goods (and reexports) and the source of a third of its primary imports in 1830 (Pollard 1974, pp. 16–17; Crouzet 1980).[13]

The peace settlements constructed a security arrangement in which the formal balance of power among the Continental states rested on a quasi-legal alliance (the Holy Alliance) among the European landed classes and the nobility against popular uprising (Imlah 1958, pp. 2–3; Gilpin 1975, pp. 81–2; Bowle 1977, p. 235). This repressive peace began to unravel with the political upheavals of 1829–34 (the anti-Bourbon July revolution of 1830 in France, Belgian independence from Holland, the Polish rebellion, agitation in Italy and Germany, and civil conflict in the Iberian states). These events signaled both the demise of European aristocracy as a political force and a shift in state power toward the " 'grand bourgeoisie' of bankers, big industrialists and sometimes top civil servants" (Hobsbawm 1962, p. 139). While political transformation occupied the resources of the great states of Europe, the British ranged overseas, consolidating the British informal empire – the privilege of hegemony. This was done by establishing strategic bases at Gibraltar, Singapore, Dover, the Cape of Good Hope, Malta, Alexandria, Vancouver Island, and later Aden and Hong Kong (Gilpin 1975, p. 82; Bowle 1977, p. 233; Southgate 1969, p. 157). In effect, Britain established military control of the oceans; command over the trading routes to the Americas and the East was the foundation

---

[12] According to Hobson (1963, p. 107), 1822–3 was the height of emigration of English skilled artisans. About 16,000 were believed to have migrated to the Continent, and most factories had English employees in some capacity.
[13] Regarding the relation with the United States, Jenks (1973, pp. 80–1) claims that British merchants hoped for a unification of the Americn West and South to maintain free trade and divert American enterprise to the development of a prosperous Mississippi Valley rather than to the American merchant marine.

of Britain's bid for the role of "workshop of the world" (Bowle 1977, p. 233).

Britain's naval power was central to securing the periphery of its world economy. Following appropriation of the French and Spanish West Indies as well as the Dutch colony of Java during the wars, Britain asserted its naval supremacy by sponsoring independence for the Latin American republics. The pattern was the same: the exercise of gunboat diplomacy to penetrate these markets and so reintegrate them into Britain's commercial empire through a liberal trade policy. Similarly in the Asian perimeter, the British state used its political and military power to incorporate the Chinese market (through the Opium Wars of 1839–42 and 1857–60) and an enlarged Indian territory (central and northern region annexation) into the global market. Not only was India destined to be the cornerstone of the late nineteenth-century world trading system, but combined with Britain's other informal empire (including the "empire of settlement," the white-settler colonies), it also underwrote Britain's bold introduction of a free trade regime into the interstate system.

The combination of formal and informal mechanisms of imperialism showed the contradictory nature of Britain's hegemonic endeavor (see Gallagher and Robinson 1953; McDonagh 1962; Platt 1968a). In attempting to unify a world market composed of regions in different stages of social development with vastly different state organizations, the British state necessarily combined liberal and mercantilist practices in its universal goal of opening markets.

This combination had its clearest example in the settler colonies. With regard to the Australian colonies, the mercantilist aspect of British policy was expressed by the *Economist* in 1850: "The colonies are of less importance to us as consuming our manufacture than as supplying us with raw produce, and affording a large field where our surplus population may both provide for themselves and minister to the wants of people at home" (cited in Goodwin 1974, p. 31).

Although the division of labor presumed here held generally for Britain's periphery,[14] the empire of settlement adopted increasingly liberal political structures in the mid-Victorian era. This "positive

---

[14] This also applied in India, which nevertheless experienced an intensification of formal control (Pares 1937).

theory of empire" was an evolving settlement strategy designed to reproduce bourgeois property relations in the colonies as a method of absorbing British working-class emigrés and retaining commercial ties with colonial economies (Pares 1937). This would decentralize power to colonial states without jeopardizing substantive imperial interests.

The ideological and programmatic justification for the extension of overseas markets for British industry stemmed from Adam Smith's advocacy of free trade as a stimulus to industrial production. The actual wellspring was Ricardian political economy, however. This generated practical schemes for expanding settlement overseas with British labor and capital to counteract decreasing profits by bringing new and fertile lands into productive use (see Winch 1965; Shaw 1970). The linking of the free-trade doctrine with the development of agricultural peripheries clearly illustrates the atavistic quality of British classical political economy (i.e., its incorporation of mercantilist relations despite its antimercantilist pretensions). Such ideological ambiguity was reflected precisely in the British state's bid for world hegemony on liberal grounds (see Semmel 1970, pp. 217–19).

These colonization schemes, the most famous of which was Wakefield's, were integral to the free-trade principle. Wakefield expressed the virtue of colonization in 1849:

It is not the land that we want, but the use of it. The use of land may be got elsewhere. It may be got by means of exchange. If, without any increase of capital or people we could purchase with manufactured goods twice as much food as we obtain now by various means, everybody here would enjoy the same prosperity as if our land were doubled or as actually happens in America and other new countries. Every fresh importation of food by means of exporting more manufactured goods, is an enlargement of the field of production: is like an acreable increase of our land: and has a tendency to abolish and prevent injurious competition. This was the best argument for the repeal of our corn laws. [from Pritchard 1968, pp. 804–5]

The ambiguity of the British hegemonic ideology was necessary to the establishment of British commercial power in an extremely uneven world market. The changing fortunes of the empire of settlement illustrated this combination insofar as political independence *followed* the organization of these regions into peripheral producing zones. Such a shift to substantive mechanisms of hegemony involved two significant processes:

1. The emergence of settler political forces that favored the liberalization and local control of resources; in effect they became
   social conduits for the growing liberal nationalist ideology in
   Europe.
2. The subsequent process of settler state building, including social
   capital formation and economic diversification.

Both processes encouraged the shifts in British trade and investment
patterns in the last half of the nineteenth century, often referred to
as Britain's "retreat" to Empire (Habakkuk 1975).

Access to this formal empire sustained British capital accumulation in the face of challenges following the Crimean War (a catalyst
of growing European diplomatic instability) (see Hayes 1975, ch.
9) and the American Civil War, which were turning points in the
national mobilization of rival states (Innis 1956, p. 354). Generally,
the European wars of the third quarter of the nineteenth century
transformed the dimensions and content of the interstate system,
at the same time confirming the significance of industrial technology
as necessary to state power (Hobsbawm 1975, pp. 80–1). The
pursuit of industrial capitalist development reorganized European
state structures and undermined the structure of the Holy Alliance
(the "hierarchies of blood and grace") with an emerging instability
among the European nation-states (Polanyi 1957, p. 9).

This fundamental shift generated the mercantilist revival in the
interstate system. This, in turn, promoted the imperial and naval
challenge to Britain's global hegemony (Bartlett 1969, pp. 182,
192), especially from Germany, which had by the early twentieth
century reestablished a German-centered Continental economic
system.[15]

Substantive elements of British hegemony

Although Britain's political and military dominance helped to construct an international division of labor that favored British capitalism, the *substantive* aspects of British hegemony shaped the
organization of the interstate system to anchor this structure. The
legacy of British hegemony (tenuous as it was) was the liberal state.

---

[15] "Round Germany as a central support the rest of the European economic system
grouped itself, and on the prosperity and enterprise of Germany the prosperity of
the rest of the Continent mainly depended" (Keynes 1971, p. 16).

Other states were not transformed to emerge in the British mold; rather, in their responses to domestic and/or international politicoeconomic pressures, they adopted certain constitutional and administrative principles that facilitated participation in the international division of labor fashioned under British hegemony. The midcentury growth of liberalism (in various national guises) created a dynamic unity in the world market.

Three interrelated processes were the substantive elements of British hegemony:[16]

1. The spread of political liberalism, where social transformation generated liberal nationalist and socialist political forces in opposition to absolutist rule. The resulting constitutional concessions (drawing on the British parliamentary model) and the elevation of bourgeois classes in state structures facilitated the link between diplomacy and trade.

2. The spread of economic liberalism, where Britain's commercial supremacy, in conjunction with nation-state formation, encouraged market integration and the universalization of a free-trade regime among states.

3. The creation, to all intents and purposes, of a self-regulating world market through the adoption by states of sterling balances in London and the gold standard as vehicles of the global division of labor and the City of London's financial power.

All three processes added new quantitative and qualitative dimensions to the world market. The liberalization of international commerce marked a midcentury cyclical expansion in which world trade increased by 80 percent in the 1850s and by 50 percent in the 1860s (Fielden, 1969, p. 92; Woodruff 1967). At the same time, the world division of labor developed as steamships and railroads opened up European hinterlands and peripheral regions overseas. The measure of this was the 50 percent increase in world crop

---

[16] These elements of substantive hegemony are derived from discussions with Giovanni Arrighi and, of course, draw on Polanyi's (1957) arguments. However, I propose that the flaw in Polanyi's construction is that it abstracts from the historical context of the market society discussed – namely, the power relations in the interstate system (in particular, British hegemony and imperial relations) and the contradictory processes of capital accumulation. Hechter (1981, pp. 420–1) comments on Polanyi's neglect of a possible "causal link between market exchange and the business cycle." The fault undoubtedly lies with Polanyi's overstatement of the nineteenth-century institutional separation of society and the political sphere.

cultivation between 1840 and 1880,[17] and the switch from international trade in luxury items to a growing world trade in agricultural produce and raw materials. This shift from colonial trading patterns to world commodity trade was reflected in the increasing domination of the staples trade by world, rather than local, prices (Woodruff 1967, p. 268). At the center of this global network was the City of London, the clearinghouse of international finance and the source of sterling as the world's currency.

As surely as British capitalism reconstructed the world market according to its own internationalist principles, the substantive aspects of British hegemony precipitated the demise of that model of the world economy. The key to this contradictory movement was the transformation of the metropolitan nation-states, which occurred along three dimensions: political, social, and world economic. National constitutionalism highlighted issues of political and territorial sovereignty, requiring industrial development to underwrite military security (as evidenced by the European and U.S. wars of the third quarter of the nineteenth century). Extension of political representation and the social impact of the 1870s depression encouraged state protectionism to temper the competitive forces of international trade. Finally, Britain's adherence to commercial liberalism maintained foreign markets and peripheral supply regions for the protected industries of rival metropolitan states.

The spread of political liberalism. Following the American and French revolutions, liberalism became the most consequential social and political ideology in midcentury Europe in the popular struggle against absolutism and in the national independence movements. These social movements promoted an ascendant bourgeoisie in the Continental states, where rulers depended increasingly on professional and commercial interests to stabilize domestic social relations and increase production and commerce for financial and military purposes.

What was the relationship between these domestic transformations and British hegemony? First, the social revolts of the late 1840s arose in the aftermath of the mid-1840s economic crisis (Droz 1967, p. 250). Popular groups (urban mainly, affected by

---

[17] Fifty percent of the increase was from the United States, Australia, and Canada (Hobsbawm 1975, p. 179).

grain shortages) and commercial classes combined to challenge the obvious shortfalls of autocratic regimes in the areas of traditional privilege and political representation (Hobsbawm 1962, pp. 359–60). These uprisings were domestically based, although their demands appealed to the historic principles of liberalism that were circulating on the Continent since the turn of the century. Nevertheless, following the military defeat of these uprisings, states instituted reforms to promote the long-run interests of the European commercial bourgeoisie. To the extent that these reforms in fact constructed the political framework for capitalism *within* states, they initially enhanced British hegemony because they reduced political controls of markets (in land and labor as well as commodities).

Although Continental political trajectories favored British commercial practice at the time, the wellspring of change had earlier origins. Nineteenth-century European social change stemmed from several centuries of political and economic transition as absolutist rule centralized once-dispersed feudal power and promoted trade and industry. Following the Napoleonic Wars, an accelerated commercialization of landed relations and the socially disintegrative process of urbanization threw into sharp relief the increasing illegitimacy of the landed and financial autocracies. Although revolutionary opposition to hereditary rule (expressed internationally in the Holy Alliance) was initially expressed throughout the Continent, the 1830 revolutions reshaped radicalism into national movements (Hobsbawm 1962, pp. 144–64). These crystallized into class-based movements focusing on systems of rule within the nation-state. At the same time, liberalism forfeited its universalism and became the reformist ideology of an emerging petit bourgeoisie of intellectuals, professionals, and small business social groups (Hobsbawm 1962, p. 166; 1975, p. 90). The social base of the nation-state had emerged and, following the 1848 revolts, made its mark on the political compromise in European absolutist states (in particular Austria-Hungary, the German empire, and Italy).

Political liberalism, in its national guise, articulated the politicomaterial interests of capitalism as it reformed state structures and, indeed, more fully tied their fortunes to the development of capitalist markets. Whereas capital itself was international, its legitimacy and dynamic as a private form of accumulation stood to gain from political reform. Reforms thus institutionalized bourgeois influence in state administrations that were still primarily ruled by traditional social elites. Given the supremacy of British commerce, to the extent that such reforms were tantamount to the *intensive* growth of the world market, British hegemony grew.

British hegemony in this sense also advanced with the active support (both ideological and diplomatic) of the British state and British business.[18] The British state supported liberal nationalist movements on the Continent (e.g., Greece, Italy, and Belgium) and sponsored anticolonial revolts in Latin America (Hutchinson 1969, pp. 152–53). Hardly a matter of internationalist principle, such intervention advanced British political and commercial interests by undermining autocracy and opening markets (Hutchinson 1969, p. 145). Such was the pragmatism of Palmerston's foreign policy (Webster 1957, pp. 81–2).

As an illustration of Britain's use of diplomacy to check autocracy and extend markets, consider the British state's Ottoman policy formulated in the 1830s. Moving to limit Russian power in the Ottoman Empire as well as in the Mediterranean generally, British diplomacy sought to strengthen the Turkish state. It manipulated Turkish access to the Egyptian economy by imposing a commercial code on Egypt in exchange for the application of a similar code within the Ottoman Empire. Such liberalization of regional trade not only checked Russian influence but also developed an important market for British manufactured goods (as well as a primary-goods supply zone). The significance of the Turkish market was that, along with South American markets, it replaced markets that had been lost to growing protectionism on the Continent in the second quarter of the nineteenth century (Bailey 1940).

While the British state forged links between diplomacy and trade by sponsoring political liberalism, those states formed or reformed by nationalist and radical social movements emulated British political practice in their adoption of constitutionalism. It is a matter of contention how directly John Bright's 1865 claim that "England is the mother of Parliaments" can be interpreted (quoted in Watson 1969, p. 101); the metaphor is ambiguous enough (see Hayes 1941, pp. 50–9; Hawgood 1960; Watson 1969). Whereas British political institutions had their own cultural distinction – not the least being an unwritten constitution – flexible principles allowed for Conti-

---

[18]See, for example, R. Graham's chapter on free trade imperialism in Latin America, in Louis (1976).

nental variation in the face of pressures for reform. It has been argued that "the British constitution offered the example of a particular institutional pattern which allowed the combination of liberal and democratic ideas with traditional and hereditary principles" (Watson 1969, p. 125). Nevertheless, the combination in the British state was peculiar to the politicocultural hegemony of a parliament-oriented aristocracy, which, in the nineteenth century, coopted the middle classes into a power block to contain the emerging working class (Anderson 1965, p. 45). European aristocracies were losing power. Here, constitutionalism initially represented a rearguard action in the eventual transformation of states into bourgeois democracies with effective working-class parties. In this sense, the British model could be only indirectly applied; as J. S. Mill remarked to de Tocqueville: "English ideas seldom make much way in the world until France has recast them in her own mould, and interpreted them to the rest of Europe" (quoted in Watson 1969, p. 125).

English liberalism, imbued with "aristocratic consciousness" (Ruggiero 1959, p. 93), expressed the historic dominance of the landed classes in a decentralized parliamentary state (and, therefore, a limited monarchy) and, in the context of *Pax Britannica*, was notable mainly for its internationalism (Anderson 1965, p. 33). European liberalism, in contrast, was more explicitly nationalistic. En route to dominance in the party systems of European states in the 1870s (Hayes 1941, pp. 66, 82), it sponsored national unification, state centralization, and military growth in coalition with conservative forces buoyed temporarily by the defeat of the 1848 revolts (Hawgood 1960, pp. 206–7). This was the period of nation-state building on the Continent, marked by reform of civil service, construction of public education systems, and integration of national markets.[19]

As the emerging liberal states committed themselves to expanding home markets for the purposes of taxation, defense, and national unity, the political framework of a growing world market developed

---

[19] As Hobsbawm (1975, p. 94) wrote:

However powerful national feelings and (as nations turned into states or the other way around) allegiances, the "nation" was not a spontaneous growth but an artefact ... It had actually to be constructed. Hence the crucial importance of the institutions which could *impose* national uniformity, which meant primarily the state, especially state education, state employment and (in countries adopting conscription) military service.

under British hegemony. Optimization of this global market, and therefore of British hegemony, required the associated policy of economic liberalism.

The spread of economic liberalism. The unilateral declaration of free trade by the British state in 1846 was an important threshold to the construction of its world hegemony. Because Britain sought to project an organizing principle into the commercial relations of the interstate system, this policy clearly revealed the state's role in fostering substantive aspects of hegemony. Whether or not it was a defensive policy (see Musson 1972; Cain and Hopkins 1980), it marked a deliberate attempt by the state to promote commercial conformity as a way of consolidating a global pattern of mercantilist relations anchored by Britain as the workshop. At the same time it expressed a new balance of social forces in the British state, in part resulting from the 1840s crisis of "textile industrialism." This was the coalition of class interests committed to expanding British industrial capitalism.

The catalyst of social change in Britain in the second quarter of the nineteenth century was the rise of the industrial classes. Commercial reforms, including trade liberalization and the repeal of anticombination and antiemigration laws, began with Colonial Secretary Huskisson in the 1820s.[20] At the same time the Manchester Chamber of Commerce pressed Prime Minister Canning to recognize the new Latin American republics and extend a free-trade policy to them (Brown 1976, p. 107). The manufacturers developed a commercial lobby following the 1832 reform and introduced "political economy" into parliamentary discourse. Landowners with financial ties to business joined the cause of free trade because they stood to gain from increasing land values as industry and mining spread (Aydelotte 1962; Semmel 1970, p. 139).

Underlying these political developments were the structural changes occurring in the British home market. During the Industrial Revolution (late eighteenth to middle nineteenth century), rationalization of the landed economy generated rural pauperism and, following the abolition of Speenhamland, urban migration (Moraze 1968, p. 142; Hobsbawm 1969, p. 98; Dovring 1966, pp. 628–36; Thompson 1963, p. 213). By 1850, the proportion of the

---

[20] This was a defensive measure against foreign competition (Schuyler 1945).

working population engaged in agriculture and fishing was 21 percent, having fallen from 34 percent in 1821 (and approximately 50 percent in 1688). Manufacturing accounted for 33 percent of Britain's work force, 22 percent of which produced textiles and clothing (Robinson 1954, pp. 444–7).[21] Food imports increased from one-seventh of total imports in the 1820s to one-third by 1850, and 90 percent of exports were manufactured goods (Robinson 1954, p. 446). The production and trading structure of the British economy revealed an increasing specialization within the world market.

The debate over the repeal of the corn laws concerned British capitalism's commercial relation to the rest of the world, which in turn related to the British social structure and political alliances in the state. While landed interests and protectionists alike espoused physiocratic notions of the natural superiority of agriculture and the importance of an "intermixture of commerce and agriculture" (quoted in Semmel 1970, p. 167), the Ricardian political economy began the liberal challenge, anticipating the workshop idea. High corn prices were not simply inflationary; "there would always be a limit to our greatness while we were growing our own supply of food," remarked Ricardo in 1822.[22] Such free-trade arguments gathered a constituency among manufacturers and merchants in the reform Parliaments of the 1830s. In the 1840s, Cobden created a social base for the Anti-Corn Law League in an alliance between manufacturers and workers, arguing not for wage reductions but for the workshop principle. This he prescribed as the panacea for British industrial crises. (Chartists extended this to a policy of reform of the national distribution of income; Semmel 1970, pp. 164–6, 169.)

Free-trade policy thus evolved under conditions of economic crisis and, intentionally or not, was a precondition for a shift in the character of world capital accumulation (as British capital goods were exported). The British state projected a free-trade policy as the cutting edge of industrial commercial hegemony into an already competitive environment. In the 1830s, British textiles faced tariffs

---

[21] Another figure is that in 1800 the rural population was 50 percent of the total population – 28 percent of rural families being agriculturists (Moraze 1968, p. 145).
[22] The statement concluded (Semmel 1970, p. 71): "But we should always be increasing wealth and power, whilst we obtained part of it from foreign countries, and devoted our manufacturers to the payment of it."

on the Continent, and by 1838 it was evident that German manufactures (cottons and hardware) were outselling British goods in
the United States (Semmel 1970, pp. 161–9). Cobden himself
understood that even though London was the "metropolis of the
moneyed world," Britain's strategic retaliation to maintain industrial
leadership – freeing trade and in so doing raising corn prices and
therefore cost structures overseas – was "absolute state necessity"
(Semmel 1970, pp. 160–1). Peel reiterated this strategy in a speech
to the House of Commons in 1846; he argued that Britain's "manufacturing and commercial preeminence" required a policy of unlimited access to cheap food (Semmel 1970, p. 150). In other words,
the international division of labor was to be shaped by the British
state (as industrial core) via a free-trade regime.

   British motives were not above suspicion in rival states, where
some perceived the apparently cosmopolitan principle of free trade
as a veiled threat to their own economic development. How, then,
was free trade successfully propagated? How was this commercial
principle embraced by Britain's rivals when some foresaw British
intentions, in the words of Friedrich List, to "erect a universal
dominion on the ruins of other nationalities" (quoted in Fielden
1969, p. 85) through commercial, rather than military, power? It
seems that beyond the abstract internationalism[23] of the idea of free
trade [far more abstract than Polanyi's (1957) pacifist and internationalist *haute finance*, though admittedly actively disseminated
by British diplomats (Platt 1968b, p. 143) and propagandists such
as Cobden (Fielden 1969, pp. 89, 91)], the adoption of free trade
was *particular* to each state. It depended largely on the intersections
of world market relations and national political structures, as well
as on political relations in the interstate system. For example, some
industrialists in France and the German Zollverein favored the freedom of import of materials and equipment inputs (Kindleberger
1975, p. 50; Fielden 1969, p. 88), whereas agrarian producers in

---

[23] Landes (1972, p. 200) wrote:

Aside from the usual pressure of selected business groups for lower tariffs and the special
political considerations that motivated, first, Napoleon III and then the government of Prussia
to seek free trade by treaty, these accords reflected a general mood of optimism and of doctrinal
acceptance, in political and intellectual if not in business circles, of the pacific as well as
economic virtues of international exchange.

Clearly, one component was mutual dependence and prosperity, which war would
undermine (nationally and internationally). See also Ratcliffe (1975, p. 144).

Prussia and the southern United States bid for commercial liberalization.[24] It is noteworthy that, in the Zollverein, producers of consumption goods favored free trade, whereas intermediate-goods and capital-goods producers were protectionist (Lambi 1963, p. 22); this suggests that commercial liberalism suited traditional industries whose markets were potentially global and whose success depended on competitive inputs supplied by the world market. (At this stage, these inputs were prominently British capital-goods exports and material reexports such as yarn.) At the same time diplomacy played its role – notably in Napoleon III's commercial treaty of 1860 with Britain to obtain license to sponsor Italian unification against Austrian domination.[25] The diplomatic and commercial ends served by free trade[26] generally marked the midcentury process of nation-state formation on the European Continent (see Kindleberger 1975, pp. 50–1; Fielden 1969, pp. 87–92).[27]

Although the combination of political factors and sectional interests favoring free trade varied for each state and therefore prohibits a general causal explanation, some general forces encouraged the spread of economic liberalism. Aside from the growing influence on the Continent of the arguments of British classical political economy (including the significant conversion of Napoleon III) (Ruggiero 1959, pp. 171, 204; Fielden 1969, p. 87; Clapham 1971, p. 475), economic liberalism had a compelling example in British commercial success in the 1850s (underwritten by gold discoveries and overseas settlement) and successful British diplomacy. The British example combined favorably with the contemporary politics of re-

---

[24] For an interesting discussion of these sectional interests, see Rubinson (1978).
[25] And to keep Austria at bay (Ratcliffe 1975, p. 146; Iliasu 1971, p. 72).
[26] For example, Ratcliffe (1975, p. 148) argues with respect to the Anglo–French commercial treaty that while

political considerations were important in the signing of the 1860 treaty ... Napoleon had other reasons for signing the treaty because the need for a new set of economic policies to relaunch growth and the possibility of lowering tariffs without gravely injuring government finance had already been impressed on him by the time Cobden and Chevalier arrived in Paris with their suggestion for a treaty of commerce... It is not, however, possible to measure the relative weight of political and economic considerations in Napoleon's decision to sign the agreement.

[27] Of course, this process was contradictory – expressing the varying political power (translated into political alliances) of different economic classes, which in turn derived from the particular conjunction of national and international market relations.

ducing trade barriers *within* Continental states (Lambi 1963, ch. 3). In addition, traditional European state ties to industry were reformulated positively as state builders deregulated markets and gained access to British technology (Fielden 1969, p. 87; Ruggiero 1959, p. 172). In this way they consolidated industrial capacity, which Hobsbawm (1975, p. 80) argues became "the decisive factor in international power."

The Cobden–Chevalier Treaty with France was the thin edge of the British state's commercial wedge. What was distinctive about this treaty was its multilateralism, its simultaneous extension to all states of the concessions extended to France (Iliasu 1971, p. 71). Britain's abolition of reciprocity requirements in its commercial relations with the world presumed commercial hegemony, as Palmerston emphasized in 1859: "When foreign countries ... find that your policy has tended to the increase of your prosperity ... they will in all probability be more likely to imitate your example than if you were to ask them to surrender an advantage which they imagine they possess" (quoted in Iliasu 1971, p. 71). This treaty became the model for enhancing British hegemony in its largest market, as Cobden himself predicted: "The effect of the treaty will be felt all over the world.... The French example will do more in two years than ours would have done in twenty" (quoted in Read 1967, p. 142).

Indeed, within five years France negotiated similar trade agreements with Belgium, the German Zollverein, Italy, Scandinavia, Austria, and Switzerland. These states in turn began similar commercial negotiations among themselves (Read 1967, p. 146). This short-lived regime of free trade was the catalyst of Continental industrialization as well as a vehicle of British capital-goods export. This strengthened both Britain's role as engineering workshop of the world and the future nationalist challenge to that status.

The self-regulating world market. Britain's bid to impose a free-trade regime in the world market depended on the monetary role of gold in facilitating the global exchange relations marking British hegemony. This system was *anchored* by the development of central banking to mediate the status of national currencies in world trade and *organized* by the City of London as the world trading center and repository of sterling balances. The adoption of the gold standard as a self-regulating mechanism in the last quarter of the century formalized this system, allowing Britain to achieve financial supremacy beyond its commercial industrial supremacy.

Founded on the great colonial staple trades of the preceding two centuries, London emerged as the financial center of Europe after the Bank of Amsterdam failed during the Napoleonic Wars (Hobson 1968, pp. 95–6).[28] At the same time European merchant banks relocated in London – perhaps the most famous being N. M. Rothschild and Sons (in 1809) (Caincross 1953, p. 90; Chapman 1977; Cowles 1975, pp. 29, 40). At this stage, the London money market's primary activity was the issue of foreign securities and merchant banking. In the decades after the Napoleonic Wars, loans flowed from London into Europe. Not only were European governments and entrepreneurs stabilizing public finance and reconstructing enterprise, respectively (Hobson 1968, p. 11), but also capital movement from Britain to Europe and the United States financed Britain's expanding export trade in lieu of an import trade curtailed by British corn tariffs (Hobson 1968, p. 99).[29] In a world market of growing exchange volume, Britain led the way, and the merchant banking capacities of London substituted the settlement of accounts by bills of exchange as a convenient alternative to precious metal transfer. This centralization of accounting operations anticipated the adoption of sterling as an international currency.[30]

In the first half of the nineteenth century, London provided a credit bridge for traders throughout the world (Jenks 1973, p. 67). This had two main sources. On the one hand, British merchant banking houses built on the staples trade, establishing a network of agents and factors (particularly in the Far East and the Americas), organizing the circulation of goods, and trading on the capital of London acceptance houses and the manufacturers (Chapman 1977, p. 46). The acceptance houses in turn settled foreign merchants'

---

[28] London became the world's bullion market following the Treaty of Methuen in 1703, which provided British access to Portuguese colonial markets, especially Brazil (Saul 1960, pp. 5–6).

[29] Jenks (1973, pp. 69–70) observes that the bulk of U.S. foreign trade in the 1830s was settled by British capital exports – that is, an increased willingness by English investors and merchant bankers to buy American securities. British export trade in the first half of the nineteenth century, dominated by cottons, iron, and steel goods, was the cutting edge of world trade, increasing from about 12 percent to 20 percent of the gross national product between 1800 and 1860, and capturing over 20 percent of world trade (Brown 1976, p. 104; Imlah 1958, pp. 190–1).

[30] Britain returned to the gold standard in 1821 (Imlah 1958, p. 11).

multilateral trade; for example, Americans drew bills on London to finance exports by British manufacturers, as well as French wine, Brazilian coffee, West Indian sugar, and tea and silk from Hong Kong (Jenks 1973, pp. 69–70). On the other hand, European merchants established international financial houses in London (German, Greek, and other) and exporting houses in northern industrial towns to promote British export trade with Europe and the Middle East, markets familiar to them.[31]

In the 1840s London suffered a growing imbalance of payments with the expansion of new peripheries that did not purchase equivalent amounts of British manufactures. Gold, necessary to settle balances, became increasingly scarce, particularly because some peripheries (notably the Far East) drained gold out of circulation (Jenks 1973, pp. 159, 161). Fortuitously or not, the gold discoveries in regions of new settlement – California (1848) and Victoria (1851) – solved the liquidity problem. Between 1849 and 1855, the stock of monetary gold in the world economy doubled (Imlah 1958, p. 157), stabilizing national currencies and encouraging industrialization while commercial confidence and prices rose.[32] Not only did gold secure Britain's free-trade policy, then, but it also strengthened considerably the development of the world division of labor. On the one hand, gold production created "large new markets out of nothing" (quoted in Hobsbawm 1975, p. 62), accelerating industrial growth in the centers of the world economy to supply goods and transport equipment (railways and shipping) and thereby enhancing Britain's metropolitan role as world financier, workshop, and steamshipper. On the other hand, gold production represented a significant reversal of liquidity distribution in the world economy, particularly in the Pacific perimeter, where it promoted social capital investment as a foundation of development beyond staple production (Innis 1956, pp. 343, 355–6). This kind of investment, though certainly important in the United States before midcentury, was

[31] Indeed, in 1836, when British merchant capital financed more than 90 percent of trade with the periphery, it accounted for only about one-third of the funds in trade with Continental Europe. Not only does this confirm the argument that the "industrialization of Britain was a *European* process," but it also demonstrates the cosmopolitan role of London as the financial center of world trading networks (quote from Chapman 1977, p. 48).

[32] Price inflation was due not directly to increases in the gold supply but to the investment boom, according to Habakkuk (1975, p. 720).

not significant elsewhere in the periphery (such as Australia) until the second half of the nineteenth century, after the transformation of the London capital market.

The transformation of the London capital market – from a merchant banking facility to supplying long-term loan capital – marked the maturing of Britain's industrial base. Whereas the rise of the discount market mobilized national savings for industrialization, the turning point in the City's transformation was the commercial involution in Britain during the 1837–42 depression (Scammell 1968; King 1972).[33] Surplus capital underwrote the railway boom, which integrated the British home market (Jenks 1973, pp. 126–7). The proliferation of railway bonds ended the concentration of London finance in Consols and foreign securities and mines, thus opening the capital market to investment in industrial securities (Caincross 1953, p. 84; Jenks 1973, p. 130). The social character of the investor changed accordingly, with the emergence of a broader investing public composed of Britain's growing commercial and professional bourgeoisie.[34] The new commercial elite speculated on, and stimulated, capital accumulation (rather than depending on the steady returns associated with traditional landed and financial holdings) by investing in public companies and private company securities, following the example of the lucrative railway dividend. The measure of this transition was the 1855 legislation that secured the limited-liability company (and the incorporation of banks in 1858) (see Rubenstein 1977a, 1977b).

The evolution of the financial corporation in Britain was not only a result of domestic socioeconomic change, but also a response to political change in Europe that altered the balance of financial power. Nation building in the metropolitan states led to the formation of capital markets, which encouraged the development of joint stock banking to mobilize investment capital for large-scale social and private projects (Landes 1972, pp. 206–7).[35] Many of these projects

[33] The London bill brokers mediated this transfer of funds from rural gentry to manufacturers (where the latter were not themselves landowners), so the bill brokers *anticipated* the function of joint stock banking when this transfer was institutionalized (Caincross 1953, p. 84).
[34] This class, which provided a more democratic constituency to the London capital market, established its presence in City politics and wealth alongside the more traditional landed and financial aristocracy (Jenks 1973, p. 130).
[35] Limited liability became legal in France in 1867 and in Germany in 1870 (Landes 1972, p. 198). See also Cameron (1953).

involved railway, industrial, and mining developments in Europe's periphery (e.g., Austria, Italy, Switzerland, Spain, Russia, and Turkey).[36] The model was the French *Credit Mobilier* established in 1852.[37] Accordingly, during the 1850s, British entrepreneurs (company promoters and contractors) and investors began to experience competition with and, indeed, exclusion from Continental projects.

The challenge of alternative European financial markets encouraged the formation of finance companies and banks in London geared to non-European lending.[38] Although European financial syndicates still raised funds in the London capital market because its facilities were second to none, British financiers reoriented their investment toward the periphery of the world economy, thus consolidating London's cosmopolitan character.[39] This shift began most evidently after the international financial panic in 1857 and led to an involution of capital financing in Europe (Platt 1980, p. 190).

What is most significant about the reorientation of British finance away from the industrial regions of Europe and the United States and toward the Empire and South America was its international thrust. British capital was developing peripheral supply zones for British *and* other industrial economies that required increasing raw material and foodstuff imports. The growing foreign orientation of the London capital market marked the global extension of the international division of labor under British hegemony.

Within this secular trend in the expansion of British capital investment in the periphery, there was a further concentration of funds

---

[36] Following Britain's lead, the advanced regions of Western Europe had "become in effect new suns of new solar systems radiating outward their exports of manufactures and capital of skill and of enterprise to awaken still new areas" (Pollard 1974, pp. 20–1).

[37] In which, incidentally, British capital participated (Jenks 1973, pp. 176, 240–7; Cameron 1953, p. 465).

[38] At the same time, the growth of financial centers overseas undermined the traditional role of merchant-bankers, thus reinforcing the shift to finance houses (Caincross 1953, p. 91).

[39] As Jenks (1973, p. 267) writes: "It was not that London was still the only center in which money could be raised upon large issues of foreign securities. . . . But none of these money markets challenged the position of London as the supreme market for commercial bills and for accommodation paper." Of course, the pivotal role of London in international finance raises the problem of determining "the proportions of foreign ownership in securities marketed in London" and therefore the problem of establishing the precise shifts in British foreign investment (Platt 1980, p. 15).

in the Dominions.[40] This coincided[41] with the 1870s depression (with corresponding financial crises and debt repudiations in such peripheral states as Turkey, Peru, and Uruguay), when colonial government securities became increasingly attractive, guaranteed as they were by the British government (Hall 1963, pp. 15, 149). Between 1875 and 1913, as loans to foreign governments decreased from 53.8 percent to 7.9 percent, those to Dominion and colonial governments increased from 9.2 percent to 17.9 percent of total loans to government authorities raised in London (Hall 1963, p. 13). In effect, this process reflected the growing *political* character of overseas finance associated with the growing mercantilism of the late nineteenth-century world economy.

The expansion of British loan capital into peripheral regions – an expression of growing British dependence on imported food-stuffs and raw materials and the foreign orientation of the London capital market – has been identified as contributing to Britain's so-called decline.[42] This confuses the issue, however, because the reorientation was significant beyond the apparent crystallization of the British economy's dependence on peripheral regions. British loan capital extended the scope of the world market for all states. First, the expansion of peripheral commodity production was not simply a bilateral event, since Britain's rivals were also importing peripheral products. Second, this growing center–periphery trade pattern depended precisely on the City's ability to settle trade balances among states indirectly (Saul 1960, pp. 45–58). The foundation of this multilateral trading system was the acceptance of sterling as "good as gold." Thus, once the gold standard spread (from the 1870s), London's manipulation of sterling balances by providing credit en-

---

[40] With regard to this, Simon (1968, pp. 28–30) takes issue with Saul and Hall (who both qualify their argument to some extent) over their thesis of a clear trend of British investment toward the Empire in the last quarter of the century. Although he disagrees with this thesis, he agrees that within the export of capital to the Empire, there was a concentration in "regions of recent settlement."

[41] Saul (1960, ch. 3 and 4) argues that colonial investment provided a countercyclical function of the British trade cycle.

[42] For example, Jenks (1973, pp. 331–5) argues that after 1875 the "secondary export of capital" was evidence of a trade gap and a shift in the terms of trade against Britain, which resulted in the growth of a rentier class preempting investment growth at home. This argument has been refuted by Imlah, who demonstrated that Britain did not have a trade surplus before 1875. Brown (1970, p. 66) added that import growth needs to be related to export growth as a consequence of free trade.

abled Britain to maintain and, indeed, extend world exchange. Profits from the Empire underwrote this function, to be sure, but the City of London's axial role in world trade reproduced Britain's world economy (Cecco 1974, p. 121).

The formal aspect of this phenomenon was due to London's prominence in exchanges among states, facilitating the system of sterling balances and thereby leading others to adopt the gold standard. This in turn disciplined them to regulate their national currencies in relation to their trading position. Thus British hegemony produced a unified system of monetary policy in the interstate system, which regulated world trade relations. Significantly enough, it also ensured the principle of constitutionalism as the political scaffolding of a unitary world economy (Polanyi 1957, pp. 252–3). It was a double movement: consolidation of metropolitan national economies as rivals and a (temporary) revitalization of the British-centered world economy.

CONCLUSION: THE DISMANTLING OF BRITISH HEGEMONY

Because British hegemony depended on the political organization of a unified world market as a condition of British capital accumulation, the question of decline must address the political subversion of that world economy. Hegemonic decline cannot be reduced to the loss of industrial superiority because this presumes equivalence in the forms of British economy and rival political economies. Similarly, identification of the London capital market's foreign orientation as a handicap to domestic industrial financing is misplaced. It ignores the historic relationship of the City with British manufacturers' extensive foreign markets as the foundation of the workshop-of-the-world character of British capitalism. This section will summarize the principal politicoeconomic contradictions of the social structure of British hegemony.

The late nineteenth-century reversal of commercial liberalism by challenger states leading to imperial rivalry was the political response to British hegemony – particularly in lieu of its world market consequences in the 1870s. These consequences were, broadly, a crisis of industrial capital accumulation manifested as a world glut of manufactured goods (such as iron and textiles) as Continental industrialization accompanied free trade (Hoffman 1933, pp. 14–16), and an agricultural crisis in Europe resulting from the competition of cheaper grains from settler regions developed with British capital (Hobsbawm 1975, p. 179).[43] The social consequences were urban distress and a conservative agrarian mobilization to counter the vicissitudes of the market (Rosenberg 1943). Economic nationalism emerged as the characteristic political response. Faced, then, with the altered balance of class forces (following industrialization) and fiscal crisis, states renegotiated their relationship to the world economy.[44]

The resulting nascent forms of state interventionism threatened the political foundations of British hegemony and were the first steps to the political redivision of the world that would lead to World War I. In Germany, for example, Bismarck's anticyclical policy (reversing his former espousal of free trade) sought to secure foreign markets for German exports to stabilize domestic politics and preserve the social hierarchy (Wehler 1970, p. 187). Such "social imperialism" was analogous to Britain's attempt to impose free trade internationally in midcentury to sustain its own economy and reduce social unrest (Foster 1974, p. 187). The methods differed, however, because of the different world-historical contexts of the states concerned and the structural differences between the British state and the Continental states discussed earlier. Whereas British state power required a liberal political organization of world markets, the logic of rivalry to British hegemony for states like Germany was the reorganization of markets along neomercantilist lines.

Nationalist reorganization of the world market coincided with what has been called the "second industrial revolution," when the capital goods industry shaped industrial development. This new phase of intensive capital accumulation provided the industrial base for newly integrated national economies. At the same time, this mode of industrial production in metropolitan states superseded the manufacturing mode associated with Britain's original creation of a world market. In other words, political and technical transcendence of the foundations of British hegemony complemented each other as world capitalism entered a new state of development.

---

[43] The United States, Canada, and Australia were the most important grain-exporting regions of settlement, but it is important also to note that European agricultural production increased during this period, which explains the squeeze on Europe's producers.

[44] See Polanyi (1957) for an argument emphasizing the altered balance of social forces in states (at the expense of accounting for the role of the depression).

In the United States and the Continental states, industrial capital accumulation was a home market phenomenon by both competitive design and technical facility. State interventionism (through central banking) reinforced the centralization of capital behind tariff walls. This development, in turn, underlay the industrial commercial challenge to British capitalism that became evident in third markets (such as South America) and even in the British market itself, where Germany and the United States exported chemicals, scientific instruments, automobiles and parts, and electrical machinery (Saul 1960, pp. 29, 37).

Increasing competition in the world market and British capitalism's slow adjustment to such competition confirmed the worst fears of the protectionists in Britain, who had long advocated a reversal of the free-trade policy to safeguard British producers from unfair competition.[45] This attitude was the basis for the movement for imperial federation in the last quarter of the nineteenth century and stemmed from the alarm at the imperial protectionism of British rivals. The conservative paper *The Standard* articulated this position in 1869:

If we do not value our colonial Empire ourselves, at least we know those who do, who are striving by all their might to do precisely that which we are called upon to undo. While we are cutting off our arms and legs and loosening our members, every other nation on earth is actively engaged in consolidating its possessions. [quoted in Bodelson 1970, p. 184]

Rivals were encountering Britain's *formal* methods of trading (via preferential banking and legal and government contracts) as they participated in the growing multilateral pattern of world trade, especially in the Empire (Stokes 1975, p. 413). This spurred rival imperialism. In effect, the mercantilist structure of British world-economic hegemony revealed itself more clearly, the greater the singularity of the world market.

The increasingly political organization of the world economy influenced the British state in spite of its historic (aristocratic) prejudice against commercial involvement (Platt 1968b; Brown 1970,

[45] It is often pointed out that the geographical redistribution of British exports toward semi- and nonindustrial markets encouraged a concentration of British production for the export of traditional industries such as textiles and iron goods, which held back British industrial development (Saville 1961, p. 58). Platt (1972, p. 124) has shown that, in addition, British manufacturers exacerbated their loss in third markets by a deliberate "decision not to go for the cheap-quality trades."

p. 106). Accordingly, both the British public and the mercantile community pressured for a selective use of diplomacy to maintain open markets in Africa and the Far East, as well as for financial intervention in China and the Middle East (Hynes, 1976, p. 973).[46] In addition, political crises in non-European states undergoing "peripheralization" (such as Egypt) encouraged more direct intervention by the British state to retain their commercial subordination (see Owen 1972).

Alongside the British state's formal responses within this repoliticized world market was the growing importance of the Empire, and particularly the Dominions, to British trade and investment. This so-called retreat to Empire emphasized the neomercantilist foundation of Britain's global economy. To a large extent, the channeling of funds toward the Empire did not represent *new* capital export after 1875, rather "a steady switching of income from one area of investment to another" (Brown 1976, p. 173). Thus, the observation that this phenomenon "can be seen as part of a continuing centralization of capital" allows a comparison between British capitalism and its rivals in the period of hegemonic decline (Brown 1976, p. 193): Whereas the centralization of capital in rival states assumed nationalistic forms, developing home markets as bases of industrial rivalry in world economy, the British response assumed a characteristic imperial dimension. Thus, in the face of political exclusion, British capital export gravitated to the most developed markets available – namely, the Dominion states, which mobilized capital for social investment in the absence of British industrial capitalist pressure on the London capital market. The Australian agrocommercial complex emerged in this context.

In conclusion, the rise and fall of British hegemony in the world economy were not simply a question of changing power relations in the interstate system. They involved a complex combination of direct and settler colonialism, gunboat diplomacy, the European trade/great power complex, and the transformation of financial institutions along with the spread of constitutional regimes that favored free trade. The construction of British hegemony itself transformed (indeed modernized) the interstate system as a consequence of the British state's bid to anchor a global division of

---

[46] See McLean (1976) for a study of the attempts by the British government to exert political control through financial investment in Turkey, Persia, and China.

labor. As I have argued, this bid was contradictory precisely because of the political subdivision of the world economy into states. Britain's attempt to impose a colonial system globally was undermined by its very encouragement of liberal states as the political infrastructure of the world economy. In the shadow of the Great Depression, the competitive pressures among states combined with social pressures within states to commit them to subdivide the world market into spheres of interest. Under these circumstances, the Dominion of self-governing Australian colonies assumed a crucial role in sustaining the British imperial economy and in turn obtained a steady stimulus to develop an integrated and liberal economy.

Part I

THE COLONIAL ECONOMY
ENTERS THE WORLD MARKET
(1788–1830)

2

THE TRANSITION FROM PENAL
TO COMMERCIAL COLONY

INTRODUCTION

The British settlement of Australia in 1788 was notably a public undertaking. Unlike former privately conducted systems of convict transportation to the North American settler colonies,[1] the expatriation of convicts to Australia under military command was a novel venture of the British Crown.[2] There is controversy among historians concerning the transition from penal to commercial status of the settlements because the initial settlements in New South Wales and Van Dieman's Land were penal colonies.[3] Interpretations differ regarding the origins, nature, and timing of this transformation. Such controversy is misdirected, however, because of its limited focus. It fails to take into account the historical origins of the colony as the projection of a metropolitan society undergoing commercial transformation. It therefore fails to recognize the immanence of

---

[1] For accounts of the system in the American South, see Smith (1947) and Handlin (1950).
[2] "New South Wales was in the unusual position of being a settlement colony governed under a system used ordinarily in only conquered or ceded colonies" (Knaplund, 1968, p. 196).
[3] For example, Shann (1930, p. 12) compares the period up to the ending of the Napoleonic Wars to communism, owing to the state's central role in economic growth. Fitzpatrick (1971, p. 230) identifies the transition from a peasant to a commercial society with the 1820s switch in land-granting policy toward the systematic favoring of the landed capitalists. Steven (1969b) considers Governor Macquarie's rule in the second decade of the nineteenth century to have liberalized society and encouraged a commercial "takeoff." Others, such as Butlin (1968) and McCarty (1964), have argued that the penal colony was in fact a dual economy, where public enterprise fostered private enterprise. More recently, Connell and Irving (1980) identify the success of colonial capitalists in obtaining a labor market in competition with state labor utilization as the catalyst of transition. Hirst (1983) argues that opposition to the convict system persisted from its inception and eventually triumphed.

35

capitalist social relations within the original colonial military-bureaucratic state.

In fact, there are very few systematic analyses of the dynamics of settler societies in terms of their origins and transformation as frontiers of European expansion. The contributions that have been made can be divided into either cultural-ideological studies or staple theories of economic growth. These theories fail to explore the connections between social relations in settler societies and the world market.

The cultural-ideological perspective derives from classical theories of social evolution developed by such writers as Weber, Durkheim, and Toennies. This perspective regards colonial settlers as embodying culturally ascendant behavioral and psychological qualities – practices and beliefs in the vanguard of social transition in Europe. The qualities the classical sociologists represented as "modern" – individualism and rationality, qualities of the market society – comprised the social psychology of the settlers. The settlers were not simply products of the society they were leaving behind; they carried the modernizing qualities in untrammeled form precisely because they were eluding the European environment where their practices were in conflict with tradition.

Indeed, Weber claimed that the "capitalist ethic" was abroad in New England settlements before the establishment of "the capitalistic order" in Europe, where "the spirit of capitalism . . . had to fight its way to supremacy against the whole world of hostile forces." In addition, this practice required an institutional support system in the form of voluntary associations such as the Protestant sects, and a compact, urban environment like New England society (Weber 1958, 1976). This he contrasted with agrarian colonies such as the American South, thereby specifying the primacy of cultural environment in capitalist genesis.

Weber was not presuming to speak for all settler colonies; indeed he was concerned with the historically specific case of New England and its peculiar cultural organization. Nevertheless, he raised the issue of the offshoot of European society and the process of fashioning settler society in isolation from traditional constraints. Characteristically, Weber analyzed only practices and their institutionalization, rather than identifying the transformation of market relations (including the development of capitalist production) as the dynamic that reproduced these practices. Necessarily, the focus was on the segment, discounting its constituency in an expanding world economy.

Louis Hartz (1964) implicitly developed Weber's theme, arguing that settler colonies were particular fragments of European society transplanted at different phases of European history. Each fragment carried in its founding settlers the ascendant social tradition of European society at that time. They proceeded, "without inhibition," to fashion new societies on these cultural premises. What was distinctive in the evolution of settler cultures was a peculiarly atavistic ideology related to the original "psychic needs" of the fragment to reconstitute itself as a discrete society. The Iberian colonies in Latin America and French Canada were fragments of the feudal phase of European history; the United States, English Canada, and South Africa were offshoots of liberal Europe in the early period of capitalism; and Australian settlement embodied the radical tradition associated with the Industrial Revolution.

Hartz's characterization of the Australian fragment is curious. He identified the origin of the radical tradition with the emigration of radical proletarians and Chartists. As a consequence, Australia developed "a democracy dedicated much less to the capitalist dream than to mateship," lacking therefore the "capitalist individualism" associated with the liberal fragments (Hartz 1964, pp. 43–4). This reveals the limitations of the Hartzian approach to fragment culture, however. Freezing cultural expression to the settlement context reifies colonial and subsequent history. Cultural ideology assumes a teleological status, and social transformation is not given the attention it warrants. In fact, the relation between the two cannot be satisfactorily explored. Insofar as social transformation and, indeed, ideological practice are shaped by international developments, the fragment thesis cannot adequately explain the trajectory of the settler society and economy.

The staple theory of economic growth has become the touchstone of growth models applicable to settler colonies. The theory derives from Harold Innis's (1956) interpretative studies of Canadian economic development, in which he focused on the production and marketing of staple commodities for export. Innis's conception did not claim the status of a systematic theory, rather he sought to account for expanding staple-commodity production within the context of a developing world division of labor facilitated by the technical capacities at hand. In addition, Innis drew empirical correlations for Canadian social and political history with the organization of production and distribution of staple commodities.

Subsequent application of the staple thesis to the economic development of settler colonies particularly has led to an inversion of the approach taken by Innis (Watkins 1963; North 1966). The framework of the world economy has been replaced by a focus on the society under investigation. Although the world economy is implicit in the assumption of international trade, it is conceived as an exogenous factor, in only external relation to the society in question. The national economy may comprise one or more regions of staple production, and the problem is posed in terms of the relation between the technology of staple-commodity production and the social and economic structure of the region. This reflects a technological determinism that dissociates a production technique from its sociohistorical setting.

J. W. McCarty (1964, 1973) has applied the staple theory to Australian colonial economic development. He catalogs the series of export commodities produced in nineteenth-century Australia, noting that some had "stronger linkage effects" in the colonial economy than others. This assessment of relative stimulus to growth is based on his claim that "the production function (or technology) of the staple industry determines the structure and growth of the economy (McCarty 1964, p. 6). In this theory, technical characteristics, rather than social forces, determined the shape of the economy. As a result, the staple theory cannot explain the transition from staple industries with weaker to those with stronger linkages, which presumably constitutes economic development. At the same time, such theory cannot address the social conflicts that emerged around issues concerning paths of economic development. The distinctive activities of settler classes and the state in developing production, markets, and the social infrastructure are thereby obscured. These are the processes that are surely decisive in explaining specific patterns of settler colony development.

Returning to the study of settler Australia, I shall analyze the social forces responsible for shaping colonial development. The British Crown specified a social organization for the settlements in its initial instructions to the colonial governor.[4] The governor's goal was to organize a prison farm and public manufactories, with an

[4] For the instructions, see *HRA*, series 1, vol. 1, p. 9.

additional subsistence farming sector for convicts on completion of their prison terms. Insofar as British political opinion disapproved of further colonization schemes following the American Revolution and the rising costs of the administration of colonial India, the Colonial Office advocated a goal of self-sufficiency.[5]

Of all the motives behind the settlement of Australia attributed to the British by historians, the need for an isolated region that could be self-sufficient was the most immediate objective (see Shaw 1976, pp. 1–5). (An expedient and strategic consequence was the preemption of French colonization in the South Pacific.) Direct commercial expectations did not motivate the foundation of white Australia; nevertheless, they were not long in appearing. By the early years of the nineteenth century, just fourteen years after settlement, the British state was encouraging wool growing as a potential export industry. Although pastoral activity was supplementary to the penal function of the colony for another decade and a half, by the 1820s the British state moved to integrate the disposal of convict labor with the expanding pastoral industry of private settlers. Under what conditions did this change of public conception come about?

It is not sufficient to see British interest in encouraging the colonial production of a staple commodity as a mere revision of expectations. It is well known that John Macarthur personally accompanied his merino wool samples to London for inspection in 1801. The point is that wealthy settlers established pastoralism on their own for both economic diversification and social differentiation. This development of the division of labor within the colony resulted from the social relations established in the initial settlement. In other words, the social organization of the penal colony bore the cultural germ and structure of an incipient market society.

In this chapter I will pursue the argument that the course of early colonial social and economic development – from penal to increasingly commercial settlement – was prefigured in the original social structure of the colony. In combination with the settlers' cultural propensities for exchange, the property relations established by the

---

[5] For a discussion of British political opinion, see Fitzpatrick (1971, pp. 34–35); and see the account of the British state's gradual takeover of the East India Company's activities in India and the corresponding establishment of a colonial administration during the late eighteenth and early nineteenth century in Mukherjee (1974, ch. 6).

colonial state (through land granting and the assignment of convict labor) fostered a market economy. Subsequent socioeconomic differentiation and the emergence of forms of settler capital in land and trade were the foundations of settler capital accumulation. Colonial Australia was not simply a fragment of British society: It *evolved* specific patterns of social relations. These social relations, initially agencies of expansion of the British state into Australia, increasingly developed the characteristics of a periphery of the British-centered economy.

THE SOCIAL STRUCTURE OF EARLY COLONIAL AUSTRALIA

Construction of the colonial state

The early settlements in Australia conformed to the requirements of military administration of a penal colony. In 1787, the English Parliament created a Court of Criminal Jurisdiction as the primary colonial legal bureaucracy, and the governor's commission granted the governor executive monopoly. A military-bureaucratic government was to be the rule for at least the first two and a half decades of the settlement, with civil rights vested practically in the governor's authority.[6] As the social organization of the colonies diversified over the next half-century or so, the monopoly of civil, political, and economic powers in the hands of the colonial governor gradually gave way to a civil court system, more representative politics, a growing market economy, and finally responsible government in the 1850s. To perceive this transformation as the *inevitable* replacement of a convict by a civilian population as the British state changed its conception of the colonies as "receptacles for offenders"[7] is too simplistic. The source of these transitions was not some inevitable

[6] Although the 1787 act did not create a civil court, the one established was hampered in its operation by the lack of appropriate officials; consequently, the governor's prerogative prevailed (Melbourne 1963, pp. 11–12, 39–44).
[7] The following is taken from a letter from Colonial Secretary Earl Bathurst, K. G., to John Thomas Bigge, Esq., Downing Street, 6th January, 1819, in J. T. Bigge, *Report of the Commissioner of Inquiry on the State of Agriculture and Trade in the Colony of New South Wales* (Adelaide: Libraries Board of South Australia, 1966), p. iii:

Not having been established with any view to territorial or commercial advantages, they must chiefly be considered as receptacles for offenders . . . So long as they continue destined by the legislature of the country to these purposes, their growth as colonies must be a secondary consideration.

realization of the rights of the free-born Englishman; rather, liberalization emerged through the social conflict generated by class formation in the settler society. As settlers began to challenge imperial power (especially economic) in colonial affairs, colonial policy incorporated an emerging British liberalism into constitutional reform.

The social organization of the penal colony was not simply founded on the military-bureaucratic monopoly of coercion over a convict population. It was also geared to the requirements of economic survival and reproduction. The most important economic resource was the land. Accordingly, the governor's primary socioeconomic function was to distribute what were called "Crown lands." As far as white settlers were concerned, then, the state initially monopolized allocation of the means of production. As far as the indigenous aboriginal population was concerned, the colonial state expropriated their lands in principle from the first landing at Sydney Cove.

Following imperial orders, the colonial state proclaimed immediate sovereignty over all lands, decreeing them to be in the possession of the Crown and their inhabitants to be trustees of the state. This action presumed the Lockean doctrine of natural law, which grounded rights to landed property in the empirical application of labor to the land. The aborigines did not apparently fulfill such conditions; their subsistence was simply one element of a total cultural relationship to the environment, including all the land and other natural phenomena. So European settlers appropriated the land for their own materialist purposes, legitimizing their actions through the kind of imperialist ideology expressed in an 1838 *Sydney Morning Herald* editorial:

This vast land was to them a common – they bestowed no labour upon the land – their ownership, their right, was nothing more than that of the Emu or the Kangaroo. They bestowed no labour upon the land and that – and that only – it is which gives a right of property to it. Where, we ask, is the man endowed with even a modicum of reasoning powers, who will assert that this great continent was ever intended by the Creator to remain an unproductive wilderness? . . . The British people . . . took possession . . . ; and they had a perfect right to do so, under the Divine authority, by which man was commanded to go forth and people, and till the land. Herein we find the right to the dominion which the British Crown, or, more properly speaking, the British people, exercise over the continent of New Holland. [quoted in Robinson and York, 1977, p. 37][8]

---

[8] For a more recent study that revises the persistent imperialist attitude of general ignorance of aboriginal responses to white intervention, see Reynolds (1982).

The reason for the unsuccessful resistance of the aborigines to the settlers' occupation of the land was their social organization. Unlike the American Indian and the New Zealand Maori, who had recognized patterns of leadership and therefore the capacity to organize military resistance, the Australian aborigines were not villagers, nor were they hierarchically organized. Consequently, the aborigines were unable to obtain any formal recognition of land rights through the process of war and treaty. This accounts for the neglect of studies of aboriginal resistance to land appropriation in Australian history.[9]

The imperial ideology of a European right to the land obtained material force through the capricious acts of vengeance by white settlers against the indigenes, whether they were actively resisting encroachment or not. The establishment of the border police system in 1834 was one culmination of such frontier conflict. Designed to mediate between settler and indigene, the border police system was in fact a coercive institution that protected settler property. In spite of trusteeship responsibilities of the colonial state with regard to the protection of aborigines' rights, appropriation of their land amounted to cultural genocide. Because the aboriginal society had no concept of property consistent with the bourgeois concept of alienable property (land, labor, or capital), juridical recognition of aboriginal right was necessarily and conveniently excluded. Limitless expropriation of the aborigine was thus integral to the introduction of English common law as a rationale for the imperial invasion of Australian land.

Hence, the founding of the colony by the British state involved the construction of specific social relations between races and within the settler population. By securing the frontier from aboriginal resistance with military force, the colonial state facilitated land appropriation by graziers who occupied fresh pastures. The original monopoly of the disposal of land and convict labor, and the pursuit

---

[9] See Rowley (1974, ch. 1). However, the official relationship to the aborigines is described in a dispatch from Lord Glenelg, colonial secretary to Governor Burke (B.S.W.) of 2 July 1837 (quoted in Robinson and York 1977, intro.):

All the natives inhabiting these territories must be considered as subjects of the Queen and as within Her Majesty's allegiance. To regard them as aliens with whom a war can exist, and against whom Her Majesty's troops may exercise belligerent rights is to deny the protection to which they derive the highest possible claim from the sovereignty which has been assumed over the whole of their ancient possessions.

of the self-sufficiency goal, constituted the early political economy of the colonial state.

Land granting and labor assignment

The initial instructions to the colonial governor specified land granting as an appropriate method of settling emancipated convicts and encouraging individual self-sufficiency. Emancipees were entitled to thirty acres of land if single and fifty if married, with an extra ten acres per child. In contrast, retired soldiers received eighty acres, and free settlers (few in number in the first two decades) 130 acres. During the military interregnum, when senior officers of the 102nd Regiment administered the colonies between 1792 (Governor Phillip departs) and 1795 (Governor Hunter arrives), military and civil officers obtained land-grant privileges and were entitled to 100 acres. Given the combination of their status, their access to foreign exchange (the corps payroll), and the conditions of military rule, officers were able to consolidate landed estates by acquiring additional lands through purchase and appropriation.[10]

The social dynamics of the colonial state thus encouraged, through the land-granting policy, an uneven distribution of landholding. The assignment of convict labor reinforced this pattern, giving rise to the first forms of agricultural capitalism in the colony. During the military interregnum, in addition to land granting to officers, the state assigned convict labor (ten assignees per officer) as free farm labor maintained at government expense but transferred from public farms (Fletcher 1969, p. 197). At the same time, the government reduced the working week for convicts, allowing them to work overtime for wages in private employment. Officers had their first wage labor force, and private economy competed with the public economy.

Exchange relations

The state did not simply allocate social resources such as land and convict labor. As public farming deteriorated, Governor Phillip established a system for public exchange with private farmers in

[10] For details, see Fletcher (1976b, ch. IV). For a contemporary account of land engrossment by officers, see Therry (1974, p. 61).

order to feed the convicts and government officials. He institutionalized a system of private commodity production and exchange, thereby creating a domestic market. This was perhaps the most far-reaching consequence of translating the goal of self-sufficiency into social practice.

The state's involvement in forming a market arose from two particular constraints. In the first place, the settlement plans, which reflected the goal of self-reliance, lacked any provision for obtaining food supplies from India, the nearest imperial outpost (Roberts 1968, p. 3). In addition, the inadequacy of unskilled convict labor for sustained production in public farming (including resistance and sabotage of production) left Governor Phillip the only recourse available – substituting private production incentives.[11] He stimulated the production of agricultural surpluses by emancipist farmers by promising a guaranteed market in the commissariat store.[12] In effect, Phillip's measure institutionalized exchange between the social poles of the settlement: the public prison sector and the emancipated population occupying land grants.

The store reproduced the domestic exchange system. (Of course there was initial *bartering* with such items as grain and spirits.[13]) The most common exchange was initially between store receipt and farm produce. Once in private hands, though, the store receipt, which retained its value as a currency until the early 1820s, facilitated the circulation of commodities and hence an internal market (Butlin 1968, p. 31). In time, because store receipts could be consolidated into Treasury bills, an accumulation of receipts provided access to the lucrative import trade. In this way the domestic market was integrated into the world market. The store receipt, as an original agent of commodity circulation in the colony, represented an early form of trading capital.

---

[11] Convict resistance to the state is discussed in Connell and Irving (1980, pp. 44–8).
[12] For example, settlers and convicts

were at liberty to dispose of such livestock, grain, or vegetables, which they might raise, as they found convenient to themselves, the property of every individual being equally secured to him, and by the same law, whether belonging to a free man or a convict. Such of the above articles as they could not otherwise dispose of, they were told, would be purchased by the commissary on the public account at a fair market-price. [Barker 1968, p. 85]

See also Dunsdorfs (1970, p. 18).
[13] This amounted to a black market involving forms of "currency," such as copper coin, promissory notes, wheat, and rum (Butlin 1968, pp. 24–5, 65–6).

The institutionalization of a market, anchored in the commissariat, established farmers as petty commodity producers. This kind of family farmer normally divides his time between the production of family consumption requirements and a surplus for exchange. The division is flexible, varying in accordance with the nonfood requirements of the farm and general market and climatic conditions.

In practice, the colonial small farmer grew maize for family consumption and wheat for the market. Maize was a more reliable, more nutritious, and greater yielding crop, more adaptable than wheat to hand hoeing, the early agricultural technique in colonial farming (Dunsdorfs 1970, p. 15). In New South Wales, subsistence production took clear priority given the predominance of maize growing. In Van Dieman's Land, however, the climate discouraged maize growing so that wheat was grown for both purposes (Dunsdorfs 1970, p. 46). Nevertheless, grain surpluses were necessary to obtain nonfood goods. Emigré Alexander Harris (1964, p. 4) observed of the poorer settlers: "wheat being the most costly grain, many eat maize from economy, selling the wheat to procure meat, sugar, tea, tobacco and clothing." Accordingly, the store traded a variety of commodities, including implements and livestock. The latter was introduced in 1804 by Governor King in an attempt to encourage private pastoral activity as well as agriculture by offering incentive premiums in livestock (a costly import) (Butlin 1968, p. 61; Dunsdorfs 1970, p. 43).

The store itself was not a producer; rather, it retailed imported goods, acting as a conduit for British manufacturers (Coghlan 1969, vol. I, p. 275). (In this capacity it was open to the public until January 1815.) Although the store marked up prices on its goods locally to generate revenue as well as cover circulation costs, it tended to stabilize prices in the colonial market against those of private traders (Coghlan 1969, vol. I, p. 136). At the same time it advanced credit in kind to settlers against future crops, thus directly promoting grain production. In many ways, then, the store had a fundamental social significance in the early settler economy.[14]

The commissariat was not simply a market for settlers' produce;

---

[14] This interpretation is at odds with Butlin's (1968, p. 44) conclusion: "It seems more accurate, therefore, to regard the Store's retail activities as the easy extension and generalization of established practice to remove technical inefficiencies in the market with no fundamental social significance."

it also functioned as the settlement's first town. Its establishment, in effect, *institutionalized* the classic social division of labor: the separation of industry (town) from agriculture (country). Under the banner of self-sufficiency, and following the failure of public farming, the state encouraged emancipist farmers to exchange surpluses with the store and thereby to become petty commodity producers.[15] At the same time, due to the public character of the settlement, public manufacturing developed first in food processing (e.g., flour milling) and the construction industry. Public industry spread from local processing to include the fabrication of imported raw materials for the local production of clothing goods, implements, and printing materials (Walsh 1969, p. 247). Many of these goods provided the nonfood supplies for the settler farmer.

The mark of precocious development of the town was the concentration of both manufactories and population in Sydney. In 1821, for example, more than 50 percent of the New South Wales population lived in the metropolitan area (Walsh 1969, p. 248; 1963a). Such unusually rapid urbanization reflected an emerging commercial, rather than a peasant, settlement. Indeed, the institutional function of the store signified the early abandonment of any possibility of settling subsistence farmers in colonial Australia.[16] This was not surprising insofar as there was little capacity for, or

[15] Nevertheless, the store was not an unlimited market for farmers. In the absence of an export market for grain, farmers were confronted with a contradiction: the government would help to settle them on grants of land, but there was no necessary correlation between the number of farmers settled and the government demand for grain. In the first place, the proportion of the population on government rations declined from the first year of settlement until, after 1804, it was not much more than one-third (Fitzpatrick 1971, p. 120; 1798: 70 percent, 1801: 50 percent, 1804: 37 percent of population on rations). In addition, the marketing situation was exacerbated by the system of subleasing land to emancipists or well-behaved assignees by large landholders, which, according to Governor King, resulted in a "superabundance of grain" (King to Camden, March 15, 1806, in *HRA*, Series 1, pp. 651–2). As far as the marketing of grain was concerned, there was a persistent problem after 1810 (Brigge, *Report of the Commissioner*, p. 23). The frequent discrepancy between supply and government demand led to the imposition of quotas on wheat sales according to criteria such as the farmer's land area under cultivation (Coghlan 1969, p. 143). However, the quota system was undermined by the problems small farmers had in gaining access to the commissariat market. We can see some of the reasons for both the tenuous character of the petty mode of production in agriculture, and the eventual shift from agriculture to pastoralism by larger producers.

[16] Fitzpatrick (1971) is the chief proponent of the view that the British were establishing a "peasantry" in Australia.

tradition of, household industry among the original farmers, given their predominantly urban origins (Robson 1965, pp. 20–2; Shaw 1966, p. 104; Rude 1978, pp. 237–41). Such propensity for sustained exchange relations symbolized the particular sociocultural heritage of the members of this new settler colony.

Private economy and socioeconomic differentiation

The private economy, as already noted, was an early competitor of the public economy. Indeed, the public economy nurtured the private economy, but the growing differentiation among settlers accounted for the success of the private economy. The origins of economic differentiation were institutional; state officers monopolized access to foreign exchange through the payroll system. Officers used these holdings (including salaries withheld from their men) to finance and control early foreign trading by importing cargoes on speculation. The first retail store opened in 1792 as an outlet for the officers' wholesaling operations (Coghlan 1969, vol. 1, p. 133). Itinerant merchants were the other outlet, acting as retail agents in rural areas. Bartering spirits for grain was pervasive, and it established a tradition of middleman activity in the grain market. In this way private trading, founded on the infamous "officers' monopoly," penetrated the public economy.[17]

Trading extended to other settlers, including emancipists like Simeon Lord and Samuel Terry, whose opportunities were provided by officers' needs for retail agents to front for them as well as the absence of established merchants in the colony. Emancipist traders acquired land through usurious relations with emancipist farmers. Many indebted farmers forfeited their land to officers and emancipist traders alike. Foreclosure was the only method of land acquisition open to emancipists, however, whereas officers and free settlers had access to land grants, in addition to private land engrossment.[18] Wentworth observed of emancipist traders that "their

[17] The officers had formed a buying cartel (indeed, they chartered a cargo ship in 1792) to eliminate, or lessen, rivalry (Barker 1968, p. 19). The resulting trading profits of the officers were often approximately 500 percent (Steven 1965, p. 36).
[18] That is, settlers with capital, and at this stage they were encouraged with land grants to employ convict labor. For example, Samuel Marsden's papers show that in the period up to 1805, his land grants totaled 1,166 acres, whereas his privately acquired land totaled 808 acres [Marsden, *Personal Papers, 1804–1838* (ML A5412-1)].

system ... is to require of the settlers mortgage securities anterior to the supply of ... articles" (quoted in Steven 1969a, p. 122). Among the emancipist farmers, early expropriation was severe; for instance, commissioners of inquiry in 1798 noted that of the seventy-three farmers settled by Governor Phillip (1788–92), only twenty-one still owned their land (Fitzpatrick 1971, p. 103). This considerable attrition rate slowed somewhat as opportunities to accumulate wealth diversified, and government intervention stabilized the small farming sector (see, for example, Fitzpatrick 1971, p. 119).

By encouraging intermediaries to peddle goods among the farming population and to establish stores in urban areas, the officers effectively competed for the settlers' business, especially in the grain market (Coghlan 1969, vol. 1, p. 135). Government intervention failed to eliminate private traders, whose more efficient distribution network, superior commodity range, and ready market for produce allowed them to compete successfully with and in the commissariat market.[19] As early as 1798, the Hawkesbury granary bought its wheat from three or four merchants only, even though there were more than 200 wheat farmers in the area (Dunsdorfs 1970, p. 21). These merchants sometimes were large landowners who sold grain grown by tenants or purchased from smaller neighbors.[20] This phenomenon paved the way for the government's acceptance of grain merchants (Dunsdorfs 1970, p. 23).

Government dealings with grain merchants marked the growing articulation of state and private economies. A further indication of this nexus was the displacement of the state's initial monopoly of the allocation of land resources as officers rapidly engrossed land.[21]

---

[19] The attempt to prevent speculative mercantile activity in the grain trade by maintaining constant prices in the commissariat market had only a moderating effect on price fluctuations in the private market, largely because of the store's inelastic demand. See Dunsdorfs (1970, p. 34) and Coghlan (1969, vol. 1, pp. 134, 137).

[20] See Bigge, *Report of the Commissioner*, p. 22.

[21] For instance, in 1796 Governor Hunter reported that 246 settlers were farming 2,747 acres, and about 20 officers were farming 2,172 acres (Fitzpatrick 1971, p. 98). Fletcher (1976b, p. 216) notes that: "The 1800 Muster Books shows that the 34 officers whose names were recorded had purchased 5,221 acres; 1,190 acres from other officers and 4,081 acres from settlers, principally non-officer members of the N.S.W. Corps."

This was the most immediate stimulus to economic and social differentiation, which eventually produced a class of exclusive graziers.

The differentiation among early settlers was most clearly expressed in unequal landholding. This much statistics show, but the process was a *relational* one. That is, the existence of a group of primarily exconvict petty commodity producers enabled the growth of large landholding capitalist farmers. The link was the marketplace, in which the latter accumulated trading profits (and sometimes obtained land and labor) through the interception of the grain market. Thus, with the penetration of public by private economy, the market evolved into a definite social structure itself, reproducing a system of economic differentiation, which in turn encouraged private capital accumulation.

In the early 1800s a further social differentiation emerged or, more precisely, a division of labor between pastoralist and agriculturist corresponding to economic differentiation. This was the beginning of the colony's pastoral economy.

Origins of colonial pastoralism

Specialization in pastoralism arose in the first decade of the nineteenth century as an increasingly distinct group of landholders shifted their capital into stock grazing. With encouragement from Britain, there was further specialization in sheep breeding for wool. This development was not due simply to the appearance of enterprising pastoralists; rather, it resulted from the particular social relations in the fifteen-year-old colony. The first pastoralists were officers with landed estates who had been displaced from commercial agriculture.

Agricultural cultivation by officers peaked in 1796 (Dunsdorfs 1970, p. 39). While small farming was being established, grain production (particularly wheat, which was the primary grain commodity) was the most profitable activity in the domestic market. The officers benefited substantially from the practice (despite imperial orders to the contrary) of the state bearing the cost of provisioning assigned labor. This reduced their costs of grain production. As sufficient numbers of small farmers were settled, thus enlarging the domestic market (the farmer population promoted both the production and circulation of commodities), opportunities expanded for officers to make trading profits.

These two developments led to the demise of officer predominance in the agricultural economy. Small holders consolidated their market position; meanwhile the imperial state set out to curtail officer abuses in the state apparatus. Governor King (1800–6), in particular, acted on these orders from Britain: "Put a stop to officers trading and dealing in spiritous liquors, destroy the oppressive monopolies that had so long existed and make a total reform in the expensive and dishonourable plans which had prevailed so long."[22]

King reduced payments by the commissariat in Treasury bills as part of a general reduction of government expenditure. The effect of this over time was to erode the officers' dominant position in internal trade (wholesaling). In turn, this gave enterprising emancipist traders the opportunity to extend their activities from retailing to wholesaling imported commodities dumped by foreign traders (Abbott 1969, pp. 165, 167). King also undermined officer farming by reducing the store price of wheat and eliminating state provisioning of privately assigned convicts.[23] Apart from diminishing the size of the commissariat market, these measures effectively reduced the profitability of officer farming.

The percentage of colonial crops cultivated by officers fell from 31.5 percent in 1796 to 5.6 percent in 1808 (Fletcher 1969, p. 199; Dunsdorfs 1970, p. 39). While agricultural activity was falling off, the officers still engaged in trade (an increasingly competitive sphere); the result was the addition of some 10,500 acres to accumulated land grants from 1800 to 1807 (Fletcher 1976b, p. 72). This land was the basis for the switch to grazing that officers made in this period.

The entry of the officers into pastoralism represented the beginnings of a rural division of labor between agriculture and grazing. At the same time, and as a condition of this development, small farmers consolidated their position as the colony's grain producers. Seventy percent of the acreage under wheat cultivation in 1804 was on farms smaller than 100 acres.[24]

Although bankruptcy and the abandonment of farms were common in the last decade of the eighteenth century (part of the process

---

[22] King to Hobart, 9 November 1802, *HRA*, Series 1, III, p. 647.
[23] Between 1800 and 1804, King reduced the number of provisioned convicts assigned to officers from 250 to 58 (Fletcher 1976b, p. 67).
[24] For statistical details, see Dunsdorfs (1970, pp. 44, 45).

of land engrossment by officers and traders), small farmers became more stable in the following decade. This stability was to a great extent due to state protection, even though the government unsuccessfully attempted to eliminate the trading monopoly (Butlin 1968, p. 44). In spite of the traders, the combination of the commissariat market and the reduction of public farming ensured the survival of the small farmer over time. Under protest from farmers (both large and small), and with the commitment to establishing a viable settler economy to reduce public expenditure, the government reconceived public farming as a sphere of employment of convicts rather than the primary source of foodstuffs (and, therefore, a competitor in the grain market) (Fletcher 1973, p. 187). With this protection, the expropriation of small farmers decreased, thus limiting the supply of free labor and depressing the return on capital and rent on land in food production. As a result, large landholders and traders diverted capital into pastoralism.

Officers were the original pastoralists for these reasons; they had no other options for investing their capital. Fortunately for them, at the very time they were switching their economy, the state was developing an interest in colonial wool growing. Not only did Governor King claim to be "well convinced from the period of my taking this Government of the great advantages that might be derived by the improvement of the fleeces,"[25] but also during the Napoleonic Wars the British state moved to establish a politically secure raw material source for British woolen manufacturers. This was in part because Spanish supplies were no longer reliable,[26] and in part because of the decline of the British wool grower – in the context of the graziers' conversion to meat production and the general premium on food production during the wars (Bischoff 1842). Thus, Governor King recorded:

In 1803 a Dispatch from Lord Hobart dated August 24, 1802, recommended an attention being paid to improve the Growth of Wool, with a view to the future Exportation of the Finest Quality of that Article for the English Market, rather than for the Employment of it in the Manufacture of the Colony which should be confined to the Coarse Cloths. [quoted in Macarthur Papers, vol. 68, p. 94 (ML A2964)]

[25] King to Camden, 10 October 1805, *HRA*, Series I, 5, p. 699.
[26] Indeed, "one of the first acts of Napoleon, after getting possession of the peninsular of Spain, was to drive into France very large flocks of the Merino Sheep" (Trimmer 1828, p. 11).

Although the state therefore took initiative to encourage pastoralism in general and wool growing in particular,[27] it emphasized the organization of such activity by landed capitalists. Governor King wrote:

Except keeping those (breeds) retained by Government in that improving state, and considering them as the stock from whence industrious individuals and new settlers are occasionally supplied, I have not considered the wool as an object for Government to attend to, beyond supplying the manufactory I have established for the employment of women, the aged, cripples, and infirm part of the inhabitants, experience having convinced me of the fallacy of appropriating public labour and expense in works of that nature, which thrive so much better when conducted by the individual who has an interest in its produce, and whose situation, unconnected with other duties, enables him to watch and turn the various changes to an improving productive account.[28]

King also developed an immigration policy that suited imperial requirements by expanding the colonial economy and providing private employment for convict labor to reduce colonial expenses. This policy encouraged settlers of "responsibility and capital" to be given special land grants (Roberts 1968, p. 13). At the same time, John Macarthur's samples of colonial wool stimulated a petition from British manufacturers to the Treasury to encourage colonial wool production (Fletcher 1976b, p. 75). Subsequently, the Committee for Trade and Foreign Plantations urged Lord Camden to organize a land grant in New South Wales to facilitate Macarthur's breeding experiments with the Spanish merino (Fitzpatrick 1971, pp. 194–5). Former officer Macarthur returned from England in 1805 with instructions for a special grant of 5,000 acres to add to his landholdings and upon which to engage in sheep farming (Coghlan 1969, vol. 1, p. 88). Macarthur's success in England had generated wider interest in the possibilities of wool growing in Australia, however, and therein lay the origin of the "gentleman settler." Thus, the beginning of significant private pastoral activity, particularly sheep raising, coincided with the arrival in New South Wales of several settlers with capital who were acquainted with stock farming (Coghlan 1969, vol. 1, p. 119). This immigration ended the dominance of officers in pastoralism.

---

[27] For example, in 1804 Governor King granted "extensive common lands" for use by settlers with small landholdings.
[28] King to Camden, 1805, *HRA*, I, 5, p. 699.

With state support for large grants of grazing land, landed capitalists undertook the development of colonial flocks to create a staple product for export (Onslow 1914, pp. 128–9). In this way pastoralism emerged from the pattern of developing social relations in the colony precisely when the British state needed an alternative supply for the British textile industry. Thus, simultaneous with colonial state encouragement of a domestic division of labor between pastoralism and agriculture, an imperial divison of labor emerged.

CONCLUSION

The object of this chapter has been to outline the social forces responsible for the development of a commercial economy in early colonial Australia. These forces originated in the structure of the Australian colonial administration. Their social content reflected the world-historical conjuncture – namely, the beginnings of the Industrial Revolution in Britain.

The colonial state's creation of an exchange nexus between the store and small farmers generated a social environment for private capital accumulation. The private economy soon surpassed the public economy, even though the state remained the primary source of the means of production (land grants and assigned labor). Indeed, the state (through its emancipist policy) reproduced the small-farming population, while also securing the conditions for private accumulation. In so doing it effectively *institutionalized* a division of labor between agriculture and pastoralism in colonial economy. At the same time, fine wool growing as a further specialization sprung from the requirements of textile production in Britain. In this way, the combination of colonial and metropolitan developments revealed a global process: the formation of an imperial division of labor as British capitalism integrated colonial Australia into the world market.

3

THE WORLD-ECONOMIC ORIGINS
OF COLONIAL WOOL GROWING

INTRODUCTION

In Chapter 2 I discussed how a potential imperial division of labor resulted from the coincidence of events and processes in Australia and Britain. This development marked the beginnings of the integration of the settler economy into the world market. Integration implied development of the settler economy to establish a productive social base for the wool-growing industry and a growing correspondence between the needs of the British textile industry and the colonial staple product.

The forging of the imperial division of labor involved the careful breeding of flocks to produce the fine wool that eventually secured colonial entry into world wool markets in the 1820s. Pioneering colonial wool growing for the world market required a special type of entrepreneur with sufficient capital to finance such a highly speculative undertaking. The pastoralist marketed his own wool clip. The distance of the Antipodes from London necessitated a long period of circulation (up to two years) for the wool to be shipped to England and the income on wool sales realized there (Blainey 1971, p. 127). The pioneer wool growers thus engaged in alternative enterprise to underwrite, and indeed facilitate, their wool-growing activities.[1] They were not merely large landed capitalists, then, but also traders with mercantile contracts in London.

In the absence of specialized wool marketing and hence commercial credit arrangements, early colonial wool growing was exclusively for wealthy landowners. These pioneers combined all phases

---

[1] Land (1965) notes the diverse economic enterprises of the early "great" planters in the eighteenth-century northern Chesapeake, for instance.

of the circuit of pastoral capital – from putting up the initial finances, to producing the wool, to marketing the commodity in London, and finally through maintaining operations during the remittance of sales revenue. The exclusive character of colonial wool growing lasted until the end of the 1820s, when colonial wool successfully penetrated the world market. Then local wool merchants encouraged smaller and specialized wool growers who had credit and access to London. Divisions in colonial society and politics – due in particular to the growth of a caste differentiation between "exclusivists" (large private settler wool growers) and "emancipists" (exconvict men of capital in trade and land) – stemmed from this pioneering of the colonial staple commodity.

TRANSFORMATION OF THE BRITISH WOOL TRADE

The final demise of England's once-prominent graziers following the Napoleonic Wars marked a turning point in the British wool trade. Methods of woolen manufacture shifted, and farming was transformed across Europe. These changes incubated colonial wool growing as a staple industry. Although colonial wools succeeded in the London market only where they met the raw material requirements of the textile industry, it was precisely the changing requirements that provided the opportunity.

During the early nineteenth century, the structure of demand in the London wool market changed decisively, with the shift from a traditional reliance on domestic supplies for woolen manufacture to an increasing reliance on imported wool (Marshall 1966, p. 123). Furthermore, between 1810 and 1840, the dominant source of these imports shifted from Spain, to Germany, to Australia.[2]

---

[2] Roberts (1970, p. 45) gives the following table on British wool imports.

Source	1810 Bales	1810 %	1830 Bales	1830 %	1840 Bales	1840 %	1850 Bales	1850 %
Australia	83	3.8	8,003	8.1	41,015	22.0	137,177	47.0
Germany	2,221	8.0	74,496	75.8	63,278	33.9	30,491	10.6
Spain	19,748	80.0	10,537	11.1	6,842	3.8	9,466	3.4
Others	3,192	8.2	5,782	5.0	74,934	40.3	114,027	39.0
Totals	25,244	100.0	98,818	100.0	186,079	100.0	291,161	100.0

The broad trend was the gradual displacement of sheep farming for wool from the European lowlands to the extensive land frontiers in the Southern Hemisphere (Australia, New Zealand, South Africa, Argentina, and Uruguay). On the one hand, such displacement reflected the advent of industrial capitalism in Europe, accompanied by the intensification of farming. This involved the reclamation and enclosure of land, which diminished the feed supply for livestock while increasing the supply of food crops for expanding urban markets (Grigg 1974, p. 176). On the other hand, the relocation of wool growing coincided with technical changes in woolen manufacture and the resulting demand for the fine strong wool of the merino sheep which was adapted to warm, dry conditions (Grigg 1974, p. 43; Lipson 1953, p. 38). The merino was the jealous monopoly of Spain until the late eighteenth century, when the relaxation of mercantilist policy led to the merino's dispersion throughout Europe and its crossing with local breeds (Clapham 1967, p. 78). Together with the restoration of local seigneurialism, this contributed to the commercial decline of the once-prized Spanish fleece in nineteenth-century wool markets (Hobsbawm 1962, p. 190). Such a decline was, of course, relative to the advance of wool-growing techniques elsewhere. As James Macarthur noted in his assessments of the London wool market in 1829:

The quantity as well as the nature of Spanish wool is greatly diminished. I mean its value as compared with German and the fine Australian wool, and I make use of the word value because I apprehend that it is not the quality of the Spanish fleece that has deteriorated but the quality of the others that has advanced, in consequence of greater care and a more improved breeding.[3]

In the London wool market, secular shifts in the structure of demand were a direct result of profound transformations in the English home market, as industrial capitalism altered both demand and supply conditions in the wool market. In the latter part of the eighteenth century, scientific developments in year-round fodder crops and rising bourgeois living standards encouraged a switch to sheep breeding for mutton. As a consequence, English wool surrendered its traditional superiority to a finer Spanish fleece (Lipson

[3] Letter, James Macarthur to William Macarthur, London, 7 November 1829, *Macarthur Papers*, vol. 35, p. 212 (ML A2931).

1953, pp. 32–3.)[4] This trend consolidated during (and after) the Napoleonic Wars as markets grew for food products such as meat and corn. The acceleration of the enclosure movement and the stimulation of high corn prices encouraged the substitution of arable land for traditional sheep pasture. Thus, Bischoff (1828, p. 39) reported (see also Trimmer 1828, p. 12):

The light and upland districts of Sussex, Kent, Wilts, etc. were, before the war, almost entirely sheep pastures, that from the high price of corn, during war, it became the immediate interest of the farmer to carry his plough upon lands where it ought not to have been seen; he sacrificed his future to the present, destroyed his pastures for fine wool sheep.

For some farmers, sheep farming became the source of manure for crops (Bischoff 1842, vol. II). The extension of fodder cropping (in combination with deliberate breeding for mutton) caused the quality of English wool to deteriorate.

The interest of the farmer is to increase the weight of the carcase of South Down sheep, by giving them food different from what they formerly fed upon. By converting the fine sweet herbage of the Downs to the succulent food produced from the arable lands, and the introduction of turnips and other green crops with the increase of the weight of the carcase of South Down sheep, the wool becomes stronger and coarser, less adapted for the purpose of carding, and the manufacture of cloth, but better adapted for the purpose of combing and the manufacture of stuffs. [Bischoff 1828, p. 42]

Such deterioration was relative to the growing bourgeois market in England, America, and Russia for improved woolen cloth manufactured from Spanish or Saxon wool, or from combinations of the latter with domestic wool (Bischoff 1842). Furthermore, the consumption of cheaper cotton cloth by the working class reduced the market for traditional coarse woolen cloths. Bischoff (1828, p. 96) claimed:

The low price of cotton, the neatness and durability of goods manufactured from it, may have reduced the demand for low wools, and if any is affected by it, British wool will feel it soonest; common observation will discover

[4] For example (Blacklock 1841, p. 106):

Mr. Bakewell succeeded in bringing his sheep to great perfection as regards form, and rapidity of fattening, by breeding in the same family for a great many years; but it was attended with considerable deterioration in the quality of the wool, and engendered a liability to disease, sufficient to deter anyone from proceeding a similar length in the same track, to what is so dubiously called improvement.

that velveteens, fustians, and heavy cotton goods are much worn now by the lower classes, and particularly by agricultural labourers, taking the place of cloth, whilst the thinner articles are used by women, instead of worsted goods.

The relative decline in the domestic wool-growing industry became the subject of intense political lobbying and conflict during the 1820s in Britain. The decline was manifested in part by a considerable decrease in domestic wool prices in the decade following 1819; the price of South Down and Cheviot wools decreased by 50 percent, for instance (Stanhope 1828, p. 3). The immediate effect was to threaten rents paid for land, which in many cases were covered by wool revenues.[5]

The political conflict involved a struggle between growers on the one hand, and merchants and manufacturers on the other. The issue was freedom in the wool trade. The growers complained that the declining prices of domestic wool resulted from the competition of imported wools. They favored protection.[6] The merchant-manufacturers, noting a general price depression except for corn, maintained that tariffs would adversely affect the wool reexport trade (a typical activity of British capitalism at that time) (Bischoff 1828, p. 17; see also Rostow 1961, pp. 112, 125). There were two reasons: First, English manufacturers increasingly used foreign wools whose utility increasingly depended on their combination with domestic wools,[7] and whose quality, they argued, had deteriorated with the changes in agrarian economy.[8] Second, duties on

---

[5] Thus, Lord Napier stated to the 1828 Select Committee on the State of the British Wool Trade: "We depend for our Rents solely upon the sale of Wool, Draught Ewes and Lambs, without any reference to cultivation" (quoted in Stanhope 1828, p. 9).

[6] For example, Lord Napier claimed "the great Importation was in the year 1825; that year prices were 10*d*. per lb. and the next year they came down to 5*d*." (quoted in Stanhope 1828, p. 20).

[7] British wools became adaptable to technical developments in worsted manufacture, as Bischoff (1828, p. 63) explained, while the quality of wool deteriorated with increasing weight of the carcass and the wool: "With the weight of the wool the length of the staple is increased, and what was applicable to clothing purposes, or the manufacture of woolen goods, has become by its length and the improvements in machinery applicable to the manufacture of worsted goods."

[8] Thus, Henry Hughes, a Blackwell Hall factor, told the Select Committee: "The heavier the carcase, the coarser the fleece. The cloth from English wool is, in fact, now unsaleable, while we can get foreign wool to offer at the prices at which we used to get English" (quoted in Bischoff 1842, vol. II).

foreign wools both limited British exports of woolen goods and encouraged foreign rivals.[9]

The struggle was not simply over whether or not domestic wool growing (the source of "natural manufacture," as wool growers maintained) should be protected and how that would affect merchants and manufacturers. It also expressed an elemental social conflict between landed and urban classes over the distribution of surplus value as profit. To illustrate, during the five years of protection, British woolen exports decreased by more than 25 percent, whereas export cloth prices fell by one-third (Bischoff 1842, vol. II; Blacklock 1841, p. 57). Bischoff (1842, vol. II) commented:

This fall in the price of cloth is in about the same ratio as the fall in price of wool, notwithstanding that labor constitutes about half the price of cloth, and that the price of labor is maintained by the monopoly of corn, which is given to the landed interest. *The profit, therefore, to the manufacturer is considerably less than it was in 1819.* [My emphasis]

A powerful and united merchant-manufacturer lobby resolved the conflict by defeating the landed interest over the protection of domestic wool growing in the unreformed Parliament of 1828. This was an early blow to the monopolistic privileges of landed property (its attempts to maintain high rents), and it also ensured the decline of home-grown wool as a significant raw material for the textile industry. Easier access to superior foreign wools resulted.

Technological developments in textile production sealed this decline, ultimately giving Australian wools a competitive edge over British wools in worsted manufacture. In the textile industry, technical change, led by the invention in 1767 of the jenny and then the mule (a catalyst for the decline of domestic spinning, Lipson 1953, p. 138), spread to weaving with the introduction of the power loom. As a result, by the mid-nineteenth century most textiles were produced in the factory. The manufacture of worsteds, which used the tougher fiber of fine wool relative to that of British coarse wool, led the transition to factory production (Lipson 1953, pp. 157, 167, 252). British wools, redefined as combing wools (coarse) for worsted manufacture in the early stages of its development, soon

---

[9] Following the imposition of duties in 1819, for instance: "It was stated in the House of Representatives of the United States of America that they were willing to pay the English for labour, but would not pay their taxes. From that period, at which the duties on the importation of British manufactures were increased, they began to manufacture for themselves" (*ibid.*).

yielded to relatively shorter-stapled wool (Australian) as combing techniques improved (see footnote 7). James Macarthur claimed in 1829 that colonial wool "combines strength with fineness in a much greater degree than any other and therefore is most suitable for combing."[10] Thus, colonial wools stole the worsted market from British wools. In addition, by supplying this expanding sector of textile manufacture, colonial wool growers gained the advantage over Saxon and Spanish supplies, which originally were short wools for the older cloth trade (Ker 1962, p. 27).[11] The longer-stapled wool from colonial flocks generally had more strength in relation to fineness, and this suited the requirements of machine technology in the British textile industry (Ker 1962, p. 29).

Thus, the type and quality of colonial wool, as a successful competitor in the London market, had to conform to the developing needs of capitalist production in the British textile industry. The precondition of colonial wool's success was the displacement of British wools – in part the outcome of political conflict between urban commercial classes and their landed rivals, who sought to sustain their privileges by fettering the wool trade. The success of the wool manufacturers and merchants in defeating the British wool growers opened the London market to colonial wools.

The expanding market for colonial wools displaced European rivals also. Market success is a competitive process and was accomplished in the wool trade by an increasingly coherent pastoral interest in Australia. Once it recognized the value of this colonial resource for both the metropolitan and the colonial economy, the British state supported the nascent grazier class with land grants and convict labor.

PASTORAL CAPITAL AND THE WOOL TRADE

In 1803 the royal flockmaster, Sir Joseph Banks, recognized the competitive quality of the first wool samples Macarthur brought to London. This was the initial market link for colonial wool because it proved its potential suitability for a mechanizing industry. The visionary Macarthur proposed to the British government:

[10] James Macarthur to William Macarthur, London, 7 November 1829, *Macarthur Papers*, 35, p. 228 (ML A2931).
[11] Worsteds manufacture diversified to "all classes of goods" (even clothing) in the late 1830s due to technical developments (James 1857).

The samples of wool brought from New South Wales having excited the particular attention of the merchants and principal English manufacturers, Captain Macarthur considers it his duty respectfully to represent to His Majesty's Ministers, that he had found, from an experience of many years, the climate of New South Wales is peculiarly adapted to the increase of fine wool'd sheep; and that from the unlimited extent of luxurient pastures with which that country abounds, millions of those animals so valuable may be raised in a few years, with but little other expense than the hire of a few shepherds. [quoted in Bischoff 1842, vol. I]

To adjust colonial wools to the specifications of the world market, wool growers needed large landholdings to guarantee the survival and steady improvement of their breeding flocks. This required the consolidation of landholdings (in some cases the outright purchase of neighboring lots) and careful fleece-breeding patterns.[12] In contrast, the contemporary practice among colonial farmers was preenclosure English methods of sheep breeding for mutton on mixed farms of unconsolidated landholdings. Indeed, in 1804 Governor King granted common lands for grazing to be used by settlers "as common lands are held and used in that part of Great Britain called England."[13] The pioneer wool growers were, then, a breed apart from other pastoralists.

Until 1811–12, the year of the first commercial shipments of colonial wool to London, only a few pastoralists such as Samuel Marsden, John Macarthur, and Alexander Riley met these criteria. All three established mercantile contact in London. Marsden (Bell 1970; Yarwood 1977, pp. 90–1, 133–5, 236–7) was the colonial pastoralist *par excellence*, involved extensively in livestock breeding, whereas Macarthur (Hainsworth 1972, pp. 159, 167) and Riley (Ker 1960) relied on their trading activities to supplement and underwrite their sheep-breeding experiments on their consolidated landholdings on the Cumberland Plain.[14] After these pioneers dem-

---

[12] Marsden, for example, in 1831 had 2,436 acres of granted land and 2,498 acres of purchased land. See *Marsden Personal Papers, 1804–38* (ML A5412-1). Graziers like Marsden usually occupied at least four times as much land for grazing.

[13] Governor King to Lord Camden, 1805, *HRA*, Series I, 5, p. 699.

[14] Thus John Macarthur wrote to his wife, Elizabeth, in 1814 (Onslow 1914):

What you report of the fall of the price of Live Stock I have long foreseen ... – this depreciation must proceed and with increased rapidity until the price is brought down to the lowest point at which stock will pay for rearing. Our Farms will then produce little besides food for the Family and servants and the Wool. That is true it is yearly becoming more valuable but it will be but a scanty provision for us all unless we can do something in the Mercantile way.

onstrated the marketability of colonial wool, other pastoralists grew fine wool by obtaining their merino stock from the flocks of the pioneers.

The most important contribution of the pioneer wool growers was their farsightedness and systematic breeding experiments at a time when colonial wools were insignificant overseas and most colonial sheep were crossbred to supply coarse wools for convict clothing manufactured in public factories. Thus, Samuel Marsden[15] wrote in 1811:

By the Admiral Gambier I have sent to England 4000 to 5000 lbs. of wool. This will be the beginning of the commerce of this new World. Many think nothing of these things now. They cannot see any advantage to be derived to them, their children, or this settlement by improving the fleeces of our Sheep. But I anticipate immense National wealth to spring from this source of Commerce in time...When I consider we have not much less than 50,000 Sheep in the settlement, and that these 50,000 Sheep will produce while I sleep or wake as many fleeces of wool. It is a National object to attend to them.

Breeding was the primary way of competing with European wools, and at this time it was the basic form of technical change in sheep farming.[16] Other secondary technical change involved the preparation of wool for the market – activities such as washing and packing. Through such adjustments, the pioneer pastoralists competed directly with foreign wool growers.

Until the late 1820s, however, as far as the London wool market was concerned, colonial wool was insignificant (especially considering that English manufacturers still obtained approximately 89 percent of their supplies from local growers), as Table 3.1 shows. Under these circumstances (even in 1819, fine-wooled sheep made

---

[15] *Marsden Family Letters, 1794–1844*, Parramatta, November 26, 1811 (ML MSS 719).
[16] This was technical change in altering and regulating natural processes for the purpose of marketing a superior product, rather than a response to the social relation of capital to labor, which characterizes technical change in the capitalist labor process. It is for this reason that I characterize pastoral enterprise in this period as primitive capital accumulation (for a discussion of this concept, see Part II).

Table 3.1: *English wool imports, 1815–22 (pounds)*

	1815	1818	1820	1822
German imports	3,137,438	8,432,327	5,113,432	11,125,114
Spanish imports	6,929,579	8,760,627	5,536,229	5,994,298
Australian imports	73,171	86,525	99,415	238,498
Total wool imports	13,640,375	24,749,570	9,789,020	19,072,365
Australian wool, % of total wool imports	0.53	0.34	1.01	0.72

Source: Ritchie (1970, p. 282).

up only 10 percent of colonial flocks), the marketing of fine wool was highly *individualized* (Ritchie 1970, p. 286).[17]

The personal consignment method of marketing wool depended on the regular exchange of trade information. Samuel Marsden's London consigning agents, for example, prompted him to add Saxon blood to his flocks to enhance his competitive position in London markets.

Mr. Marsh the Wool Broker very minutely examined the Bales ... and he states that it is evident your Flock requires improvement which can only be effected by procuring some fine rams from the flocks of Mr. Jones or Mr. Riley that have lately been sent from Europe. The long wool marked ... was very tender in the staple which is against the Wool – the sheep producing long Wool require to be well fed or the staple will not hold firm and strong for combing – it is not as for clothing Wool.[18]

There was a growing rivalry between Australian and German wool growers. ("The Germans are decidedly the only rivals we need to fear at the present time."[19]) The following letter from England by John Macarthur to his brother James in 1821 is reproduced at length.

[17] The absence of organized selling facilities in London for colonial wool rendered private selling costs approximately 20 percent of gross wool income, which limited wool marketing to individual colonial entrepreneurs who could afford the expense and speculative effort (Ker 1960, p. 41).
[18] Letter from Donaldson, Wilkinson & Co., London, 15 December 1825, *Marsden Personal Papers 1804–38* (ML A5412-1, no. 7).
[19] James Macarthur to William Macarthur, London, 7 November 1829, *Macarthur Papers*, 35 (ML A2931).

I have had the opinion of at least a dozen persons that the sheep should be washed very attentively *once* or *twice*, then allowed to run on *clean* pasture a week or *ten* days, until the wool has imbibed the grease or oil again. I am aware that you want a thick carpet of grass to prevent the sheep from becoming dirty in a few days, but as your artificial grasses increase . . . I trust you will have the necessary means of giving the sheep a run on clean sward, before they are shorn. The Germans tell me that this is their practice. . . . He (Mr. J. Maitland) . . . thought the wool of a very good description and capable of great improvement in the fineness of the fibre, by the application of the artificial means practised by the Saxons. . . . He said he had devoted much time to a consideration of the subject, and an inquiry into the cause of the rapid and singular success of the Germans – that he attributed it wholly to artificial means – to the housing of the flocks – the fineness and sweetness of the food – and the careful selection of the rams . . . [which] are considered as valuable as racehorses, and tended with as much care as the latter are at Newmarket, housed at night, exercised in the day, and even clothed in winter.[20]

The successful breeding of Saxon merinos on colonial pastures increased the quality of colonial wool, allowing it to compete with the scientifically based German fine-wool monopoly. By the end of the 1820s, colonial wool could rival the German combination of softness and strength. Success was also in part due to the beginning of deterioration of German flocks in 1829–30, when German wool growers could no longer afford to sustain their artificially created wool quality (Ker 1962, p. 45). They faced the pressure of both the losses sustained during the mid-1820s world-economic slump and rising land rents due to a growing need for arable land (Ker 1961; Heaton 1948, ch. 19). In the meantime, the costs of transporting colonial wool decreased during the 1820s; cartage costs halved and freight costs were reduced (Blainey 1971, p. 130). (As Henry Hughes told the Committee of Inquiry in 1828: "I can bring wools from Sydney or Hobart at a less expense per lb. than from Vienna or Leipzig"; quoted in Bischoff 1842, vol. II, p. 183). In fact, as a result of the system of packing developed by the Macarthurs (Hartwell 1954a, p. 120), by 1830 the average transshipment costs (in British pounds and shillings) of colonial wool to England were £3, 15s., compared with £4, 15s. for German wool (Ker 1962, p. 48).

The successful consolidation of the fine-wool stock of colonial flocks during the 1820s was declared by the London importing firm

---

[20] John Macarthur to James Macarthur, Inner Temple, August 14, 1821, *Macarthur Papers*, 15 (ML A2911).

of Messrs. Donaldson, Wilkinson & Co. in 1833: "as regards the *German* or *Spanish* wools, an unequivocal preference is now given to the importations from Australia and Van Dieman's Land, in comparison with Continental samples of a relative degree of length, or apparent fine-ness."[21]

Now, although the large pastoralists individually experimented with techniques of breeding and preparing their wools for London, during the 1820s they began to act collectively as a colonial interest. The importance of consolidating colonial flocks to anchor the industry was clear enough. It was to this end that the New South Wales Agricultural Society was founded in 1822. Members sought association for the "purposes of communicating their mutual experiences and benefiting by their reciprocal advice" and to effect "by means of a subscription fund improvements in the breed of animals" by pooling their capital and importing breeding stock (Bell 1970, p. 58). The society petitioned the British government in 1822 to remove import duties on colonial wool. This resulted in a preferential tariff of 1*d.* (penny) per pound with respect to foreign wool (6*d.* per pound) imports. It was also clear that such collective action benefited the pioneers as suppliers of the means of production to newcomers. As Wakefield noted:

Our rich sheep farmers owe their fortunes, not so much to the high price, in proportion of the cost of production, which they have hitherto obtained for wool, as to the monopoly which they have had of an article still more in demand than wool itself – namely, fine-fleeced sheep. [quote from "A Letter from Sydney," in Pritchard 1968, pp. 129–30]

This encouragement by large wool growers of colonial wool growing was a measure of the growing class organization by pastoralists. Whereas pastoralists were still furthering their individual fortunes, they were perceiving that the conditions for capital accumulation on an extended basis were indeed social.

The outcome of this process was the increased interest in colonial wool production among both English capitalists and the imperial state. The most dramatic example was the formation of the Australian Agricultural Company and its southern counterpart, the Van Dieman's Land Company. The formation of these land companies followed Imperial Commissioner Bigge's recommendations of

---

[21] Letter to Messrs. Loughnan and Hughes, London, 21 February 1833, *Marsden Personal Papers, 1804–38* (ML A5412-1, no. 7).

1822.[22] He emphasized the facility of such joint stock ventures in developing the fine-wool industry by channeling British capital into the colonies. The British government expressed its attitude in Secretary of State Earl Bathurst's dispatch to Governor Brisbane of July 13, 1824:

> His majesty has been pleased to approve the formation of the Australian Agricultural Company, from the impression that it affords every reasonable prospect of securing to that part of His Majesty's Dominions the essential advantage of the immediate introduction of a large capital, and of agricultural skill, as well as the ultimate benefit of the increase of fine wool as a valuable commodity for export. [cited in Campbell 1923, p. 114]

These land companies represented a neomercantilist imperial commitment to large-scale capital investment in colonial wool production.[23] This anticipated the pastoral expansion of the 1830s.

In summary, the pioneer wool growers founded the colonial staple industry through their combined ability to ascertain technical information from market contacts individually and to consolidate such techniques by the social initiatives they pursued. Realization of the benefits of wool-growing techniques depended on the development of wool marketing, which encouraged a proliferation of smaller, specialist wool growers.

MERCHANT CAPITAL AND THE WOOL TRADE

In addition to consolidating competitive sources of colonial fine wool through breeding, the functional differentiation of wool growing and wool marketing was decisive in establishing a viable staple industry. This differentiation marked the end of the pioneer phase and the emergence of a distinct colonial merchant class. Although merchants were not new to settler society, the division of productive and commercial activities associated with the wool industry enhanced the conditions for capital accumulation by merchants (Hainsworth 1972).

Colonial traders began to prosper in the 1800s, when commercial importing was freed from the grip of the officer monopoly. To

---

[22] J. T. Bigge was commissioned in 1819 by the British government to inquire thoroughly into the economic, social, and political state of the Australian colony of New South Wales.

[23] £1 million for the Australian Agricultural Company.

create and sustain a source of credit to finance imports, the colonial merchants sought to establish a staple commodity for export. In addition to the use of pork and sandalwood to create a Pacific trade (Hainsworth 1968) sealing proved the most beneficial temporary export staple.[24] This was because it established commercial links with London, the source of regular import goods, and it fostered the development of credit facilities in London for large colonial merchants. Whereas the "free" merchants had access to London agents so that their enterprise was primarily in foreign trade, emancipist merchants such as Simeon Lord necessarily had to spread their enterprise into shipping and colonial manufacturing. Such diversification (including land acquisition) marked an early and significant articulation of merchant capital with commodity production in the colonial economy. Historically, the settler merchant's survival and prosperity would depend on his ability to promote commodity production, rather than just commodity exchange.

Colonial merchant capital consolidated in the latter half of the 1810s, following a rationalization of trading after the post-Napoleonic War commercial depression (Steven 1969b, p. 184) and a relaxation of East India Company privileges (Ward 1948, ch. 3). Hence the formation in 1817, with state encouragement (Governor Macquarie), of the Bank of New South Wales, whose founders were "predominantly government officials and private traders" (Holder 1970, vol. 1, p. 26). (One was the emancipist Simeon Lord.) By 1820, most vessels that entered Sydney or Hobart had their import and export cargoes handled by colonial merchants, rather than by the captain or supercargo (MacMillan 1967, p. 207). As trading specialized, so did pastoralism, marking the demise of the pioneer wool-grower phase. Hannibal Macarthur remarked, "the business of a merchant is so incompatible with that of the Farmer that one or the other must be given up" (cited in Onslow 1914, p. 296).[25]

---

[24] "Temporary" because of (1) the extermination of seal colonies and (2) limited market potential in England, especially after the Jefferson Embargo Act of 1807, which eliminated the reexport trade to America (Hainsworth 1972, p. 97).

[25] Combined mercantile and pastoral activity did not disappear because the accumulation of stock and land in the hands of colonial merchants was the natural outcome of debt payments arising from local trading activity. This kind of absentee landownership as another form of mercantile speculation was the rule, however, with active mercantile farming as the exception. Fine-wool growing was a technically advanced, specialized occupation for an exceptional group of pastoral cap-

During the 1820s, colonial merchants increasingly organized wool marketing, assuming a function hitherto undertaken by the pioneer pastoralists. Regular local wool auctions began, along with regular wool market reports and local merchant solicitation of wool in the early 1820s (Hartwell 1954a; Bergman 1964, p. 407; Ker 1962, p. 42). At the same time, there was a rationalization of selling operations in London (in part at the initiative of colonial wool growers) – both to reduce costs and to obtain direct access to continually changing information regarding wool types on the London wool market. By the mid-1820s, at least three selling agents for colonial wool were in regular operation in London (Ker 1962, p. 47).

With the establishment of this mercantile nexus outside of the system of personal consignment by large growers, a system of mercantile credit appeared, which enabled smaller, specialist wool growers to begin operation. Instead of negotiating individual credit with large wool growers, British mercantile houses established credit arrangements with colonial merchants or their own merchant-factors in Australia to finance wool exporting.[26]

In effect, wool marketing could be classified by two basic methods. On the one hand, large pastoralists continued to consign their wool clip to London to be marketed by selling agents. This method relied on direct contact between grower and seller. On the other hand, smaller wool growers, who were unable to finance their activities during the long time needed for realization of their capital (i.e., transshipment to London markets), sold wool to local merchants for immediate returns. Local merchants operated through credit arrangements with London-based mercantile houses, which

italists. Not only had the number of colonial sheep owners *declined* to 136 between 1806 and 1819 (whereas there were, in 1819, 300 cattle owners), but there had also been a concentration of capital in sheep among these specialized pastoralists, with fifteen owning flocks larger than 1,000 sheep. Further differentiation shows that of the largest sheep owners, who collectively accounted for two-thirds of colonial sheep, Macarthur, Hassall, Cox, Terry, and Marsden alone owned one-third of the sheep. (Macarthur and Terry were two of the four largest sheep owners who also owned large cattle herds.) See Abbott (1971, p. 48; 1969, p. 239).

[26] Billbroking, the basis of financing foreign trade, was consolidated in the 1820s in London. See Scammell (1968, p. 124) and Steven (1965, p. 292): "By the mid-1820's the procedure was established whereby the English selling agents for colonial wool extended credit, either to the growers or to the merchants in New South Wales, who in their turn shipped the wool and turned the credit back to the producers."

made advances on anticipation of delivery of the wool clip. Merchants (particularly the factors working for British firms) also advanced credit to the producer to gain access to the wool clip and to gain the interest. The most significant development in the 1820s was the establishment of the marketing connection to facilitate the inflow of credit (money capital) in exchange for the commodity (wool). Each form of capital flowed in the opposite direction, thereby promoting regular production and reproduction of pastoral capital. This marketing framework, based on the enterprise of merchant capital, was strengthened during the late 1820s depression.

The crisis in the colonial economy followed the tightening of the English money market after the collapse of South American mining speculations in 1825 (Jenks 1973, p. 57). In addition, due to the fixed sterling exchange standard institutionalized in the colonies in 1825 and the rapid flight of Spanish dollars during the transition to British specie, currency and credit in the colonies became extremely scarce (Butlin 1968, pp. 143, 167–8). Foreign merchants aggravated this situation by dumping cargo and calling in debts (MacMillan 1967, pp. 203, 238). Insolvent colonial merchants were unable to advance loans to pastoralists, who were affected by the halving of wool prices following the financial squeeze and the reduction of British duties on wool imports from the Continent in 1824. The wool price slump especially affected pastoralists who had invested in flocks during the preceding boom.[27] A severe two-year drought after 1827 further exacerbated their situation, eventually forcing them to sell stock they could no longer feed. This resulted in the culling of colonial flocks.

The 1820s depression clearly revealed the growing integration of the colonial and metropolitan economy, where wool exports and capital inflow from Britain rose and fell together in this early trade cycle (Hartwell 1956, p. 56). As a result of this commercial depression, there developed in the wool trade two significant trends.

1. Enhanced functions of merchants as an intermediary in the wool trade. The shortage of credit in London compelled the wool growers, who previously consigned wool directly to London agents, to sell locally to merchants (Ker 1962, p. 42). The lack

[27] In 1822–5, prices ranged from 2/ – to 3/6 per pound. In 1826–31, estimated prices were – 1826: 1.75*s*.; 1827: 1.19*s*.; 1828: 0.98*s*.; 1829: 1.26*s*.; 1830: 0.78*s*.; 1831: 1.08*s*. (Hartwell 1956, p. 56).

of alternative financial institutions to supply credit (the first colonial banks were not prepared to lend to producers) reinforced
this producer-merchant relationship.
2. Improved position of the fine-wool breeder. This was due to
the tendency for fine-wool prices to be sustained through the
slump – at least at a sufficient level to promote specialization in
fine-wool growing (Ker 1960, p. 216).[28] This, and culling,
caused a general improvement in colonial flock standards during
the latter years of the 1820s, enhanced by the capital investment
by large pastoralists in stock imports (Beever 1965, p. 102; Ker
1960, pp. 216–17; 1962, pp. 41–5). As noted earlier, although
wool prices undermined the coarser wool growers in Britain,
the competitive position of fine-wool growing was advanced in
the world market.

In this way, the commercial depression consolidated the technically advanced sector of pastoral production – namely, fine-wool
specialization. At the same time, pastoral capital was further concentrated among the large fine-wool growers. These pastoralists
anchored the expansion of pastoralism in the 1830s by providing
a pool of fine-wooled sheep as means of production for newcomer
pastoralists. As argued in this section, the condition for this process
was the system of marketing relationships forged by merchant capital in the 1820s.

LANDED CAPITAL AND THE STATE

State policy was also instrumental in the development of pastoral
capital. The policy of the colonial state toward land granting
changed from an initial attempt to settle an emancipist small-farming population to the active sanction of large landholding in the
1820s. This change accommodated an intensified postwar transportation policy to the structure of landholding in the colony. As
the number and size of landed estates increased, the economies of
assigning convict labor to estate farmers became obvious. This reinforced a state commitment to landed capital.

Estate farming developed under pressure to extend pastoral prop-

---

[28] See also Fogarty, (1968, p. 122): "In 1827 compared to 1825, fine and coarse
wools were 10–20% lower in price while middle-quality wools were 30–40%
lower."

Table 3.2: *Grants issued, 1812–20*

Size of holdings (acres)	No. of grants	% of total	No. of acres	% of total area
Less than 200	39	15.32	5,226	3.45
200–499	93	36.46	27,410	18.10
500–999	81	31.76	49,440	32.65
1,000 and over	42	16.46	69,360	45.80
Totals	255	100.00	151,436	100.00

Source: Robinson (1969, p. 99).

erties as livestock accumulated. The government's differential land-granting policy sustained this process, as Table 3.2 shows. Meanwhile, land was acquired through extralegal means, thus furthering the process of concentration.[29]

Table 3.2 conceals the impact of the period following the Napoleonic wars. After the war Britain faced two problems. First, the interest rate on the national debt comprised 60 percent of the government's annual income (Ritchie 1967, p. 29). Second, considerable social dislocation followed the demobilization of roughly 250,000 soldiers during an agricultural crisis.[30] This crisis involved not merely the postwar agricultural slump (following a wartime boom), but also the more far-reaching reorganization of agriculture by the enclosure movement, which expropriated small landholders

[29] As Commissioner Bigge claimed:

A practice has for some time prevailed of allowing individuals to consolidate under one grant, several small allotments that had been occupied by the first grantees, and sold by them before they had been able to obtain the grant, or to comply with the conditions of it. This system is convenient to the large capitalists, and has led to the accumulation of a considerable quantity of land in their hands; but it affords an irresistible temptation to the small settlers to abandon the cultivation of land, as well as to abuse the indulgences that are bestowed by the Crown for the express purpose of maintaining that cultivation.

[Quote from *Report of the Commissioner of Inquiry, on the State of Agriculture and Trade in the Colony of New South Wales* (Adelaide: Libraries Board of South Australia, 1966), p. 36.]

[30] Thus (Hobsbawm and Rude 1968, p. 72):

The demobilisation of anything up to 250,000 men from the armed forces within a short period swamped the rural labour market, which was already glutted with excess labour, with even greater numbers of the unemployable. All this at a time when the labourer was peculiarly denuded of protection. The Speenhamland policy had opted for relief rather than high wage-rates and in so doing taken away the labourer's safest guarantee, a living wage, and substituted the much weaker one of the minimum family income for paupers.

and threatened yeoman farming. In combination with the secular demise of domestic industry, these forces accelerated rural depopulation and placed acute stress on urban resources. Crime also increased with greater urban concentration (Kiddle 1967, p. 26; Shaw 1966, ch. 7, 8), and there was an increasing incidence of offenses against property (Fitzpatrick 1971, p. 239 fn.).

The response of the British government to these problems led to policy changes that encouraged colonial landed property. Under pressure from a growing free-trade lobby, the treasury instituted a policy of financial retrenchment in New South Wales in 1817. The colonial state responded with a policy that encouraged the assignment of convicts to landowners to reduce public expenditures. This policy coincided with a greatly increased inflow of convicts, as Britain attempted to relieve economic and social pressures by accelerating the transportation program.[31] Table 3.3 records the increased convict transportation to Australia.

How to dispose of the increased number of convicts was the problem that faced Colonial Secretary Earl Bathurst. In 1819 he commissioned J. T. Bigge to investigate. As a result of Bigge's recommendations, the Colonial Office resolved to sponsor the pastoral industry with the regular assignment of convict labor. This would both disperse the convicts throughout the colony (using distance as a form of punishment) and enhance commercial development (Ritchie 1970, pp. 65, 294).[32] Land regulations in the mid-1820s ended the tradition of accommodating the small farmer (Jeans 1966). Whereas provisions were made for grants of less than 320 acres (Coghlan 1969, vol. 1, p. 230),[33] the new regulations

---

[31] An additional reason for the greater volume of transported convicts was the commutation of capital punishment into exile in this period (Shaw 1966, p. 147). Free emigration also relieved British socioeconomic pressures. Settlement schemes in Canada and South Africa and the proximity of North America drew most free immigrants. See Carrothers (1966, p. 305). The few settlers who moved to Australia emigrated with capital to escape declining economic circumstances, some pursuing fine-wool growing (Ritchie 1967, p. 34).

[32] With respect to the execution of assignment policy, it was estimated that 70 percent of convicts were assigned to private capital in 1826–8 in Enclosure No. 50, Darling to Goderich, 11 June 1830, HRA, Series I, XVI, p. 270.

[33] Fitzpatrick (1971, p. 230), wrote: "One hundred and one grants were made or confirmed by Darling in 1828, aggregating more than 150,000 acres. Ten of them averaged 67 acres, another eight, 354 acres. The remaining 83 averaged nearly 2000 acres per grant. The small-holder was vanishing from the colonial scene."

Table 3.3: *Convicts transported to Australia, 1812–30*

Year of ship's arrival	From Great Britain		From Ireland	
	Male	Female	Male	Female
1812	400	126	—	—
1813	401	—	147	54
1814	706	239	219	98
1815	700	110	214	69
1816	732	102	370	84
1817	1,501	103	320	89
1818	2,333	227	689	101
1819	1,864	—	842	—
1820	3,003	268	640	78
1821	2,083	103	484	80
1822	1,461	108	852	—
1823	1,579	222	837	97
1824	1,368	90	320	109
1825	1,342	390	905	113
1826	1,162	100	902	100
1827	2,225	562	745	161
1828	2,625	271	755	274
1829	2,942	501	1,177	177
1830	4,036	363	698	319

Source: Data are from Shaw (1966, pp. 365–6).

encouraged large landholders with grants in proportion to capital up to the 2,560 maximum acreage, with an option to buy or rent adjacent Crown land (Jeans 1966, p. 206).

In response to the graziers' needs for fresh pastures, the lands outside the Cumberland Plain were officially opened in 1820 (Perry 1963, p. 33). State policy accelerated this extension of the wool-growing frontier. Between 1822 and 1828, the 600,000 acres of land grants made in 1788–1821 increased fourfold, with several hundred square miles actually sold (Fitzpatrick 1971, p. 299). Table 3.4 shows this expansion.

The enormous growth of the frontier beyond the Cumberland Plain included within it large sheep runs, smaller cattle runs, and a mixed-farming region in the Hunter Valley (Perry 1963, p. 123). Nevertheless, in spite of this heterogeneity, overall the large sheep-grazing pastoralist predominated. In 1828, 40 percent of land-

Table 3.4: *Distribution of alienated land, 1821–8*

	1821		1825		1828	
	Acres	%	Acres	%	Acres	%
Cumberland Plain	378,308	99.2	595,543	74.5	435,550	15.8
Outside Cumberland Plain	3,158	0.8	198,124	25.5	2,331,383	84.2
Totals (New South Wales)	381,466	100.0	773,667	100.0	2,776,933	100.0

Source: Perry (1963, p. 131)

owners owned more than 2,000 acres; their total holdings consti-
tuting 76.7 percent of the acres held and 68 percent of the sheep.[34]

In summary, the policy shift in the 1820s toward encouraging
large landholding with assigned labor aided the development of an
increasingly coherent pastoralist class. As the frontier expanded and
more finances were needed, the exclusivist pastoralists established
their own Bank of Australia in 1826 (Bergman 1964, p. 414). As
a competitor of the Bank of New South Wales (1817), this new
"merino" bank symbolized a further attempt by the exclusivist graziers to permanently differentiate themselves from emancipist merchants and financiers. They based their aristocratic pretensions on
their near-monopoly of large landholdings (a consequence of land-
grant patronage) as well as their political leadership through exclusive representation in the newly created Legislative Council.[35]

CONCLUSION

This chapter explored the politicoeconomic forces involved in the
consolidation of the colonial wool-growing industry. Of course, the
early development of pastoralism depended on the enterprise of the

[34] Figures are based on 1828 census data (unamended) for Hunter Valley, western
districts, and southwestern districts (including Illawarra) in Perry (1963, pp. 137–
45).
[35] In 1817, there were only three emancipists (Samuel Terry, D'Arcy Wentworth,
and William Redfern) in the top twenty land users (by area occupied for grazing);
in 1828, the same proportion applied, but with John Grant substituting for emancipist Wentworth. See the national hierarchies of land users in 1818 and 1828
constructed by Denholm (1972, pp. 369–72).

pioneers. Their resources (both financial and social) were essential to their success in the following:

1. Sustaining contact with London agents for technical and marketing advice. This allowed them to produce wools to match the changing needs of woolen manufacture and to compete successfully with, and displace, European competitors.
2. Maintaining their enterprise over the long turnover time of their pastoral capital.
3. Gaining a political presence in the colony to obtain state assistance through land policy and the assignment of convict labor.

Pastoralists benefited from a growing interest by the imperial state in promoting a neomercantilist solution to its own social problems – that is, exporting surplus population in exchange for wool imports.

Whereas fine-wool growing anchored the colonial pastoral industry, the development of colonial merchant capital helped to spread the industry. Not only did merchants become the colonial intermediaries of the London market, but also their entry into the wool trade reduced the turnover time of pastoral capital (through local sales and credit operations). This encouraged the proliferation of smaller, specialized pastoralists, thus preparing the ground for the 1830s "squatting rush" – the subject of the following chapters.

Part II

THE SQUATTING PHASE OF PASTORALISM (1830S AND 1840S)

4

SQUATTING AND COLONIAL POLITICS

INTRODUCTION

During the 1830s, extensive squatting on the frontier and increased profits in the wool trade transformed colonial social organization and politics. The success of colonial wool in the world market consolidated a pastoral economy, contradicting the reformed imperial policy toward colonial development. Although in 1831 the Colonial Office had instituted reforms for "systematic colonization," wholly *unsystematic* occupation of Crown lands beyond official boundaries followed. A paradox emerged: A mercantilist relationship with the imperial economy strengthened with the burgeoning wool trade, whereas politically antimercantilist forces developed in both the colony and the imperial state. In the latter, the growing problem of unemployed labor necessitated a reconceptualization of the settler colony as a host to free, rather than convict, labor. This was the source of the so-called positive theory of empire, which anticipated self-government. It was also consistent with the liberal reform currents within Britain, as commercial and manufacturing classes challenged the monopoly of political power in the hands of the landed classes.

Within colonial Australia political transition combined two movements. On the one hand, emancipists solidified democratic opposition to the patriarchal structure of the colonial state, in which the exclusive pastoral gentry aspired to aristocratic rule through their privileged relationship to the governor. On the other hand, the impact of squatting, in conjunction with the cessation of convict labor at the end of the 1830s, undermined the social organization of a colonial aristocracy. As the landed economy shifted to extensive squatting and the Colonial Office encouraged middle-class emigrés and a free labor force to replace convict labor, the props of the landed aristocracy disappeared.

Nevertheless, these changes did not quickly end the neomercantilist conceptions of the large wool growers. By combining squatting with their landowning, they attempted in the 1840s to forge a domestic political alliance to support their appeals to Britain to retain Australia as a wool-growing periphery. Although they were successful economically, it was at a political cost within colonial society from the late 1840s on. This chapter addresses the transformations that eventually weakened the social legitimacy of pastoralism as the center of the colonial economy.

ORIGINS OF THE MERCANTILIST–LIBERAL SOCIAL DIVISION

As suggested in Chapter 2, settling the exconvict population as small landholders released forces of social differentiation that contradicted the penal nature of the colony. These social relations assumed two forms: (1) the establishment of capitalist production relations, which provided an entrepreneurial dynamic to colonial society; and (2) a social antagonism between emancipists and free settlers, centered around access to civil privileges. Governor Macquarie's encouragement of emancipist enterprise first articulated this antagonism, which developed as emancipist entrepreneurs asserted their civil rights.

The latter phenomenon drew attention to the character of the colonial state. Until the 1820s, the governor was the sole executive and legislative authority in the colony. It was a government founded on overt military power, backed by a system of magistrates who dispensed the law in the various localities.[1] Originally composed of civil and military officers, the magistracy extended as the settlement expanded, devolving increasingly upon men of capital, such as merchants, and, in the outlying regions, the large landowning gentry. Necessarily, as the settlement expanded and assigned convict labor

---

[1] Governor Darling wrote to Huskisson: "I am importuned incessantly to form Benches of Magistrates in the remote and newly settled parts of the Country, the Settlers and Magistrates declaring the measure indispensable to the preservation of their property" (letter, 24 March 1828, *HRA*, Series I, XIV, p. 38). For a discussion of the metropolitan source of this system, see Anderson (1965).

was dispersed, the local magistrates coordinated convict discipline with their supervision of local markets and resolution of land disputes among the settlers. The administration of justice was arbitrary, depending on individual magistrates whose powers were "large and almost irresponsible, as far as related to . . . rule over the convict population" (Therry 1863). The magistracy not only exercised effective coercion in a society with bonded labor and few civil traditions, but it also was part of the nexus of patronage through which the governor secured informal private support. After Macquarie, emancipists were denied appointment to the magistracy, just as they were by and large excluded from obtaining land grants. Consequently, whereas the state and the exclusive graziers meshed in this patronage system, emancipists became the irritant.

The conflict between emancipists and exclusivists became a struggle to reform the administration of the colony, with the emancipists demanding civil rights. However, the struggle must also be seen as a growing claim by emancipist capital for equivalent access to political power, given its contribution to the economy. At first, this claim was secondary to the general demands for legal equality that began in the early 1820s.

Although emancipists were the first consequential social minority in colonial reform politics, they were not the only claimants. There were recommendations to liberalize the legal system and reduce the military character of the state as early as 1812. In 1819, when Alexander Riley (magistrate and landholding merchant) appeared before a House of Commons inquiry into colonial administration, he argued that constitutional reform and trial by jury would attract immigrants and traders to the colony (Melbourne 1963, pp. 50, 54). In fact, he represented commercial interests that were increasingly frustrated with the limitations of an autocratic state. As an expression of this discontent, in 1819 some 1,260 free settlers forwarded a petition to the House of Commons, stating that there was "a great number of free respectable inhabitants, sufficient and perfectly competent for jurymen, by whose property, exertions and labour the country had been cleared and cultivated, towns built, and a thriving colony . . . reared up and established" (quoted in Melbourne 1963, p. 62). They demanded not only trial by jury, but also measures to liberalize trade and shipping regulations, taxation laws, and so forth. The Imperial Parliament, in the process of instituting economic reforms, resisted granting trial by jury; the colonial secretary considered that the principle of peer trial was not feasible in a penal culture (Melbourne 1963, p. 43).

A civil court system was not firmly established with the principle of trial by jury, and the emancipist population remained second-class citizens. This status became the focus of the emancipist movement, which included some free settlers. William Wentworth, the spokesman for the emancipists, laid out their political program in his book, *Statistical Account of the British Settlements in Australia* (1820), which became the basis for the Whig opposition in the Imperial Parliament, where general colonial reform was under consideration (Schuyler 1945, p. 98). Indeed, in 1821, the emancipists sent a petition for reform to London. Arguing the preponderance of their aggregate wealth and therefore their significant economic contribution to the colony, they requested complete restoration of their civil rights (Melbourne 1963, pp. 72–3).

The reforms demanded at this stage from both free settlers and emancipists did not include a representative legislature of any kind. The exclusives thought constitutional change would threaten the patronage system, which they sought to formalize by establishing an advisory council of their members. Meanwhile, emancipists were primarily concerned with civil rights, with trial by jury being basic to such rights, particularly the right to possess and convey property (Melbourne 1963, p. 90). Such were the positions of each social group throughout the 1820s.

During this period, the Imperial Parliament instituted reforms as it saw fit to accommodate the colonial social hierarchy. The British Parliamentary Act of 1823 established a Legislative Council and a Supreme Court with limited, or discretionary, trial-by-jury powers (Melbourne 1963, pp. 99–100). This act marked the beginning of British parliamentary involvement in colonial legislation, establishing the legality of the governor's continuing executive supremacy. Not only would he consult with an Executive Council of high-ranking officials, but also his legislation obtained *legal* continuity through the creation of a Legislative Council of half a dozen or so nominated members. Although the size of the Legislative Council was increased to a maximum of fifteen nominated members in 1828, its function as a legislative forum was not essentially altered, except that it could veto the governor's intended legislation (Melbourne 1963, p. 154). The 1828 act also granted the optional use of juries in civil cases.

The reforms of the 1820s rationalized, rather than liberalized, the colonial regime. Exposing the governor's legislative procedures to limited public scrutiny lowered his executive profile and provided some checks on his authority. In spite of concessions allowing wealthy settlers an advisory role, the British state retained its authority in those areas that vitally concerned the creation of a colonial periphery – namely, the disposal of land and convict labor (Melbourne 1963, p. 168). The colonial state continued to be an autocratic regime under imperial authority. Although the council did include settlers, the governor nominated them, notably from the exclusivist faction. In other words, the British state maintained a mercantilist political structure that served the imperial division of labor (premised on transported labor).

Within the colony, this political structure obtained legitimacy through a mercantilist ideology, representing pastoral capitalists (with state support) as the nucleus of a productive peripheral society geared to metropolitan needs. John Macarthur affirmed this ideology in the following proposal to the Bigge Commission in 1820:

If His Majesty's Government propose to retain this colony, as a dependency of Great Britain, there is no time to be lost in establishing a body of really respectable settlers – men of real Capital – not merely adventurers. They should have Estates of at least 10,000 acres, with reserves antiguous of equal extent – such a body of Proprietors would in a few years become wealthy, and with the support of the Government powerful as an Aristocracy. – The democratic multitude would look upon their large possessions with Envy, and upon the Proprietors with hatred – as this democratic feeling had already taken deep root in the Colony, in consequence of the absurd and mischievous policy, pursued by Governor *Macquarie* – and as there is already a strong combination amongst that class of persons, it cannot be too soon opposed with vigour. – If forty or fifty proprietors, such as I have described, were settled in the Country, they would soon discover that there could be no secure enjoyment of their Estates but from the protection of Government. As the population increases, the aristocratic body should be augmented: and as fine woolled sheep will increase, in a few years, with surprising rapidity, the New Settlers, with Capital, would find no difficulty to stock their Estates. They – i.e., the new aristocracy – would maintain a large body of domestic Servants and labourers: and from their numerous flocks supply Great Britain, so abundantly with Wool of the finest quality that the price must considerably diminish. – This point once attained what nation would export a yard of fine cloth at the price the English Manufacturer could produce it aided as he would be by cheap wool, machinery, capital and skill. – In return for the Wool exported from hence British Manufactures to an immense amount would be consumed in the Colony, and as the carcase of the sheep will be of no value off the Estate in which it is produced the Proprietors would be desirous to take as many convicts as possible. These men would produce Bread for themselves and their surplus labour would be directed to clearing, fencing, and draining, so that every year the estates would become capable of supporting more sheep and the proprietors in circumstances to provide for more Labourers to carry on his improvements. Surely these are points entitled to the most serious attention of Government – they present the double advantage of giving Great Britain the most extensive monopoly that any Nation ever enjoyed and that upon the most unexceptionable principles namely supplying other people cheaper than they can be supplied elsewhere, and there is a certainty of an increasing demand for the labour of any number of convicts or paupers Great Britain and Ireland may send forth.[2]

Such an ideology expressed, at one level, the gentry's political self-conceptions formed during the 1820s when all immigrant labor was bonded and the imperial state sanctioned landed estates. At another level, the mercantilist vision of a wool-growing periphery was prophetic. However, history would prove it to be anachronistic. The British consolidation of a primary-producing periphery was, in the nineteenth century, also a step toward the elaboration of a liberal world-economic regime as British industrial capitalism matured. In the settlement colonies especially, the aristocracy would be challenged by British state policy as well as by emigrés seeking a liberal social and economic environment. Whereas wool growing would continue to dominate the colonial economy, it would also exacerbate nascent social currents opposed to the exclusivist aristocratic vision and supporting a broader, more liberal conception of colonial development. Stemming from the transformations of the 1830s, these new social forces in both town (urban workers, craftsmen, professionals, and merchants) and country (leaseholding squatters and small farmers) eventually challenged those who upheld a mercantilist vision.

REFORM IN BRITISH COLONIAL POLICY

The 1831 Ripon Regulations sought to reverse colonial landholding patterns by abolishing the land grant system. The system

---

[2] *Macarthur Papers*, Vol. 1, pp. 64–7 (ML A2897).

nourished political patronage and encouraged landed oligarchy to the detriment of a productive rural economy in the colonies.[3] Furthermore, landholding was highly differentiated, often speculative, and therefore dispersed.[4] The imposition of land sales, in the view of imperial authorities, would concentrate land settlement and, as a consequence, agriculture.[5] At the same time, the authorities wanted to initiate a uniform pattern of settlement by cultivators throughout the Empire. In Australia, in particular, they expected such rationalization of settlement to reduce imperial expense. In fact, the Ripon Regulations did initiate the kind of colonial land policy that Wakefield and the systematic colonizers advocated in this period as a deliberate step toward self-government.[6] Colonial self-sufficiency required a domestic market, which would emerge from an internally consistent division of labor. The solution was to guarantee a wage labor force by pricing land, and thus "to prevent labourers from turning into landowners too soon." Regular land sales would, in turn, concentrate settlement.[7]

The motives behind this imperial social engineering go beyond

---

[3] For a discussion of this in relation to North America, see Teeple (1972).
[4] For example, Sir George Murray wrote to Governor Darling: "The practice however of Individuals accumulating large Tracts of Country in their possession appears already to have led to very serious evils, and is, of itself, one which weighs most heavily on the Colony from so many Proprietors, who have been admitted to that indulgence, having allowed large portions of their Grants to remain in the same uncultivated state as when they received them" (Enclosure No. 89, 25 October 1830, *HRA*, Series I, XV, p. 803).
[5] Secretary of State Goderich wrote (*HRA*, Series I, XVI, p. 21):

What is now required is to check this extreme facility (land-granting) and to encourage the formation of a class of labourers for hire, as the only means of creating a market for the agricultural produce of the colony, of effecting various improvements, and of prosecuting the many branches of industry which are now neglected, while, at the same time, by enabling the agriculturalist to apply the great principle of the division of labour, his produce will be increased and afforded at a more reasonable rate.

[6] See, for example, Burroughs (1967), Mills (1974), Roberts (1968), and Morrell (1966). For a critical discussion of the notion of a direct link, see Philipp (1960), Burroughs (1965).
[7] Wakefield wrote:

The division of employments ... increases the produce of industry. But it can never take place without combination of labour. Combination of labour is a condition of all the improvements of industry ... The principle of combination of labour ... seems in old countries like a natural property of labour. But in colonies the case is totally different. There, the difficulty of inducing a number of people to combine their labour for any purpose, meets the capitalist in every step of his endeavours, and in every line of industry. [quote from "The Art of Colonization," in Pritchard 1968, p. 847]

the rationalization of either colonial land tenure systems or colonial administration. They arose from the growing policy need to co-ordinate colonial development with trends in the social transformation of Britain during the Industrial Revolution. This need was both material and ideological. In material terms, there was the social pressure of a growing mass of people displaced by the uneven development of a market society. Agriculture was persistently depressed following the war, with deteriorating conditions for tenant farming. At the same time, land enclosures, which lasted until mid-century, consolidated tenant farms into estates and eliminated cottagers' customary rights to the common lands.[8] On top of this, rural outworkers forfeited their looms and livelihood as they lost to the competition of machine production (Thompson 1968, ch. 9). Finally, the survival of the Speenhamland System until 1834 bound the dispossessed to local parishes under the "right to live" principle, thereby fostering "pauperization" (see Polanyi 1957, ch. 7; Hobsbawm and Rude 1968, p. 220). The social unrest generated by these dislocations led to parliamentary concern with emigration in the 1820s (see Mills 1974, ch. 2). This was the decade in which emigration schemes to Canadian and South African colonies amounted to what Wakefield would later call "shovelling out paupers" (Pritchard 1968, p. 381). The Australian equivalent was an acceleration of transportation in the 1820s, and then in 1832 a scheme to assist poor immigrants organized by the Land and Emigration Commission and established within the framework of the Ripon Regulations (Sherington 1980, pp. 36–8).

Meanwhile, because of depressed prices, English landowners exacted more rents from tenant farmers, and Scottish graziers engrossed tenant farms.[9] Wakefield drew attention to the high turnover of tenant farmers in his 1833 discussion of the "uneasiness of the middle class": "there are very many farms which have ruined two or three tenants since 1815. No one pretends that the rent of farming is lower . . . at this time rents are, by some, supposed to be the cause, or at least one cause of agricultural distress" (quoted in Prit-

---

[8] See Saville (1969), Lazonick (1974), Dovring (1966), Thompson (1963), Thompson (1968), and Hobsbawm and Rude (1968).
[9] Thompson (1963, p. 220) details rent increases during the period 1790–1829 as ranging between 20–30 percent and 300 percent on farms and 50 percent and 175 percent on estates.

chard 1968, p. 357). These yeomen of the rural economy were precisely the new middle-class element in the colonization schemes designed to establish capitalist agriculture in the empire of settlement.

From the early days the Colonial Office expected that colonial rural economy would replicate the trends of English estates, which used mixed farming as an integrated method of agriculture. Commercially productive landlords combined crop rotation (allowing fodder cropping) with animal husbandry to supply food to growing, and protected, urban markets. In Australia, Governor King tried to encourage mixed farming in the early 1800s, after the colony had a stable livestock herd and sufficient farmers with capital. This did not last, however, because sheep-breeding goals differed in the two countries. As English wool deteriorated with the altered pastures of the mixed farmer, colonial pastoralists specialized in wool-bearing sheep for the British wool trade, given the colony's limited internal market, labor scarcity, and seemingly boundless natural pasture. Agriculture and pastoralism separated into distinct productive and social spheres, the former lagging behind the latter in productivity.[10] Governor Macquarie deplored the lack of agricultural skills and practice in colonial Australia in his critical report on colonial graziers, implying a social parasitism in their enterprise.[11] The imperial authorities contrasted the "wild and uncultivated state of grazing land" with the potential improving occupancy of land "by an industrious and thriving population" in 1826.[12]

The ideological undercurrents in these critical observations of the colonial landed economy expressed a political groundswell against powerful landed classes in settlement colonies as well as in Britain. The struggle turned on the commercially monopolistic practices of wealthy landholders, who used their social and political power to restrain the development of capitalist markets. In Britain the anti-Corn Law struggle challenged landlord protectionism, which raised

---

[10] Noting the absence of skilled colonial farmers who combined fodder cropping and the fertilization of cultivated lands, contemporary Atkinson (1826) wrote: "it may be safely stated that folding fatting sheep upon green crops would be the greatest improvement that could be introduced into the agriculture of New South Wales … many proprietors are of the opinion that it is injurious both to the sheep and their fleeces to fold them upon cultivated lands."

[11] See Governor Macquarie's (1814) comments on colonial grazing in comparison with British farming patterns in *HRA* Series I, VIII, p. 303.

[12] Additional Royal Instructions to Darling, 26 August 1826, *HRA*, Series I, XII, pp. 502–3.

corn prices and therefore wage costs of the emerging manufacturing sector. The Anti-Corn Law League argued that the costs to British commerce affected social prosperity. Laissez-faire policy required the circumscription of landed power in the economy. In the 1830s, such political currents resulted in parliamentary reforms, spear-headed by the Whigs, some of whom were aristocrats with family connections among City merchants and provincial industrialists. These reforms advanced bourgeois interests as they diverted working-class unrest.[13]

Opposition to a landed monopoly found its way into colonial land regulations via the Colonial Office, which was influenced by the arguments of classical political economists for colonization as a liberal extension of British economy. Some notions concerning the extension of British social arrangements into the colonies came from the colonial reformers, led by Wakefield (see Mills 1974, ch. 7; Morrell 1966, pp. 6–14). They performed the historic role of translating classical political economy into practical colonization schemes (Robbins 1958, p. 144). Although classical theory posited colonization as a logical remedy for declining profits (Smith), overpopulation (Wilmot-Horton, Torrens), or scarce land (Ricardo), its success required that mercantilist political structures be dismantled. In particular, protectionism and imperial preference systems fettered free trade, thus contributing to the misallocation of imperial resources and unnecessary administrative expense.[14] In addition, the reformers opposed the expense and militarism of the traditional colonial system, including its oligarchical forms of colonial government. Their reformulations of systematic colonial settlement proposed less hierarchical and fluid social structures, favorable to liberal capitalist development. Wakefield identified the absence of landed property (and, therefore, an open frontier) in the colonies as the cause of settlement dispersion, which limited an adequate division of labor upon which to found a viable society (see footnote 7). From this followed his proposition of regulating the supply of land by pricing it, which in turn would guarantee an agricultural labor force.

[13] See, for example, Anderson (1965), Thompson (1968, ch. 16), and Moore (1968, p. 33).
[14] See Schuyler (1945, pp. 50–78), Shaw (1970), and Winch (1965). Australia, incidentally, was not considered commercially significant at this time to require the imposition of British preference. See LaNauze (1948).

The practical consequence of land sales, which had the blessing of the British government because it resolved the problem of imperial expenses, was that the revenue would finance working-class emigration. At the same time, and of great significance to the colonial reformers, the colonization scheme was a civilizing plan designed to attract middle-class emigrés, especially farmers who were experiencing social decline in Britain. The planners expected to stabilize the colonial social structure, thus ending the arbitrary practice of simply shoveling out paupers. In this way settlement colonies would become an agricultural periphery complementing metropolitan needs, while evolving into self-governing societies in the British political mold. This was the context in which imperial policy projected the themes of "informal empire" into its relations with settlement colonies such as Australia. Nevertheless, this dismantling of the formal infrastructure of the old mercantilist colonial system was at cross-purposes with the impact of the world market in the colonial political economy.

COLONIAL SOCIETY IN THE 1830s

"Squatting," initially referring to the illegal occupations of Crown land by landless men of ill fame ("bush harpies") who preyed on others' livestock (Roberts 1970, p. 58), achieved social legitimacy as landowning graziers advanced their flocks into the unsettled districts en masse.[15] Responding to land pricing and the constant need for open pasture, the squatters overrode the Colonial Office's attempt to confine settlement within official boundaries.

Who were the squatters? Basically, the graziers involved in squatting were new emigrés, sometimes representing companies floated in Britain (significant in the Port Phillip region), landholders from the settled districts (that is, the colonial gentry), and overseers for absentee flockowners from urban centers. Many emigré squatters considered their venture to be temporary, expecting the profits to restore or enhance their social status at home. Thus, John Robertson observed of Port Phillip squatters in the 1840s (from McBride 1898, pp. 24–5):

---

[15] This was itself an extension of prior land use patterns practiced by landholding graziers in the 1820s within the so-called settled districts.

Numbers of the young gentlemen who came out to this colony about that time, with a few hundred pounds, took up runs with 300, 400 and 500 sheep, clubbed together, and expected to make fortunes in a few years, from the way they spoke, and the way in which they managed their sheep farms.

With respect to the social origins of the squatters, Governor Gipps was at pains to distinguish them from "those who bear the same name in America, and who are generally persons of mean repute and of small means, who have taken unauthorised possession of patches of land." He went on to establish their credentials:

Among the Squatters of New South Wales are the wealthiest of the Land, occupying with the permission of Government thousands and tens of thousands of acres; Young men of good Family and connexions in England, Officers of the Army and Navy, Graduates of Oxford and Cambridge are also in no small number amongst them.[16]

Apart from established stock, many emigré squatters were from the hard-pressed landed and mercantile classes in Britain following the European war and economic crisis (Collier 1911, p. 72; MacMillan 1967, pp. 298, 369). There were also squatters from other classes, as Crown Lands Commissioner Captain Fyans's three-fold classification of Port Phillip squatters suggests (from McBride 1898, pp. 119–21, emphasis added):

The squatting population consists of such various classes of persons that is impossible to speak of it as a body. Many of the squatters are *gentlemen*, worthy and excellent men, of undoubted character and well connected at home ... Another class of squatters is a kind of *shop-boys* ... Another class consists of old *shepherds*. I have known this class to grow rich, the master poor, and in time the worthy would become the licensed squatter.

The social differentiation among squatters was sharp. In the early period of settlement of the squatting frontier, the line was well drawn between *genteel* and *common* origins, as evidenced by the exclusiveness of tavern accommodation to the former (Billis and Kenyon 1930, p. 83).

The squatting movement wrought considerable change in the colonial social structure; it affected the balance of political forces and reformulated conceptions of colonial development. Squatting diluted the clear social hierarchy dominated by the pastoral gentry.

[16] Gipps to Russell, Despatch No. 192, 19 December 1840, *HRA*, Series I, XXI, p. 130.

At the same time it undermined the tidy quantitative relation between labor (emigration) and land (emigration funds) envisaged by the Colonial Office. Continual labor shortages on the frontier revealed the rigidity of this scheme.[17] During the 1830s assigned labor filled this gap, but with the abolition of convict transportation in 1840, wool growers confronted an intransigent Colonial Office. Reduced land sales during the early 1840s depression exacerbated the labor shortage, which was unrelieved by the growers' resort to temporary contract and coolie labor schemes. These events necessarily focused attention on the labor supply system and, eventually, on the political control of the colonial state. Although this is running ahead, it does relate to why the exclusivists conceded to the transformation of social relations in the colony and reformulated their goals in interest rather than moral terms.[18]

The first major setback to the exclusivist gentry was Governor Bourke's rationalization of land occupation procedures. The gentry saw squatters as usurpers of their established system of landowning. Specifically, squatters threatened land values and weakened the labor emigration scheme because they did not generate land revenue (Buckley 1957, pp. 92–3; Roe 1965, ch. 2, 3). Having tried the vigilante method against convict squatters ("stock raiders"), the exclusivists attempted to use their status as magistrates to regulate squatting (Roberts 1970, ch. 4). Bourke short-circuited their position by establishing a Crown Land Commission to regulate squatting through a licensing system. During the 1830s this new public bureaucracy was not totally effective in replacing the gentry's power. This was partly a problem of distance, because abuses in frontier regions were hard to control, and partly because licensing often relied on the magistracy (Roberts 1970, p. 132). As Roger Therry (1863) observed: "A certificate of character from the nearest magistrate, and of the *bona fide* purpose of the applicant to maintain stock, was required to be produced before a commissioner of Crown Lands."

Bourke nevertheless managed to blunt the monopolistic pretensions of the landowning gentry by legally sanctioning squatting. He established a bureaucratic method of assigning and disciplining

[17] See Morrell (1966, p. 87) and the squatters' statements on labor scarcity in Chapter 7.
[18] This point is made also by Connell and Irving (1980, ch. 2). I acknowledge their emphasis of it in "A Reply ...," *Intervention* 16 (1982): 34.

convicts to replace the patronage system, thus guaranteeing squatter access to convict labor (Roberts 1970, p. 18; Therry 1863).[19] Although Bourke thereby legalized squatting, which contradicted imperial designs for land settlement, he upheld the ideological principles of imperial policy. The license system fulfilled the imperial desire to reserve the land for "respectable occupation" against occupation by a potential working class (Roberts 1970, p. 84), and it restrained colonial oligarchy.[20] Bourke's actions were an acceptable mediation of imperial policy, since distance compelled a certain autonomy of government practice.[21] It was certainly pragmatic to sanction squatting for commercial reasons and to save the expense of trying to restrain it.[22] Bourke's approach to squatting, in fact, symbolized his

---

[19] Governor Bourke's new act of council concerning convicts "defined the law: it abolished the administration of justice in the private houses of magistrates: it established petty sessions, whose proceedings were open to public observation: it encouraged the convict to an amended course of life, by passing a law enacted for his protection as well as his punishment and it restricted the excessive and capricious use of the lash" (Therry 1863). Indeed, Bourke's pragmatic liberalism included a desire to bring the convict labor system – so much a part of the landed economy – to an end gradually. Thus, he wrote to Lord Stanley (from Enclosure No. 1, 15 January 1834, HRA, Series I, XVII, p. 314):

Regarding however the advancement and prosperity of this Colony as now placed on foundations, which cannot be shaken, I am strongly impressed with the belief that the manner and morals of the People would be much improved, and ultimately their wealth and happiness would be much augmented by a gradual relinquishment of the Services of Convicts. Yet I am well aware that this sentiment is not generally prevalent among the Settlers.

[20] The licensing system was, incidentally, also instituted "to prevent pauper free or freed men from squatting" and was supported by the establishment of a border police force (quote from John Jamison in Buckley 1957, p. 86).
[21] Colonial governors applied their own theories of government, sometimes rather eccentric ones, and they were too far away and too much the source of all the official information reaching England to make effective supervision of their actions or policies possible (Manning 1965, p. 89). See also Cell (1970, pp. 45–6).
[22] Thus, Bourke wrote in a dispatch to the secretary of state:

The proprietors, settlers, and owners of thousands of acres of land soon find, from the increase of their flocks and herds, that it becomes necessary to send their stock beyond the boundaries of location, and to form what is termed "new stations": otherwise, the only alternative left to them would be either to restrain the increase of their stock, or find artificial food for it. The first of these courses would be a great falling off in the supply of wool: and as to the artificial food, from the uncertainty of the seasons and the light character of the soil, it would be found quite impracticable. Besides, either course would seem to be the rejection of the bounty of Providence, that spreads, with a prodigal hand, its magnificent carpet of bright green sward over the boundless plains, and clothes the depths of the valleys with abundant grass. Moreover, the restraint on dispersion would entail an expense in the management which could not profitably repay the Government. [quoted in Therry 1863, p. 131.]

opposition to privilege in colonial society, in particular his aversion to the exclusive clique whose dominance in the council frustrated his Whig conceptions of colonial government. He complained that "the evil of legislating for the whole community by means of a Council composed of one party exists at this moment in full force, and is only checked by the power possessed by the head of government to prevent the introduction of any bills but such as he approves" (quoted in Melbourne 1963, p. 174).

The antagonism was mutual; Bourke's regulation of squatting threatened the colonial political structure advocated by the gentry. His reforms threatened gentry power in the state, which resulted from previous Tory patronage in civil appointments (Roe 1965, p. 154). Squatting particularly undermined the idea of a landowning oligarchy. Although some of the gentry engaged in squatting, their economic and social base was in estate farming in the settled, freehold districts (see Chapter 6). Such estates, involving intensive mixed farming and often modeled on village communities with tenant farming, inverted the squatter pattern of extensive, specialized farming (Roe 1965, p. 48). The landed estates served as fattening ground for inland cattle en route to Sydney markets, and it is not unlikely that they also supplied provisions other than stock for their up-country squatting runs. This connection of squatting to landowning was the only acceptable form of squatting to the exclusivist pastoralists.[23] As they petitioned the British Parliament:

Let the energies of the Colony continue to flow in the course indicated by Providence, and in due time concentration will follow as a natural result. The riches gathered in the wilderness will be stored in the towns and villages. Successive races will go forth in quest of the wealth yielded by the fleece, and will return with their acquisitions to the resorts of social life. [Roe 1965, p. 51]

These antagonisms crystallized around the constitutional issues raised in the renewal of the Australian Government Act in 1836. The gentry saw Bourke as champion of the liberal cause; James Mudie (1837) (a landowning magistrate) characterized him as "the real darling of his convict faction and of the felonry." They favored

The Colonial Office, recognizing it as a phenomenon replicated in other British colonies and difficult to prevent, resigned itself to squatting and attempted to regulate it. See Burroughs (1967, pp. 152–3).
[23] This point is made by Roe (1965).

continued restrictions of emancipist civil rights as a precaution "indispensably necessary to guard the administration of justice from sinister and contaminating influence."[24] Furthermore, their exclusivism extended to the franchise issue, which was imminent. They were determined to hold the line against the taint of the convict.

> Your Petitioners would entreat your Honorable House to bear in mind that, from the facility of acquiring wealth in New South Wales by dishonest and disreputable practices, the possession of property affords but slight proof of good character ... if it be proposed to confer free institutions upon this community, property ought not to form the sole standard for the regulation of the elective and representative franchise.[25]

The formation of a liberal party in 1835, the Australian Patriotic Association (APA), to represent the emancipist and progressive opinion in the colony put the exclusivist faction on the defensive. The party gained Governor Bourke's tacit support, as he was committed to civilian juries and the emancipist vote. Nevertheless, although the APA publicly demanded a representative legislature "upon a wide and liberal basis,"[26] its leader Wentworth was by no means a leveler in the matter of franchise qualifications; property was an important component. The intensity of the struggle between exclusivist and emancipist interests thus concerned political representation in the Legislative Council. At this stage, demands were absent on both sides for responsible self-government and the disposal of Crown lands. The area of contention was the social character of the colonial state, with the gentry fighting a rearguard action against the forces of liberal capitalism.

The imperial authorities, supported by Bourke's pragmatic attitude toward this social infighting, postponed a decision until 1842; they simply renewed the 1828 act. Attention shifted from constitutional reform to the question of labor supply.[27] In particular, replacing convict transportation with the emigration of free labor on a wider scale appeared to be an appropriate way to relieve the British labor market and promote civil society in Australia. The

---

[24] Petition from Members of Council and others to House of Commons (Enclosure A2), *HRA*, Series I, XVIII, p. 396.
[25] *Ibid.*, p. 397.
[26] Petition from Free Inhabitants (Enclosure B), *HRA*, Series I, XVIII, p. 400.
[27] Melbourne (1963, p. 272) suggests that the delay in colonial constitutional reform in fact reflected the growing influence of the Wakefieldians in the House and their ability to switch attention to the issue of transportation.

British decision to abolish transportation was not simply an offshoot of the antislavery and reform ideology of the 1830s. It arose out of the combination of growing Wakefieldian influence within the Colonial Office and domestic social pressure.[28] Following the 1834 New Poor Law, the Whig government faced rising political expressions of the social distress among Britain's unemployed and laboring poor (for example, Chartism) and general alarm among the propertied classes. Relief would dovetail with boosting free immigration to colonial Australia.

The growing threat to abolish transportation was influential in dissolving the social division between exclusivists and emancipists. They now had a common interest – namely, preserving their pattern of accumulation by maintaining an adequate supply of labor. The imperial intention to switch from bond to wage labor was not a straightforward solution, given the difficulty of attracting wage labor to the squatting frontier. A substitution of this kind would not only incur greater operating expense, but also affect the immigration formula. This was clearly stated by the New South Wales Legislative Council's Committee on Immigration (1838): "The sudden discontinuance of transportation and assignment, by depriving the colonists of convict labor, must necessarily curtail their means of purchasing Crown lands, and consequently the supply of funds for the purpose of immigration."[29]

Under these circumstances, the potential political alliance between the gentry and pastoral representatives of the liberal forces marked the emergence of squatting as a material force in colonial politics. Because squatting involved the majority of wool growers (and their financiers) and tied their fortunes to assigned labor, British manipulation of the land–labour relation rankled the colonists. This metropolitan–colonial conflict of interest shaped the 1828 act, in which the imperial state retained power to administer land and, therefore, power to appropriate land revenue. The conflict materialized in 1834, when the British treasury suggested that expenses of penal administration could be financed from colonial land fund surpluses. To members of the Legislative Council, this rather broad interpretation of the land–labour relation represented a misappro-

---

[28] Ritchie (1976) suggests that decision making was related to the growing influence of the Wakefield lobby in the House. See also Mills (1974, ch. 10).
[29] *V&P, NSW*, 1838, Committee on Immigration, Report.

priation of emigration funds (Melbourne 1963, pp. 181–3).[30] Moreover, such practice threatened the long-term colonial capacities to finance immigrant labor, given the limited future of the transportation system.

The future of convict labor in Australia concerned not only the material interests of wool growers and wool traders, but also the social composition of the colony. Although some exclusivists recognized the inevitability of an economy based on wage labor,[31] the immediate labor scarcity produced demands for a continued supply of assigned labor and a need to forge an alliance with the emancipists to secure pastoral capital.

Conceding to civil and political rights for emancipists was one thing, but the mercantilist practice of assigning convict labor compromised British plans for promoting a liberal state. As Charles Buller, member of the House of Commons and the Molesworth Committee on Transportation, emphasized:

If the inhabitants of the colony insist on the supply of convict labour as the most essential of their privileges, I am sure that this country, were it inclined on other grounds to accede to that demand, would accompany that concession by declaring that the continuance of transportation is incompatible with the establishment of representative government. [quoted in Melbourne 1963, p. 228]

[30] In 1836 the exclusive faction petitioned Parliament (*HRA*, Series I, XVIII, p. 363):

Your Petitioners have observed, with unfeigned sorrow, the proposed application of a large proportion of the funds arising from the sale of Crown lands to other purposes than the encouragement of Emigration, notwithstanding the faith of the Government was virtually pledged that the revenue arising from this source should be exclusively devoted to that important subject: and your Petitioners would, with great deference, submit to Your Majesty that the expenditure of these funds in the introduction into the Colony of industrious and well-conducted families of the labouring classes presents the most obvious and powerful means of rescuing the Colony from its present state of moral debasement.

[31] For example, in 1835 Hannibal Macarthur, a premier grower, stated (*V&P*, *NSW*, 1835, Committee on Immigration, Minutes of Evidence, June 11, 1835):

By the present system of convict discipline, there is not a sufficient restraint upon these men, to prevent the indulgence of their vicious propensities. It is therefore desirable to obtain free men at liberal wages for all agricultural purposes, as the stoppage of wages for losses occasioned by neglect of duty operates as a better check on the free, than on the present convict discipline on the bond.

James Macarthur, of the same notable family, stated in 1837–8 that "free labour must be cheaper in the end than slave or forced labour" (quoted in Fitzpatrick 1969, p. 58).

These sentiments echoed within the colony among urban workers who opposed transportation because it undercut their market interests (Melbourne 1963, p. 230; Fletcher 1976a, pp. 140–1). Such opposition marked the emergence of an articulate urban radicalism, which distinguished itself increasingly from the popular posturing of wealthy emancipists involved in the staple industry (Irving 1963, pp. 20–1). This kind of political liberalism was the first step toward creating a representative state, even though its claims were limited to political rights for the propertied classes. It took more than a decade before an enlarged social base of nonpropertied classes demanding reforms carried the franchise to laborers (and, incidentally, an alternative to the conception of colonial Australia as a pastoral periphery gained legitimacy). In the meantime, the issue of representation converged with the growing crisis of control over the landed economy.

Colonial opposition to dismantling the transportation system was also a protest over the British government's method of handing down the decision. Pastoralists were increasingly frustrated with their powerlessness over the disposal of land and therefore the labor supply. [In fact, recognizing the vulnerability of the squatting system, Governor Bourke attempted to convince the Colonial Office to phase out the assignment of convict labor gradually (Ritchie 1976, p. 161).] When Governor Gipps (1839) proposed a taxation system to finance penal administration, the Legislative Council rejected the bill on the grounds that Britain should contribute to penal expenses, and also that the council was insufficiently representative to pass laws legislating taxation (Melbourne 1963, p. 185).[32] This was a turning point in colonial politics, where exclusivists began to compromise with the liberal position on representation.

The alliance of gentry and liberal (pastoral) interests became a united front demanding self-government as a Wakefieldian perspective in imperial policy strengthened. Paradoxically, the independence demands of the settlers rested on premises quite alien to the systematic colonizers, who for a brief period had considerable influence at the Colonial Office. The antiimperialism of the colonists was political only, because they comprised growers and financiers

---

[32] One other significant change was the abolition of military juries by Gipps in 1839, thus removing a source of contention for emancipists (Fletcher 1976a, p. 140).

involved in a staple-producing economy and sought to preserve a mercantilist form of colonial economic development.

The early demands of settlers for political independence from the imperial regulators, then, focused on Wakefieldian practice. The Colonial Office had raised land prices in New South Wales from 5*s*. (shillings) to 12*s*. per acre in 1838. It argued that prosperity justified higher land values, and these in turn would expand free immigration to compensate for the abolition of labor transportation (Burroughs 1965, p. 209). Then in 1842 the price rose again to £1 per acre in the midst of economic crisis. In 1839 there was strong colonial opposition to the imperial Land and Emigration Commission's proposal to dismember New South Wales (including squatting districts) into three territories and to price land in the southern and northern regions to encourage investment. Pastoralists considered this a thinly veiled threat to their central New South Wales squatting runs in the future, especially because these runs had been serviced with land revenues from the Port Phillip district, which would finance itself under the proposal.[33] In effect, the proposal threatened divisions between New South Wales and Port Phillip pastoralists.

The response of settlers to this proposal demonstrated the growing pastoral alliance against Britain's power over land administration. It also revealed the capitulation of the exclusivists to liberal ideology for the sake of a united front. As the *Australian* reported a public statement by James Macarthur:

> One particular reason why he feared the result of an evil consequence from the proposed division of the colony was that it might probably render the voice of its inhabitants less powerful in their divided state than they were in their present concentrated position and thus operate as a means of retarding the grants of free legislative institutions. [quoted in Melbourne 1963, p. 259]

Constitutional reform now shifted from being an issue of internal division to an issue between the pastoral alliance and the imperial

---

[33] Gipps communicated this fear to Lord Russell thus:

They are consequently greatly alarmed at the prospect which the system of selling land at a fixed Price, with an unrestrained right of selection, seems to open to them, of having the land of which they have been so long in possession, or the best portions of them . . . wrested from them by anyone who may be able to get before them to the Land Office.

[From Correspondence respecting the sale of Crown Lands at a Fixed Price, and the Division of the Territory into Three Districts, *V&P, NSW*, 10/5/42].

state (and its representative, the governor), especially concerning land administration. This shift was reinforced by the 1842 act granting colonial representative government. The colonial state legislature was now composed of an elected majority based on a property-owning electorate, including emancipists, and weighted in favor of country districts. The British government reserved powers of land administration, however (including its revenue – 50 percent of which was for emigration). Thus, the settler Legislative Council was hamstrung in precisely the policy that concerned its majority of large landowning members. This politicoeconomic contradiction dominated 1840s politics but at the same time transformed them again. Out of the pastoral alliance arose an emboldened faction of large landowning squatters. They attempted to maneuver in the political currents of the 1840s toward a hegemonic position within the colony and to obtain preemptive rights to the land they leased. This was a rearguard monopolistic action by a social group whose interests would be compromised with self-government. The extremity of their demands, in conjunction with the exposure of the limits of squatting in the colonial economy by the 1840s depression, precipitated an opposition, led by urban liberal interests, to the wool growers' monopoly of landed economy. This is the subject of Chapter 9. The intervening chapters are a theoretical analysis of the contradictions of pastoralism as a staple industry in this period.

CONCLUSION

The 1830s contained a double, and contradictory, challenge to the social pretensions of the pastoral gentry in colonial Australia. Each emanated from the imperial relationship and demonstrated the ambiguities of the construction of British hegemony. On the one hand, the Colonial Office, staffed increasingly with systematic colonizers, projected contemporary British liberal reformism. Translated into imperial policy, the reforms checked colonial landowning oligarchies by encouraging capitalist agriculture supported by emigration policies attached to land regulations. Self-sufficiency (and future self-government) and a site for surplus British labor were the objectives. As a corollary, in Australia, the withdrawal of gentry monopoly of assigned labor and then the abolition of labor transportation undermined the patriarchal economy of the gentry. Discarding their social exclusivism and conceding to the extension of citizenship, they cast their political lot with their squatting neighbors. This was their first conversion into alliance politics to preserve their economy. Because of their participation in squatting, the reformed framework of imperial administration had challenged their social foundations circuitously.

On the other hand, the profitability of squatting, the product of world market forces (the development of peripheral commodity production), invalidated the gentry's claim to the top of the social hierarchy by introducing new social groups into the colony. Again, joining with the squatters, the gentry invested their future in a pastoral alliance aimed at preserving the mercantilist privileges of colonial wool growing through state concessions. This move contained the elements of a revived oligarchism, resting on the legitimacy of squatting, but now devoid of the stable hierarchy that once supported the gentry. Squatting focused the neomercantilist character (and consequences) of colonial pastoralism. This became the object of a decisive challenge by an urban-based alliance committed to a liberal colonial economy and society – reflecting the midcentury ascendancy of political and economic liberalism established under British hegemony.

5

MERCHANTS AND GROWERS

The 1830s and 1840s in colonial Australia are commonly called the "squatting age," when colonial entrepreneurs "put everything into four legs." The resulting pastoral boom extended the land frontier rapidly, with squatters occupying seemingly boundless Crown land (beyond the official boundaries) for a minimal license fee. Wool exports increased from 1,967,309 pounds in 1830 to 41,426,655 pounds in 1850, accounting for almost 50 percent of Britain's wool supply (Coghlan 1969, vol. I, p. 276).

Traditional interpretations of this period of colonial development stress pastoralism as a successful staple industry and the reciprocal attraction to Australia of banking capital and labor. The image of the growing "Australian economy, hitched to a wool waggon" misconceives what was fundamentally a world-economic process, however (Fitzpatrick 1969, p. 33).[2] Colonial wool was grown as an

---

[1] I am indebted for the conceptual framework of this chapter to the work of Richard Garrett (1976).

[2] As with most accounts, however, the conditions of propulsion of the wool wagon are never specified beyond the positivist observation of expanding demand in the wool market. The notable exception is Barnard (1958), who traces the evolution of different patterns of capital inflow according to the particular patterns of wool marketing through the nineteenth century. It is remarkable that this work remains the sole study of the relationships involved in the wool trade and finance in the nineteenth century. Even more remarkable is the subsequent failure to elaborate Barnard's insight into the sources of finance that are appropriate to particular patterns of marketing. This would conceivably give a more comprehensive understanding of the structural impact of the wool industry on colonial economic development. Nevertheless, it is not surprising that Barnard's work has not been elaborated upon, because its implicit metropolitan-colonial framework has been minimized in the recent historiography of Australia. Barnard's study itself

industrial commodity, and hence the growth of pastoralism consolidated an imperial division of labor. The dominant agent of this relationship, London-based merchant capital, secured colonial wool as a raw material for the textile industry in Britain. By advancing commercial credit to producers in return for their wool clip, merchant-financiers sponsored the squatting expansion.

We saw in Chapter 3 that pioneer pastoralists had sufficient capital to sustain their operations during the time between shearing and the remittance of income from London wool sales, a delay that might last two years. The pioneer combined both productive and commercial functions in his enterprise. Alongside these individual concerns, a second form of pastoralism emerged by the 1830s, with the involvement of colonial merchants in the wool trade. They organized the commercial sphere, facilitating the entry of smaller specialized wool growers, who were able to realize the value of their wool clip when it reached Sydney, and thereby obtain financing for the next production cycle.

Although these two forms of wool marketing remained during the squatting age, a third, and predominant, form arose that reflected the entry of British capital en masse from the mid-1830s. Agents consigned wool to London and drew bills on London agents, making the London capital market the source of capital. This form comprised two processes. First, large growers such as Niel Black of Port Phillip initially consigned to their partners in London, who centralized the accounting operations of the pastoral enterprise. Second, mercantile agents in the colony consigned wool delivered to them as a condition of commercial advancing to growers. This latter system of factoring became the dominant form of consignment by the 1840s (Barnard 1958, p. 97). On a world-economic scale, though with local consequence, London merchant banking thus challenged colonial merchants.

The expansion of the factoring system (dependent as it was on a chain of credit from London) expressed the increasing integration of colonial production with the metropolitan economy. This intensification of the imperial division of labor converted colonial Aus-

---

has an essentially institutional focus – on empirical marketing patterns – rather than being an analysis of the origins of, and dynamic in, metropolitan-colonial exchange relations as an essential part of development of the capitalist world economy.

tralia into a consequential periphery of the capitalist world economy. At the same time, the social organization of wool growing as a staple industry set limits on the character of the settler economy.

IMPERIAL COMMERCE AND THE LONDON MONEY MARKET

Staple production in Australia depended on an expanding supply of commercial credit channeled from London to the colonial producer. The availability of commercial credit was a direct outcome of the development of British capitalism, which was expressed in the growing financial sophistication of the City of London as the hub of internal and external commerce. Specifically, the rising importance of the London discount market in the 1830s marked the institutionalization of merchant capital as *money-dealing capital* and a new stage in the development of commercial credit.[3]

The London discount market originated in the unification of a decentralized system of country banking as industrial regions sought transfers of funds from agricultural regions (Jenks 1973, p. 21). Given the Bank of England's legal monopoly of joint stock banking, thus prohibiting branch banking, these surplus transfers required intermediaries in London (where country bankers traditionally maintained balances with private bankers) (Cameron 1967, p. 20; King 1972, p. 7). The increased velocity of the circulation of commercial paper between London and the country banks, as industrial banks sought accommodation in excess of their London balances, encouraged the development of billbroking (Scammell 1968, p. 126). In turn, the bill broker dealt with London merchants. Bill brokers discounted their bills at London banks and thus covered any unequal demand and supply of bills in the country banking system. Bill brokers, who initially traded on commission, offered more favorable conditions than the Bank of England. The real consolidation of billbroking, however, came after the financial crisis of 1825, when London banks ended their practice of paying interest on the London deposits of the country banks, and also shifted their banking practices away from bill dealing toward maintaining greater liquidity in reserves (including Bank of England deposits). This prompted country banks to redirect their London deposits to the

---

[3] For a discussion of this specialization, see Marx (1966, vol. III, ch. XIX).

bill brokers at low call money rates (Cameron 1967, p. 31). Additionally, the previous practice of London banks of rediscounting bills at the Bank of England was transferred, by 1829, to the prominent bill brokers, who obtained the privilege of "discount accounts" or "final resort" facilities at the Bank (Scammell 1968, p. 133).

Thus, an organized discount market emerged by the 1830s, anchored by the Bank of England in its newly acquired responsibility as "effective public treasury of the United Kingdom" (Clapham 1945, vol. II, p. 132). The operating freedom of the bill market, epitomized in the exemption of short-dated bills from usury laws, was guaranteed by the bill brokers' rediscount facilities at the Bank. At the same time, the Bank of England became the ultimate source of commercial credit, and the bill merchants' activities shifted to bill *dealing* rather than bill *broking* – a distinction that expresses the consolidation of a discount market. This was the foundation of mercantile credit (i.e., money-dealing capital). Henceforth, foreign merchants drew indirectly on London facilities rather than relying on direct connections in London. Bill dealing thus universalized credit.

While the London discount market consolidated in the 1830s, British industrial capitalism emerged and the drive to expand world commerce intensified. The development of export markets beyond the traditional Empire markets in such regions as Southeast Asia, Australia, Brazil, Argentina, and the west coast of Africa depended on the encouragement of export staples in these regions (Mathias 1969, p. 245). The existing system of commercial advancing was the key to this expansion of peripheral commodity production. As the Standing Committee on the Law of Agents and Factors reported in 1823,

by far the greater part of our commerce is aided by advances at some period . . . and in many instances there is, first, an advance by the foreign shipper or consignor to the foreign proprietor, then an advance by the consignee [in Britain] to the consignor . . . and subsequently an advance by some capitalist to the factor [the British consignee, who was not the legal owner of the goods] in consequence of the difficulty of finding a ready and advantageous sale. [quoted in Clapham 1959, p. 256]

As the report indicated, the functions of merchant-trader and money lending were often combined and, indeed, merchant-bankers increasingly specialized in commercial advancing by discounting bills of exchange.[4] Dealing in commercial bills, they guaranteed the credit of the importer-consignee, speeding the turnover of commodities and expanding world commerce.[5] The nineteenth-century world division of labor thus developed around the discount market.

Mercantile promotion of staple commodity production through the agency of commercial credit was the mainspring of Australian wool growing from the 1830s. The consignment system encroached increasingly on the practice of local wool sales and became predominant in the wool trade by the 1860s. At this time, and indeed for half a century more, the major institutions in the foreign exchange market, and therefore in discounting bills in London, were the imperial banks.

BRITISH BANKING CAPITAL IN THE COLONIAL ECONOMY

The entry of British banking capital into the colonial economy en masse in the 1830s was attracted by, and indeed facilitated, the pastoral boom of the 1830s. The following advice from Van Dieman's Land merchant and banker Charles Swanston to an intending Scottish absentee investor describes contemporary investment opportunity.

Your ideas are just the same as those of all men who have never visited a colony just arising from the wilderness. You are anxious to build mills and make salt and to lay out money that will never bring you in any return. It is with these English ideas that too many emigrants and all companies yet formed have ruined themselves. In a young colony we must go step by step and not get into manhood before we can run on our legs. And when money can be otherwise more advantageously laid out as it can be here in land, in sheep and cattle, in bank shares, or lent on mortgages, mills and salt must be left to the miller and small capitalists who, by their personal labour and with few or no servants make their trades answer. Cultivation also, beyond cultivating for home consumption, does not pay the great landholder and lord of flocks. It suits the purpose of the small farmer and gives him a moderate income after paying his expenses. Wool is the great point to be attended to and the secondary object to the great landholder is the breed of cattle for market. But the breed of sheep and gradual improvement of the *fleece* is the source from whence ultimately a

[4] For a summary of the rise of the merchant-banker, see Landes (1969, ch. 1).
[5] As Clapham (1959, p. 261) writes: "They lent their names to importers and accepted bills drawn against consignments from abroad, so rendering the bills much more marketable and, by their knowledge of the parties concerned, facilitating and safeguarding the whole course of trade."

certain return can only be expected for any great outlay of capital. [quoted in Butlin 1968, p. 232]

In addition to private investment agents like Swanston, British capital entered the colonies through the contemporary joint stock company in the form of mortgage and trading companies, and predominantly through the three imperial banks established in the colonies at this time: Bank of Australasia (1834–1951), Union Bank (1837–1951), and Bank of South Australia (1836–92).

The appearance of the imperial bank in the colonial economy marked legislative changes in financial operations in both England and New South Wales. In England, in 1826 joint stock banking was authorized beyond a sixty-five-mile radius of London, following the failure of sixty banks in the financial crisis (Cameron 1967, p. 27). Amendment of the 1826 act in 1833, despite opposition from City financiers, permitted joint stock banking in London (though forbidding the issue of bank notes) (Powell 1966, p. 310; Cameron 1967, p. 29). The subsequent proliferation of joint stock banks (through deposit banking) reflected an increasing centralization of surplus funds in the domestic economy (Clapham 1959, p. 511). At the same time, imperial joint stock banking performed a similar function in the Empire; it was a source of commercial expansion on a global scale. In Australia, by 1855 "there were nine joint-stock banks with offices in London . . . – the Bank of Australasia, Bank of British North America, Colonial Bank, English, Scottish, and Australian Bank, Ionian Bank, London Chartered Bank of Australia, Oriental Bank, South Australian Banking Company, and the Union Bank of Australia" (Powell 1966, p. 312).

In colonial Australia, the passage of the Forbes Act of 1834 by the New South Wales Legislative Council encouraged imperial banking. This act disqualified English money laws in New South Wales, allowing flexible interest rates on loans (with a maximum recoverable rate of 8 percent where no prior agreement existed). Because of the relatively low paid-up capitalization of existing colonial banks in the mainland colonies and the low cost of gathering English deposits, potential high rates of interest in Australia made the colonies an attractive investment sphere (Baster 1929, p. 12). Thus, by 1840 there were seven banks (colonial and imperial) with paid-up capital of £2,300,000 and two English mortgage loan companies (Butlin 1968, p. 117).

Profit considerations aside, the shortage of colonial currency and its uneven circulation due to irregular trading operations necessitated a limited liability arrangement to protect shareholders (Baster 1929, pp. 3–4). The system of Royal charter on which the Bank of England was based guaranteed this, and the Bank of Australasia was the first such chartered colonial bank. The principle of imperial banks financed by English capital and directed from London was readily endorsed by an 1840 edition of *Atlas*, an English financial journal.

The benefits resulting from such establishment are incalculable, not merely in a mercantile or financial point of view, for they are also of the utmost social and political utility. They prevent the necessity for the transfer of bullion from one country to another; lower the rates of interest by supplying capital whenever it can be advantageously employed; steady and equalise the exchanges; give confidence to all engaged in distant trading operations: induce the merchant to direct all his skill, energy and means, to the production and transfer of profitable commodities, leaving to the banker the intermediate agency between the buyer and seller of goods, while the powerful and enduring tie of mutual self-interest binds in an indissoluble and peculiarly pleasing union the distant dependency and the parent state. It is surprising that these colonial banks have not long ago been established ... All the colonial banks have been profitable investments for their shareholders and the dividends range from 6 per cent to 9 per cent per annum, with every prospect of increase. [quoted in Baster 1929, p. 18]

More specifically, the 1837 prospectus of the Union Bank claimed:

The Directors are fully persuaded that in no part of the world can capital be more advantageously or more securely employed than in Australia, where the Bank Interest is 8 per cent and the current rate considerably higher, and where the dividends of the Colonial Banks have hitherto averaged fully 15 per cent per annum ... A local currency based upon a capital affording unquestionable security is much wanted and loudly called for. [quoted in Baster 1929, p. 65]

The entry of imperial banks into the colonial economy had a salutary effect on local banks. Initially, colonial bank loans underwrote the early 1830s pastoral expansion; in fact, in the first half of the 1830s New South Wales bank loans increased by 600–700 percent, quadrupling again in the next four years (Butlin 1968, p. 228). From 1836 to 1840, the proportion of bank loans and discounts to deposits rose from about 170 percent to almost 200 percent (Holder 1970, p. 116). The rapid expansion of loans reflected the intense competition that arose with the arrival of the English banks. The latter, showing the way in branch and deposit banking as well as taking over the foreign exchange market from the commissariat, compelled local banks to transform their formerly conservative practices.[6]

Bank competition for deposits in the 1830s boom was alluded to in Alexander Harris's (1964, p. 156) advice to the intending settler: "The banks will give him very high interest for his ready money – at least double what he would get in England." The high rate of interest offered by banks reflected two phenomena: (1) the general shortage of currency in the colonial economy, and (2) the specific shortages resulting from the intensified demand for deposits caused by competition between banks under the new stimulus of deposit banking (Hartwell 1954a, p. 117).

Before the mid-1830s local banks had operated on shareholder capital, but the entry of imperial banks compelled the colonial banks to engage in deposit banking. This centralized local capital as a supplement to capital raised in Britain for financing the expansion of wool production.

Raising capital in Britain and through local deposits, the colonial bank was the principal facility for channeling capital to the producer by discounting merchants' bills of exchange. In this period, direct bank loans were not a routine banking practice. Imperial banks were forbidden to discount commercial paper (e.g., bills of lading for wool exports) and to make mortgage loans on land (Baster 1929, p. 40), and colonial banks were averse to making extensive loans to producers, arguing that risks were too high where pastoral capital was not secure. The colonial banks preferred to conduct business with merchants, who would then lend to wool growers.

MERCHANT CAPITAL AND WOOL GROWING

The large-scale intervention of merchant capital into the pastoral industry stemmed from the long-distance character of the wool trade and the regulation of production by natural processes. For the wool grower, who sheared once a year, production time was on average twelve months. In addition, the realization period on the wool clip

---

[6] Thus, "the British banks in a matter of months converted a government-dominated, uncompetitive and primitive exchange market into a highly competitive, private enterprise market, fully linked with London, and for its day a highly mature system" (Butlin 1963, p. 85).

was approximately twelve months – an eight-month journey from station to London market and a further four months for the reflux of payment.[7] Thus the turnover time of pastoral capital averaged two years. Because of this delay and the continuous shepherding needed during the growing period, the producer required liquid capital in advance. As Henry Marsh put it to the 1842 Immigration Committee: "To carry on sheep farming it would be necessary to have a floating capital equal to an average of about one year and a quarter's expenses."[8]

Merchant capital met this requirement. Intervention involved commercial advancing, but the patterns differed according to the origins of the pastoral enterprise. When the enterprise was a partnership or company originally established in England (which many of the new 1830s squatters were), the accounts and therefore commercial advancing were located with an agent in London, just as the imperial banks' operations were. Otherwise, a mercantile agent in one of the colonial port cities kept business accounts for the individual squatter, and the grower either sold or consigned his wool to or through that agent. The consignment of wool through a local factor was an increasing tendency through this period.

Advancing to the producer took at least two primary forms: (1) commercial advances against the realization of wool revenues extended by merchants to consigning growers, and (2) the provision of general short-term credit to the grower to cover current operating expenses.

The first advancing involved setting up the intending squatter. In most cases the newcomer obtained initial finances from mercantile or financial agents in the port city. Because squatting land carried a minimal license fee (after 1836, £10 per annum), the major outlay was for stock (cf. Harris 1964, p. 161). Normally financed through a credit arrangement called the "thirds" system, this involved either liberal advances on future returns or sponsorship of a squatter by a financier acting as absentee pastoralist. The former arrangement enabled the intending squatter with £1,000 of capital in the bank to obtain on credit livestock worth £3,600, or, in return for pasture,

---

[7] This depended, of course, on the distance from farm to port city, the delay on the wharves, and the delay in London before the sale. See Roberts (1970, p. 345), Barnard (1958, p. 96), and Blainey (1971, p. 131).

[8] *V&P, NSW*, 1842, Committee on Immigration, Minutes of Evidence, 20 July 1842.

the intending squatter (tenant) would guarantee the landowner a third of his flock and the increase (Harris 1964, p. 161; Fitzpatrick 1969, p. 281). Another variant, a frequent arrangement during the 1830s boom, involved the financing of a pastoral enterprise by a Sydney capitalist in return for one-third of the profits (Roberts 1976, p. 281). Such liberal credit provisions constituted the foundation of many small and medium-sized squatting enterprises. The merchants' relation to the grower was akin to a putting-out system, especially where credit was tied to the delivery of the wool clip.

The operating costs for the grower were chiefly for supplies and labor, with the wage bill amounting to 90 percent of annual costs (Blainey 1971, p. 131).[9] Generally, pastoralists paid their employees annually, not with money but with a bill of exchange on city merchants. This bill, the "order," was the primary currency of the interior. It acknowledged a debt drawn sometimes on the local storekeeper, but more commonly on a city merchant (Butlin 1968, pp. 288–90). Although the order system was convenient for geographical reasons,[10] its use was further evidence of the fundamental credit basis of the squatting system. A settler named Haygarth described the credit nexus thus:

It is usual for proprietors of stations "up the country" to keep an account current with a Sydney merchant or agent, from whom they also purchase

---

[9] Such operating expenses, as well as the "thirds" relation established with his mercantile agents, R. Campbell Jnr. and Co. of Sydney, is evidenced in Henry Dangar's letter draft to his father:

Melbourne   August 15, 1842
Henry Dangar
My Dear Father,
Found run at Moonee Ponds, . . . I will have no expenses but wages which are now £25 for Shepherd – 14 for servant Girl/ milks cows, washes, cooks. Allowance to a man per week is

  10 lbs. flour @ £20/1,000 lbs.
  10 lbs. meat
  2 lbs. sugar ¼ lbs. tea.

other expenses: licence fee of £10 p. a. and 1*d*. head tax on sheep, 3*d*. on cattle + £10 for stuffs to keep sheep clean.
   My stock at present consists of 600 ewes that will begin to lamb 1st of next month and which will cost me 12/- per head (£100 cash − £100 − 3 mth £100 6 mth) shear them in Oct/Nov. and expect to get sufficient wool off them then to pay 12 mo's expenses.
[from M393 Australian Joint Copying Project misc, Dixon Library, University of New England, NSW, Australia]
[10] Butlin (1968, p. 289) wrote: ". . . which meant that in New South Wales stocks of cash could only be obtained at infrequent intervals and must therefore be dangerously large."

their annual supplies, and, when discharging any debt in the interior, they simply draw an "order" upon him for the amount: their produce is likewise intrusted to his charge, and he either sells it in Sydney, purchases it himself from the settler, or ships it to England, as may be most advisable from the state of the market. [quoted in Butlin 1968, p. 290]

Operating on such a pervasive credit basis, it was rational for the grower to consolidate his debt and conduct business with one mercantile agent. Merchants actively encouraged this practice with liberal advancing, but on condition that they control the wool clip. They either purchased the wool and consigned it for resale in London or simply consigned the wool (see Butlin 1947, p. 176; Barnard 1958, p. 117). Wool was the squatter's only collateral. To the merchant it was also a valuable commodity, and the wool bill was either a foreign-exchange earner or a means of settling accounts with English creditors. Hence, control over its marketing augmented the general importing capacity and therefore accumulation. The long-term interest of merchants, then, was to establish a credit relationship with the grower to enlarge, over time, the servicing of his enterprise.

Merchants competed for pastoral agency. Competition involved mainly services, such as attractive credit arrangements, often on a personal basis rather than through commissions.[11] Such competition bred money lending involving short-term advances to growers. In this way, merchants forged an *active*, rather than a passive, relationship to pastoralism, whereby credit expanded wool production.

The prominence of commercial credit in the development of Australian wool growing affected the location of wool sales. With the rapid involvement of metropolitan capital from the mid-1830s, the wool market shifted from colony to metropole, the source of credit. Consignment marketing increased as colonial selling facilities proved inadequate and colonial banks could not accommodate larger cash discounts for merchants during the long period of wool marketing. Hence, local merchants switched from wool buying to wool factoring. Their own ability to advance credit to the grower depended on the system of discounting bills of exchange drawn on London at local imperial banks with London accounts. During the 1840s, 30–40 percent of the wool clip was consigned (rising to 80 percent

---

[11] In fact, Barnard claims that commission charges remained stable until the 1870s, when banks entered the consignment-factoring business on a large scale (1958, pp. 114–15, 125).

by the 1860s), 50 percent was resold in London on behalf of colonial merchants, and large growers with accounts at London mercantile houses shipped the small remainder directly (Barnard 1958, pp. 47, 137).

Consignment marketing (both for pioneer pastoralists and for wealthy emigré pastoralists of the 1830s) was conducted initially through a London mercantile house. Growers consigned to their English agents, drawing bills on them in turn. Thus, Niel Black, resident squatter and manager of Niel Black and Company, received the following letter from the parent company of Gladstone, Serjeantson and Company concerning consignment:

Niel Black, Esq.   Liverpool
June 6, 1844
Dear Sir,
    On your return to Port Phillip we authorize you to draw upon us at your discretion against consignments of wool to our address and we engage to accept and at maturity pay such bills, it being understood that these Drafts are to be accompanied by the Bills of Lading. You will also take care to give us timely advice that we may provide the necessary Insurance and that in the event of the wool when sold by us, not realizing the amount you may have advanced, after paying the . . . and charges, the loss if any to be born equally by you and us.
Gladstone and Serjeantson

Accounting operations were appropriately centralized with the parent company, as the following account illustrates:

Account sales of Bales Wool and Indemnity from Port Phillip to London on account of Messrs Niel Black and Co.

1842			
Sept. 20 Sale of 20 Bales Wool			
		Revenue:	263.18.4
Charges			
To Marine Insurance		7.11.6	
Public Sales Exp		6.8	
Warehouse Charges		3.10.0	
Freight	30.10.11		
Primage	1.10.7	32. 1.6	
Brokerage		2.13.0	
Commission @ 4%	10. 2.0		
			56.14.8
Net proceeds			208. 3.8

Source: Black Papers (MS 8996).

Commercial advances for operating expenses were made to Niel Black & Co., in addition to commercial advancing on wool in transit, as the following letter [Black Papers (MS 8996)] illustrates:

Niel Black, Esq.   Liverpool
June 6, 1844

We hereby authorize you to draw upon us in the usual way from Port Phillip to the extent of £1,500. Fifteen hundred pounds. We engage to accept and pay your drafts on us to this extent.
yours . . .
Gladstone and Serjeantson

Alongside this rather exclusive method confined to only the largest graziers grew the system of consignment through a local factor. The trend was away from the dominance of the *general* colonial merchant and local sales toward the consolidation of consignment in the hands of specialized mercantile agencies with regular English connections. The relationship between mercantile houses in metropole and colony took several forms: interlocking partnerships or close commercial-financial ties, relocation of a branch of an English house in Australia (e.g., J. B. Montefiore & Co.), and relocation or establishment of a branch of an Australian firm in London (e.g., Dalgety, Elder Smith) (Barnard 1958, pp. 61, 121).

The increased availability of metropolitan capital for colonial staple production fostered a growing division of labor in the wool trade. Although colonial merchants purchased a relatively declining share of the wool clip, they assumed the consignment agency on an increasing scale. Some companies that combined wool buying and wool factoring such as Elder Smith & Co. Ltd. (1839), Dalgety, Borrodaile & Co. (1846), T. S. Mort (1843), and Richard Goldsborough (1848), developed over the next half-century into large-scale pastoral finance companies, with commercial interests extending into associated activities, such as banking, railroads, refrigeration, shipping, mining, and sugar refining (Barnard 1958, pp. 57–8; Fitzpatrick 1969, pp. 403–6).[12]

Banks also acted as consignment agents, though not without some hesitation to involve themselves in hitherto unorthodox commercial banking practice (Butlin 1968, pp. 506–8). Whereas the

---

[12] These were the large merchant and finance capitals that became consequential in the struggle of colonial commercial capital to subordinate pastoral capital in the latter half of the nineteenth century and so develop a local division of labor.

banking system as a rule was not involved in general credit operations with producers, it was sometimes prepared (after 1845) to
accept a bill of lading as sufficient security upon which to make
advances. Evidence of this practice is supplied by a letter to Niel
Black from the Bank of Australasia (Black Papers).

Bank of Australasia   Melbourne
6th Jan, 1844
Sir,
   In reply to your letter of this day, in reference to your Draft on England
for £500, and other matters connected therewith – regret extremely that
any misunderstanding should have arisen in our negotiation, and with a
view to prevent any inconvenience, I beg to state that the Bank will honor
your Drafts for the amount of the bill namely – £500, on the understanding
that your Drafts shall be negotiated against Bills of Lading for Wool, to
that extent. I am
Sir
Your obedient Servant
Geo. Molson
Ass. Manager
Niel Black, Esq.
Melbourne

   During this period, the bank policy of generally avoiding credit
relations with producers reflected not only British convention with
respect to mortgage lending but also the contingent character of
squatting, where tenure security was not guaranteed and growers
were indeed dependent on credit. It also reflected the domination of
colonial banking by merchants. The banks argued (through a
spokesman such as George Griffiths, director of the Union Bank,
but also a merchant):

The paper of merchants and shopkeepers is preferred to that of settlers
. . . because their operations are much more under our congizance. . . . I
believe the object of discounting mercantile bills in preference to settlers'
is that the Bank believes the merchants are better acquainted with the
resources of the settler than the bank can possibly be.[13]

To which William Bradley (agriculturalist and grazier) responded:

I imagine the reason why the settler has so small a share of accommodation
granted by the Bank arose from the Bank Directors being themselves

---

[13] V&P, NSW, 1843, Committee on Monetary Confusion, Minutes of Evidence,
15 September 1843.

merchants, and that they had a fellow feeling in accommodating each other.[14]

It was to the advantage of merchant capital to secure credit operations with growers, thereby gaining both access to the wool clip and the ability to supply the grower. This centralized the commercial and financial requirements of the pastoralist in particular factoring agencies. Such a relationship was the condition of merchant capital accumulation.

Even with the introduction in 1843 of preferable liens on wool and mortgages on stock as a response to the 1840s depression (see Chapter 9), this merchant–grower relationship did not immediately change. These legislative measures provided the producer with legal security, when previously squatters had no independent means (except those who also owned land in the settled districts) of raising loans apart from the credit nexus with their consigning agent. They also enabled the producer, on the security of his livestock and wool, to gain legal access to bank loans, and thereby to organize financial operations in advance. The liens on wool permitted the pastoralist to obtain commercial credit before shearing. Nevertheless, banks were still reluctant to accept liens from producers without merchant intervention (see Butlin 1968, p. 344; Barnard 1958, p. 118). What developed was that merchants dealt in liens, passing them on to banks as a method of obtaining bank loans, and the bank accepted the security of the merchant's name. Once again, the merchant earned interest on advances against the liens. The liens in turn secured pastoral agency, thereby perpetuating the growers' dependency on merchant capital.

IMPACT ON THE COLONIAL ECONOMY

Until the middle to late 1840s, when pastoralists were able to secure commercial advances with wool liens and stock mortgages and squatters gained temporary title to the land they occupied, the wool clip was their sole economic security (except for pastoralists who owned freehold land). In other words, for most growers access to credit necessitated a contract with the merchant-financier for delivery of their wool. Merchants cultivated this relationship because it was to their commercial advantage to maintain a credit nexus. Con-

[14] *Ibid.*, 21 September 1843.

sequently, inherent in the wool trade was a tendency for merchants to speculate on future wool markets through money lending. This was widely considered a cause of the early 1840s depression – the liberal financial accommodations in the late 1830s by merchants and banks particularly. The following remarks in a letter from London importers Robert Brooks and Co. Ltd. [Letters (FM4 2348)] illustrate this point:

Cornhill, 13th March, 1841
Mr. James Cain.
Dr Sir,
    You will be surprised perhaps to hear that Messrs Montefiore Bros. of this city have suspended their payments: their embarrassments have arisen from the heavy Drafts upon them from their Sydney establishments although at the same time they have scarcely any capital of their own employed ... The Messrs Montefiore have for a long time been endeavouring to become large importers of Wool into this Country, and have adopted a system of advancing on Wool while growing on the Sheep's back, this extraordinary way of doing business has led to their present embarrassment.

    Mercantile engrossment of colonial pastoralism via the imperial relationship encouraged a specialized system of production resembling a staple economy. For the individual grower, dependence on short-term credit precluded flexibility of operation in the market; he was tied into a semibarter arrangement of supplies obtained on credit in return for wool. As a rule, debt tied producers to particular commercial agents. Commercial advancing thus invested merchants with a good deal of social power. On the one hand, merchants commanded the market, as Samuel Lyons told the 1843 Committee on Monetary Confusion:

The merchant has been in the habit of supplying settlers with merchandise and charging interest upon the amount of their purchases after a given time. They charge what price they please for their articles, because the settlers have not money to go into the market and buy for themselves.[15]

    On the other hand, financial arrangements, combined with the insecurity of land tenure, denied growers access to the banks and therefore to longer-term loans. This discouraged fixed capital investment in the pastoral regions. In addition, the desire of financiers to obtain wool reduced the available credit for other industries and

[15] V&P, NSW, 1843, Committee on Monetary Confusion, Minutes of Evidence, October 21, 1843.

thus impeded the production of varied commodities in the colony. Agriculture particularly suffered. The pastoral boom superimposed economic constraints upon the original social constraints on agriculture. Colonial self-sufficiency in grain production came only in the late 1840s, and then as a result of regional development, especially in South Australia. The policy of pricing Crown land in the 1830s and the *system* of pastoral economy both conspired against agriculture. (Land lots of 640 acres in particular reduced access for small cultivators.) Squatters spread over vast regions of the interior, which therefore lacked towns and transportation systems to encourage agriculture on the frontier. At the same time, squatters tended to produce their own grain. Shepherding requirements attracted many small farmers away from coastal agriculture with high wage inducements, which in turn inflated production costs in agriculture, since it was labor-intensive.[16] (For further discussion of this phenomenon, see Chapter 6.)

The dependence of the colonial economy on pastoralism and the wool trade was shown dramatically in the early 1840s economic depression. In the shake-up that followed, opposition to the social and economic limits of squatting developed. This would signal the beginnings of a vigorous urban-based capitalism committed to alternative patterns of capital accumulation for settlers as it moved to bring pastoralism under its financial and political control.

CONCLUSION

The expansion of colonial wool growing in the 1830s and 1840s was also the development of a periphery of the world economy. The source of expansion, then, was not local but the colonial relation. In particular, the maturing of the London discount market allowed a British mercantile system to be consolidated on a global scale. This was the framework within which squatting occurred. Merchant capital secured the relation between the squatting frontier and the British textile industry.

From the colonial perspective and for most growers, the year-long production cycle and the long-distance character of the wool

---

[16] See Dunsdorfs (1970, p. 85). Also see Governor Darling's discussion of the discriminatory effects on small farmers of large-scale squatting on leased Crown lands in Darling to Murray, Enclosure no. 2, 6 July 1829, *HRA*, Series I, XV, pp. 63–6.

trade necessitated commercial credit for continuous pastoral capital. Merchant capital met this requirement. It took two forms: commercial or trading capital and money-dealing capital. Commercial advancing was an active process in which merchants competed for pastoral agency to obtain the wool clip, which provided access to London credit to expand their commercial operations.

Merchants established a credit nexus with growers and so extended the pastoral frontier. Because wool was an increasingly valuable commodity in the world market, commercial credit from London mushroomed, channeled through a growing colonial banking system (with London accounts). Such metropolitan involvement in the wool trade promoted wool consignment to the London markets. Whereas the short-term effect of consignment marketing was to induce colonial merchants to add wool factoring to their buying operations, the long-term effect was to expel many of them, as metropolitan houses engrossed the wool trade. The 1840s crisis hastened this tendency. Colonial merchants thus joined growing settler opposition to the socioeconomic limits of a staple economy.

6

PASTORAL ENTERPRISE IN THE COLONIAL ECONOMY

INTRODUCTION

Colonial wool growing developed within the expanding British mercantile system. Indeed, as a makeshift form of land use, squatting accommodated well the liberal supply of commercial credit from London. From this perspective, wool growing simply enhanced financial and commercial fortunes. In world-economic terms, such temporary occupation of the imperial land frontier represented a large-scale "putting-out" system, organized around the wool trade by an international merchant banking community.

This mercantile putting-out relationship appeared *within* the colonial society as the squatting system advanced beyond the settled regions. The latter was a source of fine-wooled flocks and commercial credit in particular. To be sure, the origins of credit were ultimately metropolitan, but a local commercial apparatus of merchants and factors in port cities organized the financial and trading sphere. The social geography of the colony in this period thus conformed to the enclave-like relationships of the squatting system; market relations were largely confined to the coastal towns, which serviced a specialized rural hinterland.

The object of this chapter is to examine the relationship between the character of wool production in this period and the social division of labor in the colony.

THE SQUATTING "SWARM"

The squatting phase of colonial wool growing began in 1829 as flockowners breached the boundaries of the official "Nineteen Counties" to create a new land frontier called the "unsettled districts."

119

The squatting expansion resembled patterns begun during the 1820s when, to gain access to cheap, fresh pastures, graziers obtained a limited tenure ("ticket of occupation") by paying a minimal rent for the right to graze their flocks on Crown land over which they had no legal rights. In 1836 Governor Bourke officially recognized the squatter, instituting the £10 occupation license to graze on land beyond the Nineteen Counties. This land was soon divided into various commissioners' districts. License to squat was counterposed to the system of land sales in the "settled districts" instituted in 1831. Subsequent raising of the minimum price of land from 5s. to 12s. per acre in 1838 (and then £1 per acre in 1842) accelerated the squatting phenomenon.[1]

The expansion pattern of the squatting frontier was a radiating arc out from the original Nineteen Counties clustered around Sydney on the east coast of Australia. By midcentury, grazing lands spread from the hinterlands of Adelaide to those of Brisbane (the Darling Downs), 200 miles and more from the connecting coastline (Roe 1976, p. 101). The relationship between the coastal settlements and the squatting frontier was represented by Governor Gipps thus: "The *older settlements have under [squatting] become the Hive, from which swarms of Sheep and Cattle have been driven* to give a value to the lands of Port Phillip and South Australia, which without them would to this day have been an unprofitable wilderness."[2] The owners of the hive, the original landholders of exclusive stock, undoubtedly profited by supplying new pastoralists with their means of production. This sale of surplus stock by the pioneer graziers

---

[1]Compare Coghlan (1969, vol. 1, pp 384–5):

At the rate of interest current at the time, a capital expenditure of 12s. per acre would require a return of 1s. per annum, and as it was estimated that 3 acres of new land were required to maintain one sheep, the burden imposed by the purchase of land was equivalent to 3s. per sheep, which, in the depressed condition of trade after 1840, it was impossible for the industry to bear. The natural course for newly arrived settlers, who desired to become flockmasters, was therefore to go beyond the boundries and endeavour to obtain land without the initial outlay of purchase; and the distressing events of the years 1841–1843 had brought about the bankruptcy of so many persons, who were formerly the holders of extensive possessions, that those among them who were able to submit to the hardships of pioneering, were also disposed to betake themselves beyond the boundaries, with the hope of retrieving their fortunes. Almost all classes of pastoralists had therefore become interested in squatting.

[2]Gipps to Russell, 19 December 1840, *HRA*, Series I, XXI, p. 133 [emphasis added].

Table 6.1: *Register of leases of Crown lands, 1831–42*

Name	Date	Leasehold (acres)	County
William Cox	Aug. 27, 1831	3,120	Roxburgh
Wm. Cox, Jr.	April 1833	1,000, 640, 640, 640	
		1,100, 640, 640, 640	Brisbane
R. Campbell, Sr.	Aug. 11, 1832	1,370	Murray
	Oct. 30, 1833	1,280, 640, 640, 640	
		1,280, 640	Murray
Wm. Lawson	June 25, 1831	1,280	Bligh
	Feb. 26, 1832	640	Bligh
S. Terry	Apr. 10, 1833	10,880	Murray
W. C. Wentworth	Nov. 30, 1832	1,670, 1,360, 850	Camden
		976, 512, 528, 692	
		560, 850	

was both a supplementary source of income,[3] and a method of diffusing stock breeding throughout the frontier and thereby maintaining a reasonable standard of colonial wool.

Governor Gipps's image of the original hive and the squatting swarm emphasizes the basic difference between the freehold estates and the squatting runs.[4] The former were the province of the established landowners – the pioneer wool growers. Many of these landowners were also squatters, but their role of supplying stock for the squatting expansion led them also to engross leasehold land within the settled districts. This form of accumulation is shown in Table 6.1.[5]

The squatting runs, however, increasingly produced most of the wool for export in the 1830s and 1840s. By 1839, 694 squatting runs grazed about one-third of the colonial livestock. The returns for 1843 show that nearly two-thirds of colonial sheep were de-

[3] This is discussed in Chapter 7. Wakefield (from Pritchard 1968, pp. 129–30) claimed that Macarthur profited more from this production of the means of production than from wool sales.

[4] Within the two district categories, there was further regional differentiation. Here we are concerned with the broader unevenness between original settlements and their hinterland – a more obvious *relational* differentiation.

[5] *Register of Leases of Crown Lands, 1831–42* (NSW SA 2/2235).

Table 6.2: *Number of laborers, 1851 census*

Location	Agricultural/ horticultural laborers	Shepherds, stockmen, and other managers of livestock[a]	Total
Settled districts	12,441	6,426	18,867
Squatting districts	387	9,193	9,580
Totals	12,828	15,619	28,447

[a]Includes salaried overseers as managers.

pastured beyond the boundaries. In 1847–8 the respective proportions for New South Wales and the Port Phillip region were 56 percent and 85 percent of the sheep beyond the boundaries (Coghlan 1969, vol. I, p. 597); by 1850 three-quarters of the cattle and four-fifths of the sheep grazed in the squatting regions.

The rural labor force was distributed between the two regions as shown in Table 6.2 (Dunsdorfs 1970, p. 90). Thus, whereas more than half the pastoral labor force was tending livestock in the squatting runs, the agricultural labor force was overwhelmingly concentrated in the established areas of settlement. A dual process was under way in this period: the squatting frontier had dramatic *extensive* growth, while a more *intensive* process of settlement (largely urban based) proceeded gradually in the settled districts, where 70 percent of the colonial population lived in 1850 (Jeans 1972, p. 117).

THE LANDED ESTATE: THE "HIVE" OF PASTORALISM

In addition to extensive occupation of land in the squatting regions, landowners developed their own landed estates. The profits of pastoralism allowed them to accumulate more freehold land (see Appendix 1), and they improved their farms.[6] Improvement meant

---

[6] Estates such as those in Cumberland were

run by the old landed gentry who built fine houses from the profits of their up-country pastoral stations . . . the estates of such men as William Macarthur of Camden, George Cox of Winbourn, Hannibal Macarthur of the Vineyard, were not run for pleasure but for profit. Most were improving farmers, growing wheat, hay and vines, and reserving the pastures as resting and fattening grounds for inland cattle on their way to Sydney. [Jeans 1972, p. 126]

either the production of an array of market commodities or greater self-sufficiency. Of course, it is likely that some estates supplied provisions other than stock for their up-country runs.

Since the "Colonial Returns of Crops and Produce" aggregate cultivation for the various districts, it is difficult to establish the amount of estate production of, say, grain for the market. It is most likely that production for the grain market depended on location. For example, the *Australian Dictionary of Biography* (vol. 2, p. 195) has the following to say about Thomas Potter Macqueen's Segenhoe estate, which was in the largest inland agricultural region, the Hunter River Valley: "Between 1825 and 1838 he spent at least £42,000 on plant, stock and improvements on Segenhoe, and firmly established the Hunter Valley's reputation for efficient agriculture. During the drought in 1827–30 Segenhoe was the main source of grain for the whole valley."

Segenhoe had a labor force of about 160 convicts, some of whose families Macqueen had brought from England, settling them as tenant farmers on the estate. Indeed, for the Committee on Immigration in 1835, Macqueen presented his tenancy arrangements as follows:[7]

Wages and allowances I have proposed:
Labourer, man and wife
    20 lbs Beef
    20 lbs Wheaten Flour
    ¼ lb Tea
    2 lbs Sugar
    2 oz Tobacco; weekly
    2 quarts of warm milk daily
Snug cottage and garden rent free, and for the man £15 p.a., the woman according to her abilities, and the children the same.

The very size of the estate labor force makes it likely that self-sufficiency was the predominant goal of the improving farmer. The absence of an established rural market in the pastoral regions, undeveloped transportation (Dunsdorfs 1970, pp. 65–7), and, most important, the price fluctuations in the Sydney grain markets encouraged agricultural self-sufficiency on estates (Jeans 1972, p. 125).

The pattern of land use in colonial pastoralism, being very dis-

---

[7] Evidence of T. P. Macqueen, "Committee on Immigration," June 4, 1835, *V&P, NSW.*

persed, confined cultivation to the coastal regions while transportation lines lagged behind the flocks.. Because the coastal regions had the poorest soils and suffered the greatest hazards of grain rust and blight, the Sydney market depended on imports of grain from Tasmania, India, the Cape, and Valparaiso (Dunsdorfs 1970, p. 67). The state withdrew from this market, so merchant monopolies of the grain trade led to "periodic fluctuations of great violence ... even in normal years" (Coghlan 1969, vol. 1, p. 279).

To reduce unpredictable expenses that would interfere with calculating income from pastoral production, the estate farmer found it more profitable to use the estate's resources to supply his own food requirements.[8] This was possible given the seasonal nature of some of the pastoral jobs (e.g., lambing, washing, shearing). It also was appropriate to the contemporary English model of mixed farming; the colonial estates emulated the village community style.[9] Thus, Macarthur's Camden estate had many cottages for tenant farmers, a school, and a benefit society (Roe 1965, p. 48).[10] William Cox's "large estate at Clarendon near Windsor had all the appearance of a self-contained village. Over fifty convict servants acted as smiths, tanners, harness makers, wool sorters, weavers, butchers, tailors, and herdsmen" (*Australian Dictionary*, vol. 1, p. 259). Finally, Alexander Harris (1964, p. 72) observed of the pioneer estate farmer:

Like almost all the old settlers he had a great many farms, as well as cattle and sheep stations, in various parts of the colony, hundreds of miles from each other; he also, as usual, had at the home farm his smithy, flour-mill, tailors', shoemakers', harnessmakers', and carpenters' shops, tannery, cloth-factory, tobacco sheds, brick-kilns, saw-pits, etc., etc., and all the necessary

[8] This idea is from Garrett (1976, ch. 3).
[9] Compare also the organization of large cotton plantations in the South of the United States; see Genovese (1961, 1976).
[10] The following illustrates the tenancy arrangements by the Macarthurs:

... that we will give you during good behavior for three years, that you may be in our service, Fifteen pounds per annum, a cottage rent free, a plot of ground for a garden, 7 lbs. of meat and 11 pounds of flour per week, also the privilege of keeping a cow with Pigs and poultry on condition of their getting into no mischief, and being solely for your own use, and after 5 years should you continue that time in our service, we will establish each of you as a tenant on fertile land taking the rent either in labour or in produce and during the first 6 months in our service to give your wife one half of the above allowance of provisions.

[from Memo of agreement between the undersigned Emigrants (*per* Ship Brothers) and Messrs. James, William and Edward Macarthur, April 11, 1837, *Macarthur Papers*, vol. 22, p. 118 (ML A2819)]

tradesmen for these various occupations. Probably on his establishments there were altogether nearly or quite 200 men; some free, some bond.

This diversified pattern of farming required considerable investment in fixed capital. The following itemization of expenditures for improving his 2,560 acre (only) land grant was submitted by Peter Cunningham, Surgeon Royal Navy to the Colonial Office, in a request for an additional land grant to accommodate expanding livestock holdings:

Improvements on grant[11]

Stone Cottage shingled	£ 160
Stone Milk Dairy	40
Cheese Dairy shingled with ten stone presses	100
Cheese Store and two dry stores (shingled)	110
A Barn shingled	110
Stock Yard, milking pales and Calf shed	120
Garden Cottage and Garden	100
Four miles and ¾ of fencing	300
Out buildings for men, pig sties etc.	100
Ninety Acres of land in Cultivation	100
Implements of husbandry	130
	£ 1,370

Such intensive development of estates contrasted significantly with the seminomadic operation of the squatter. Much of the finances for farming improvement, however, came from squatting, building on the legacy of former land grant practices. The difference was that the specialized squatter had only the credit relation with the merchant to sustain his enterprise, whereas the estate farmer could diversify and limit his dependence on the financier.

THE SQUATTING RUN

Squatters' runs – numbering 1,866 in 1846–9 (Roberts 1970, p. 362) – were by no means equal or equivalent in size (see Appendix 2). J. D. Lang observed in 1845 that even in 1837 in Port Phillip squatters could be divided into two classes: "first those with a small capital, say £1500 or £2000, or more commonly two in company each with half that amount, and second, those with large sums from £5000 upwards" (quoted in Kiddle 1967, p. 38). Lang's first class

[11] Memorial of Mr. Peter Cunningham: Enclosure in Despatch of Under Secretary Hay to Governor Darling, 21 October 1830, *HRA*, Series I, XV, p. 798.

normally ran a flock of 500 to 600 sheep and was the largest group of small pastoral capitals (approximately 50 percent) (Abbott 1971, p. 68). Here, the enterprise was typically petit bourgeois, with the squatter constantly supervising production. This contrasted with the large sheep runs – the core of the squatting expansion of this period (see Barnard 1958, pp. 48, 75; Roberts 1970, pp. 304–5). These runs were increasingly financed through partnerships between colonial investor-operators and British absentee owners.

After 1834 British mercantile capital not only fostered such large-scale enterprise, but also underwrote mushrooming local credit relations. This encouraged staple commodity production across the board; the differences in the size of pastoral capitals and, therefore, the source of capital (local or metropolitan) was reflected in alternative patterns of wool marketing. (Either the small grower sold his wool to a local merchant for ready cash, or the large grower consigned his wool on account or through a local merchant-factor.) The point is, however, that the short-term advancing by commercial capital both reduced the significance of economies of scale and centralized the servicing of pastoral capital in the port cities.

In spite of size differences, until the late 1840s fixed capital investment in runs, and therefore in production, was generally insignificant.[12] The normal construction on the run included movable hurdles used to fold sheep at night, several slab or bark huts for the squatter and his labor force, and a temporary wool shed for shearing and storage. Materials for these buildings were entirely local (see Kiddle 1967, p. 54, for details). Primarily due to the insecurity of land tenure, the makeshift style reflected the liberal conditions of credit, which encouraged speculative growing. Permanent fencing did not make sense, and squatters "gained an uneasy security" by claiming more land than they immediately needed (Kiddle 1967, p. 50). The resulting pattern of land use was described to Lord Stanley by George Hyde of Green Hills, Port Phillip.

The tenure by which the Squatter holds lands from the Crown . . . is one by which it is defrauded of the just rentage of the land, while it most

---

[12] For example, "even squatters with substantial capital behind them usually contented themselves with camp dwellings which would either be abandoned or hastily reassembled if it became necessary to move the station" (Kiddle 1967, p. 54); and see Roberts (1970, pp. 283–4). Also, "settlers jostled for position around the water-holes and creeks, refusing to spend money in digging wells when they had no secure tenure in land" (Kiddle 1967, p. 49).

pointedly retards the progress of the Colony, impoverishes its resources, and prevents the employment of emigrant families, a class who stand most in need. I have my Lord been in new countries all my life, and I can with confidence assert I never saw such perfect discomfort and determination to retard all manner of improvement as among the squatters; the reason assigned is no other than the uncertainty of holding the land; thus proving it to be the most effectual plan of keeping the Country in its present waste state.[13]

Extensive land use by squatters resulted in a general disregard for improving pastures. Given the contemporary accounts concerning the destruction over time of pasture by sheep grazing, especially during the squatting phase, it is clear that wool growers had two options: find fresh pastures or enclose paddocks to which scientific methods of improvement could be applied, such as using artificial grasses. Characteristically, squatters chose the first option. Pasture destruction through unsystematic grazing (exacerbated by careless shepherding) as well as nonreplacement of essential chemicals removed from the soil through grazing[14] compelled continued movement onto fresh pastures (see Gardner 1854, vol. 1; McBride 1898, pp. 34–5).

At the same time, given the speculative environment, little care was taken to improve and preserve flock breeds. When purchasing stock at central stock sales or sometimes directly from other growers in the interior, the squatters' chief concern was to buy breeding sheep that would bring a quick return.

PASTORAL COMMODITIES

The speculative environment stemmed from wool being produced purely as an article of exchange in the world market.[15] Wool was not the only product the grazier offered for sale, however. Livestock, both sheep and cattle, were potential sources of supplementary income. In the colonial market, sales of sheep tallow and sheep to

---

[13] *Despatches*, June 4, 1842 (ML A1290).
[14] For example, Gardner (1854, vol. 1, p. 108) states that the distinctive feature of wool, qua animal product, is the significant content of sulfur in it: five parts to every 100. Furthermore, he estimated that 3,000 tons of gypsum were removed from the soils of Great Britain per year through sheep grazing, the consequence being declining soil fertility and declining wool yields.
[15] In the 1840s, wool accounted for two-thirds of the total value of colonial exports (Coghlan 1969, vol. 1, p. 504).

prospective pastoralists provided current revenue for the pastoralist. There was a colonial market for beef, but demand lagged behind supply (beef on the hoof), partly because of the English taste for mutton and partly because population growth lagged behind the growth of cattle herds. In fact, salt beef and cattle products such as hides, bones, and tallow (in addition to sheep tallow) were exported (Coghlan 1969, vol. 1, p. 505).

Generally, small pastoralists grazed cattle because they were cheaper to buy and manage (Jeans 1972, p. 149).[16] This was also an *initial* pastoral enterprise.[17] For some, cattle remained a significant source of supplementary income (Jeans 1972, p. 147; Buxton 1967, ch. 1). The point is that wool growing was the permanent form of commodity production, whereas supplementary sheep and cattle sales were variable market ventures by the pastoralist, often in response to market conditions (e.g., the price relative to wool prices, the rate of expansion of squatting, and the availability of credit).[18]

SOCIAL RELATIONS IN SQUATTING

Social relations in squatting included both permanent and seasonal labor forces supervised by the squatter or his overseer. There was generally an inflexible labor force requirement for each run beyond a certain minimum size. As Hodgson (1846, p. 49) remarked:

It scarcely pays a man to keep less than 5,000 sheep; for he is obliged to have a station, huts, woolshed, paddocks, store, dray and bullock-driver; and by a slight increase of capital, he might be doing much better, and might have a much larger establishment, at very slight additional expense. Therefore you generally hear of partnerships.

[16] See the table by Peel (1974, p. 19), which indicates differential capitals in sheep and cattle raising in Port Phillip, where the tendency was for landed proprietors who hired labor to concentrate in sheep, whereas tenant farmers with less labor concentrated in cattle.

[17] This is to some extent confirmed by Collier (1911, p. 70), writing of the nineteenth century after 1850:

The average station went through four different stages. First, it was a fattening station, with a choice herd of cattle; for all its improvements, a stock-yard and a hut. It was valued at £30. Next it was advertised as fully improved, fenced, and subdivided sheep property. Thirdly, it was a valuable pastoral estate of 35,000 acres freehold. Finally, it consisted of rich agricultural land, divided to suit intending farmers.

[18] See Kenyon (1926, p. 206). See my discussion of this in Chapter 7.

The amount of land required for grazing increased proportionately with the growth of flocks. This was true for large and small pastoral capitals alike, as the report of the commissioner for Crown lands made clear.[19]

The large occupiers, each on an average, depasture for £10 per annum, 21,726 sheep, or 2,716 head of cattle. The small occupiers 1,214 sheep, or 152 head of cattle. It will be further seen, that the proportion of land to stock is very nearly the same in both cases, that is to say, the large and the small occupiers hold each about 6½ acres of land for each sheep, or about 52 acres for each herd of cattle.

The production technique did not alter with the size of the enterprise; that is, capital accumulation neither was based in nor generated technical change.

The wool-growing technique was overwhelmingly labor-intensive, with 90 percent of current expenses committed to labor costs (Blainey 1971, p. 131). For the squatter, the cost, and consequently the supply, of labor was of fundamental importance to the profitability and reproduction of his enterprise. Alexander Harris (1964, p. 225) observed: "The rich find labour so scarce and stock-holding so profitable that they naturally throw all of their force of labour into the latter and have none comparatively left for agriculture." As the pastoral frontier extended, squatters were compelled to offer higher wages (Blainey 1971, p. 131).

For the most part, the size of the squatter's labor force varied with the size and number of sheep flocks. Estimates of the ratio of shepherds to flocks vary. Government statistician Coghlan (1969, vol. 1, p. 434) claimed a normal ratio for the 1840s of one shepherd for 400 sheep, with the charge being increased to 800–900 sheep where labor was scarce, though in these circumstances "flocks did not receive proper attention, with the result that disease became common and wool deteriorated." Coghlan qualified his ultimate solution of extensive fencing with a reference to an immediate remedy of improving the quality of shepherds (i.e., nonconvict labor). This was not an unreasonable qualification, given that in the 1850s the ratio had moved to three nonconvict shepherds for 4,000 sheep. However, in the period under examination, convicts were frequently the only labor available for remote squatting districts.

[19] "Depasturing Regulations," in Correspondence Relative to Crown Lands, *British Parliamentary Papers*, vol. 19, p. 438.

Another estimate of the labor/capital ratio is one shepherd for 600 sheep in the late 1830s, with one hutkeeper-watchman for every two flocks (hutkeepers conducted the night shift of watching hurdled flocks) (Roberts 1970, p. 282). A further estimate is that in the mid-1820s there was one shepherd per 800 sheep, and by 1845 one shepherd per 1,500–2,000 sheep (Peel 1974, p. 33). Finally, Edward Curr (1883, p. 38), from his squatting experiences in Port Phillip, wrote:

Experience in New South Wales led to the size of a flock per shepherd to be limited to 500–700 sheep. This practice developed out of the scrubby land there, and the decision of the country police magistrate to determine that a shepherd would not be held responsible for flocks which exceeded 520. This custom was imported into Port Phillip, in spite of its rich open plains and free shepherds as well as the belief that larger numbers of sheep defiled the grass.

The differences among these estimates suggest differences between ideal and practice, which varied according to farm size, geographical regions, and so forth. However, the *real* differences in the labor/capital ratio, particularly over time, reflect the squatters' sole technical change in response to market conditions – namely, the adjustment of his capital (sheep) to his available labor force.[20] This was a requirement especially in the 1840s when the labor scarcity was aggravated by the decrease in bond labor, since transportation to the mainland ended in 1840.

In addition to shepherds and hutkeepers, the squatter required as part of his regular labor force an overseer and a bullock driver. For a run of about 2,000 sheep, then, there was an estimated labor requirement of seven men (Roberts 1970, p. 282; Curr 1883, p. 36). During the 1830s this labor force was employed on an annual basis (Butlin 1968, p. 342), receiving wages annually following shearing and provisioned during the year with basic farm-store rations [10 lb. flour, 2 lb. sugar, ¼ lb. tea, and 12 lb. meat per week (Kenyon 1926, p. 216)]. Otherwise, any part-time or seasonal labor (e.g., splitters for any construction tasks, sheep washers, and shearers) worked on weekly or piece-rate wage contracts (Peel 1974, p. 22).

Securing enough shepherds was a constant problem for squatters,

[20] Adjustments to this ratio in relation to capital accumulation are more fully discussed in Chapter 7.

who either offered incentives for free laborers or obtained assigned labor. Shepherd's wages were sufficiently high (and increasing during the 1830s boom) to attract new settlers away from small farming, and sometimes squatters gave them a cow and two acres to cultivate (Kiddle 1967, p. 51; Dunsdorfs 1970, pp. 84–5; Coghlan 1969, vol. 1, p. 204).

Even when money wages were higher, however, employers used their monopoly of station stores to undermine the real wage increase; as Hodgson (1846, p. 45) claimed: "I *have* given £40 a year to men; but when I did so, I raised the price of my stores, which they *must* buy; so that, while they imagined themselves richer, they were perhaps receiving less." Because of the increasing labor scarcity, the market for free labor became a seller's market, and the former system of yearly contracts gave way to a more limited period of employment (Roberts 1970, p. 319), confirming Harris's observation (1964, p. 67): "It may be as well to notice ... a peculiar characteristic of the free labouring population of Australia: it is in a state of constant migration."

The alternative use of convict labor was a growing trend during the 1830s expansion.[21] Bond labor was considerably cheaper to the squatter; wages were not customary (not being legally recognized), and the cost of maintaining assigned labor was approximately two-thirds that of paying wages and provisioning free labor (see Appendix 3). The state prescribed board for assigned convicts in 1826.

The weekly ration ... was 12lbs. of wheat or 9lbs. of seconds flour (of which 3lbs. of wheat or 2lbs. of flour might be replaced by 3½lbs. of maize or barley meal), 7lbs. of beef or mutton or 4½lbs. of salt pork, 2oz. of salt and 2oz. of soap. The yearly allowance of clothing consisted of 2 frocks or jackets, three shirts, two pairs of trousers, three pairs of shoes, and one hat or cap, and the employer was also bound to provide one good blanket and a palliase or wool mattress for the use of each servant. [Coghlan 1969, vol.1, p. 182]

Employers did not necessarily adhere to the prescription, especially because there was no social regulation of employment. As Harris (1964, pp. 66–7) observed of the employment of assigned labor:

There was no restraint on their personal liberty beyond that of fear of consequences if they left the farm or neglected the work; their huts were

---

[21] See the table in B.C. Fitzpatrick (1969, p. 93).

at the edge of the piece of tobacco ground, and were merely a few upright sheets of bark with interstices of many inches and only part of a roof – in short many a countryman in England provides his pig a snugger shelter. In fine weather this would matter but little, but in the wet it must have been the source of much discomfort. They received no wages but were provided with a scanty suit of shop clothing at certain seasons specified by law; and also every Saturday afternoon with as much coarse beef and flour as would just keep them till the same period of the succeeding week. Occasionally their master opened his heart so far as to give them a little tobacco, tea, and sugar beyond the allowance ordered by law. Altogether their cost might be about half that of free labourers; whilst between fear of being flogged and hope of getting a little indulgence in the matter of rations, their labour was nearly or quite equal – so that the master's clear gain was just the wages a free servant would have been paid over and above his ration at the same kind of work.

It is difficult to assess the efficiency of convict labor when in many cases bond labor was the only type squatters could obtain for the demoralizing work of shepherding.[22] It is in this context that the complaints from both sides about the conditions of assigned labor should be considered. The employers' attitude was generally similar to the following description by Governor Bourke in a dispatch to the Colonial Office:[23]

The Convict generally does as little as he can, not unfrequently robs his Master. Much of his time is passed in the road to or returning from Hospital, or to a Justice to Complain the Master's Charges against him for negligence, drunkenness or insubordination. Many also are unfit for labour of any sort.

Although, as Collier (1911, p. 108) remarked, squatters sometimes "sought to disarm opposition" by alleging that "convict labour . . . was not cheap labour," it clearly was in pecuniary terms. Compared with the *impersonal* power of capital over labor inherent in a labor market, however, the particular relation between assignee and pastoralist had a fundamental flaw, as articulated by Hannibal Macarthur (cited also on p. 96):[24]

By the present system of convict discipline, there is not a sufficient restraint upon these men, to prevent the indulgence of their vicious propensities.

[22] Large numbers of exconvicts continued to work in the squatting districts (Burroughs 1967, p. 113).
[23] Governor Bourke to Viscount Goderich, No. 53, April 30, 1832, *HRA*, Series I, XVI, p. 625.
[24] Evidence of H. H. Macarthur, "Committee on Immigration 1835", June 11, 1835, *V&P, NSW*. Also see Appendix 3.

It is therefore desirable to obtain free men at liberal wages for all agricultural purposes, as the stoppage of wages occasioned by neglect of duty operates as a better check on the free, than the present convict discipline on the bond.

An arbitrary law with respect to labor relations prevailed in the squatting districts, despite the police magistrate system. There was generally an alliance between magistrate and employer, as the following statement by Governor Bourke suggests:[25]

Although the condition of the convict is that of a slave, it has not been thought desirable to give to the Master a power of personally inflicting punishment; a most extensive Summary jurisdiction over prisoners is however given to Magistrates, who, with the exception of those who are Stipendary, are always themselves Settlers directly interested in maintaining the strictest subordination, and in exacting the most laborious exertion which the Law permits on the part of assigned Servants.

Until 1840 there was no legal regulation of labor relations in the squatting districts. The employee, bond or free, was subject to the squatter's caprices. The 1828 Masters and Servants' Act had provided for "the better regulation of servants, labourers, and work people," but not in the regions beyond the Nineteen Counties (Fitzpatrick 1969, p. 94). Eventually the Legislative Council's Immigration Committee demanded appropriate legislation for the squatting districts, no doubt because of the end of convict transportation and the need to remove further barriers to free labor immigration into the pastoral economy. Accordingly, the revised act of 1840 provided for labor service in return for adequate provisioning by the squatter as well as disciplinary measures against each party for failure to meet the contract (see Kiddle 1967, p. 51). Remoteness, official corruption, and *lumpen* resistance to discipline on the part of convicts and exconvicts, however, combined to create conflict and capricious discipline of the labor force (see Curr 1883, p. 438; Kiddle 1967, ch. 6).

THE SQUATTING SYSTEM AND THE COLONIAL MARKET

The squatting system had a minimal effect on the extension of a colonial market, which was still concentrated in the coastal urban

[25] Gov. Bourke to Stanley, No. 1, January 15, 1834, *HRA*, Series I, XVII, p. 822.

centers. This stemmed from the social character of wool growing as part of a large-scale putting-out arrangement. There were two main components of the exchange relations that supported the squatting run: (1) the consumption requirements of the enterprise, and (2) the marketing of the staple commodity.

Consumption requirements

As a labor-intensive unit of production, the station had minimal capital-goods requirements. The main item of capital investment was a bullock dray, and supplementary nonfood items included saddles, shears, a wool press (sometimes), household utensils, clothing, tobacco, and rum (part of the wage). Such basic requirements were scarcely sufficient to sustain country towns as artisanal and supply centers. Extensive patterns of land use reinforced this limitation.

Given the minimal needs for capital goods, what effect did the pastoral labor force have on the development of a consumption-goods market? The first point to be made is that the regular pastoral labor force in this period did not fully constitute a wage-earning proletariat for the following reasons:

1. A considerable portion of the work force was assigned labor that received primarily wages in kind from the pastoralist; it had little need of a market.
2. The bulk of pastoral labor wages were paid annually, and then in credit notes (chiefly on urban centers).
3. Day-to-day rations were provided by station owners as part of the requirement of the Masters and Servants' Act (Kiddle 1967, p. 51). This was supplemented on large runs by the store system, whereby employers stocked consumer items ranging from axes to cabbage-tree hats.[26]

---

[26] Thus

a well-stocked store, besides being supplied with all manner of foodstuffs and general needs such as axes, writing paper, bags and so forth was stocked as a "reach-me-down" as well. Black hats, black coats, white shirts and trousers, check trousers, coloured waistcoats, coloured cotton jackets, handkerchiefs, cloth caps, even in one instance a toothbrush are listed among the usual stores in 1843. In the dusty, cobwebbed corners would be the bushmen's remedies for all ills: gleaming blue bottles of castor oil, brown bottles of pain-killer. But as a rule station hands cared little for the refinements of coloured waistcoats and toothbrushes. Their wants were heavy boots, canvas trousers, serge shirts and cabbage-tree hats. [Kiddle 1967, p. 59]

Such relations between squatters and their labor force precluded a viable rural market for consumption goods. The market for these goods was concentrated in the coastal towns, where squatters purchased their annual requirements on account with their mercantile agents. Following shearing, some laborers journeyed to the coast to cash their orders and indulge in their annual spree.

Some rations were homegrown, such as mutton, grains, and vegetables. Larger squatting runs grew and milled their own grain crops, but these were primarily for immediate consumption on the farm.[27] The stipulation of the Pastoral License forbidding crop cultivation beyond the needs of the station's work force reflected and reinforced this. Surplus foodstuff production was not feasible economically because (1) there were no staple foodstuffs markets in the squatting regions, and (2) the scarce labor force was required for year-round flock management. Thus, William Lawson declared, "The extent of my cultivation, and agricultural as well as other improvements, has been greatly circumscribed by the . . . deficiency (of labour)." John Blaxland confirmed: "The want of labour has now become so alarming, that we have not men to plant our crops, or gather in what little may be grown of hay or corn."[28] There were exceptions to this, of course, with some larger stations diversifying their food production for local sale.[29] Such sales, however, constituted surplus production from a basic attempt at self-sufficiency on the run. Settlement was too dispersed for such local exchange to develop into an expanding rural market at this stage.

Where small towns did appear in the squatting regions, they grew in response to a growing itinerant population, much of which constituted the mobile labor force referred to earlier. Small towns consisting of inns and stores emerged, not as marketplaces for the products of the farm, nor primarily as supply centers, but as centers

---

[27] Evidence of this practice as integral to pastoral pioneering is in "Abstract of the Returns of Stock and Cultivation at Pt. Phillip, to accompany the Census Returns of 1836," in *Census Returns of the Province of Victoria for 1836 and 1838* (Microfilm No. 28385, The Genealogical Society of the Church of Latter-Day Saints, Salt Lake City, Utah). See also Harris (1964, p. 205) and Coghlan (1969, vol. 1, p. 506).

[28] Evidence to the Committee on Immigration, 1837, *V&P, NSW*.

[29] Such as the activity of a Port Phillip squatter's wife (Kiddle 1967, p. 91): "When her mother sent her a spinning wheel from Scotland it was well used in making cloth for the family's clothing. But her chief work was to raise poultry, manage the dairy, sell her butter and cheeses at a profit and buy pigs to fatten."

for travelers. It has been suggested that small squatters obtained provisions from local stores (Jeans 1972, p. 143), and this is confirmed by Alexander Harris's account of his own family's venture into up-country storekeeping.[30] Neither account completes the market nexus of the small squatter. Undoubtedly, the small or newcomer squatter in need of immediate cash from his wool clip, and probably unable to afford a bullock dray, sold his clip combined with that of a larger neighbor. [Although it has been suggested by Barnard (1958, p. 50), Harris does not mention wool handling as an enterprise or barter function of the storekeeper.] Typically, the immediate cash sale would discount the small squatter's income, which then faced the inflated prices of goods sold through the country store (for example, Harris 1964, p. 203).

This petty provisioning was not sufficient activity for rural town development. Nevertheless, once squatters gained secure tenure (1847) and instituted basic improvements on their stations (especially around the homestead), towns began to concentrate on the hitherto itinerant artisan. In 1849, for example, Albury, "largest and best equipped of the road settlements," contained "inns, stores, a steam flourmill, blacksmith, undertaker, builder, tailor, and shoemaker" (Jeans 1972, p. 145).

The marketing pattern of the staple

The bullock dray, the primary item of capital investment, was significant in the squatting system. It was the essential mode of commodity transportation before the railroad and in the absence of a river system connecting the coast to the hinterland. Transportation arrangements were essentially individual, connecting grower and merchant. This individualist mode of commodity transportation, in addition to the great expense of transportation (in excess of 100 percent of equivalent costs in England), made it profitable to carry provisions as ballast on the up-country journey (Burroughs 1967, p. 107 fn; Dunsdorfs 1970, p. 67). Such provisions covered operating needs between annual clips and were invariably supplied by the mercantile agent. It was a simple exchange, then, reflecting the

---

[30] "A large proportion of our sales ... were to settlers, and therefore wholesale" (Harris 1964, p. 204).

enclave character of the squatter's run (in relation to the surrounding frontier).

In summary, during the squatting period the wool producer participated in market relations specific to the organization and financing of the wool trade. The social character of wool production and wool circulation generated a pattern of exchange resembling a putting-out system of commodity production *within* the colonial economy. This pattern in turn both limited the development of a rural market and concentrated commercial activity in the port cities.

UNEVEN REGIONAL DEVELOPMENT

The squatting regions in this period consisted essentially of a hinterland spread of sheep runs connected to coastal commercial centers by the ubiquitous bullock dray, the lifeline of squatter economy. Town and hinterland expanded in symbiotic relation.[31] In the Port Phillip region where, in 1841, the urban population was almost double that of the rural population,[32] the town–hinterland relation was sharper than that in New South Wales, where prior agricultural settlement and freehold patterns in the settled districts intervened between the town and the squatting frontier.

In New South Wales, the source of colonial pastoralism and accordingly the stock-breeding base from which the pastoral frontier of the 1830s spread inland, there was a considerable contrast in economic diversification between settled and squatting regions (Mansfield 1847, p. 117). In the latter, for instance, shepherds made up more than half the population and a third of the occupations. Conversely, in the settled districts, the occupational category "commerce, trade, etc.," grew from 12.6 percent to 21.7 percent of the

---

[31] Blainey (1964, pp. 125–6) comments on the town-country relation as it developed in Port Phillip in the 1830s and 1840s:

The more wealth that came from wool and the more people that settled in the pastoral areas, the more work there was in the port for bankers, government officials, sailors, and wharf labourers, professional men, domestic servants, artisans, blacksmiths, shopkeepers and the merchants that handled wool and supplied the inland sheep stations. As town populations swelled, farms multiplied around Melbourne and Geelong to serve mainly the local market. After the region had been settled for only 17 years, manufacturing-commerce was the biggest employer of labour in Victoria, and the wool industry – still the great export – was also being challenged as an employer of labour by agriculture and domestic service.

[32] See the table in Peel (1974, p. 17): urban population: 5,539; rural population: 2,989.

population between 1841 and 1846. The latter trend focuses attention to the growth of urban capitalism.

This development is shown in Table 6.3. (Note also the divergent trend in the whole colony during the height of the squatting boom, 1836, when the population beyond the boundaries was increasing relatively.[33])

The significant extent of urbanization in colonial Australia resulted from the original military-bureaucratic character of the penal settlement and, later, the servicing of the pastoral frontier. Some urban manufacturing developed, in spite of a continuing dependence on manufactured imports due to colonial subordination to British commercial hegemony. Local manufacturing had both geographical and social stimuli. Distance, of course, encouraged domestically oriented manufacturing, and emancipist traders were some of the most successful early manufacturers.[34] Precluded from land grants, they created markets by developing industries to process rural products and by servicing both urban settlements and the growing rural economy. As pastoralism developed, so did adjunct industries in the urban centers.[35]

If we now consider industrial establishments outside of Sydney, during the 1840s grain milling in particular and manufacturing in general were expanding in the settled districts. For example, between 1840 and 1849, the number of steam mills increased from 26 to 70 and water mills from 23 to 41.[36] Similarly, breweries increased from 11 to 31, soap and candle works from 5 to 19, tanneries from 16 to 72, hat manufacturing from 1 to 5, and iron and brass foundaries from 6 to 16.[37] An examination of the return

---

[33] See Mansfield (1847, pp. 14–15). Note that the data for 1833, 1836, and 1841 exclude penal settlements and crews, and the 1846 data exclude crews of colonial vessels.

[34] As Blainey (1971, p. 137) writes: "The ocean was Australia's first tariff wall." See also Coghlan (1969, vol. 1, p. 511).

[35] See *Returns of Mills, Manufactories, etc., 1831–41* (NSWSA 4/7267).

[36] Return of the Number of Mills for Grinding or Dressing Grain in the Colony of New South Wales (Including Port Phillip), 1840–49 inclusive, *V&P, NSW*, 1850.

[37] Return of the Number of Manufactories, etc., in the Colony of New South Wales (including Port Phillip) from the year 1840–49 inclusive, *V&P, NSW*, 1850.

Table 6.3: *Total urban and rural population, 1833–46*

Classes		Population (and %)			
		1833	1836	1841	1846
1. Middle districts	Urban	23,776 (40.5)	28,740 (38.7)	48,585 (42.3)	69,932 (54.7)
	Rural	34,875 (59.5)	45,533 (61.3)	66,217 (57.7)	84,602 (45.3)
2. Port Phillip district	Urban			4,933 (42.0)	15,041 (45.7)
	Rural			6,805 (58.0)	17,838 (54.3)
3. The whole colony	Urban			53,517 (42.3)	84,973 (45.5)
	Rural			73,022 (57.7)	102,440 (54.7)

of mills and manufactories reveals that many of these processing establishments were owned by the landowners, thus attesting to the development of their estates (*Returns of Mills,* . . . *1831–41*).

In contrast, the squatting districts of the middle district had no manufactory establishments at all and only a sparse distribution of mills (*Returns of Mills,* . . . *1842–50*).

Superimposed on these differences between settled and unsettled districts was a further economic regionalism in the grain market. Grain supplies to the urban population came from combinations of local, interregional, and international trade. In the pastoral regions of New South Wales, including the Port Phillip district, land carriage costs prohibited agriculture beyond urban environments, except in the case of the Hunter Valley where there was water transportation. In the Sydney market, grain imports from Van Dieman's Land (as well as supplies from the Cape, India, and Valparaiso) competed successfully against locally grown grain (Burroughs 1967, p. 106).[38] This reflected the continuing paucity of capital in agriculture in the staple economy, as well as labor displacement, which resulted in small-scale and technically backward cultivation by petty producers.

The superior ability of pastoralism to attract capital and labor (not to mention its tendency to cover its own agricultural requirements) was a function of the competition between markets – one a world market based on industrial expansion and the other decidedly local (at least before the abolition of the Corn Laws). It was in large part because of this distinction that a natural colonial regionalism emerged to complement the specialized wool-growing east coast. Thus, Van Dieman's Land developed initially as a granary, with its favorable temperate climate, abundant and accessible fertile land, and an advantageous river system to the coast (Rimmer 1969, p. 327). The continuing grain deficiency in New South Wales encouraged wheat exports from Van Dieman's Land and, later in

---

[38] For example, 7s./6d. per bushel versus 4s./5d. per imported bushel. Compare Coghlan (1969, vol. 1, p. 281).

the 1830s, from South Australia.[39] Settled in 1838, South Australia was exporting grain (regionally and overseas) by 1843 (Dunsdorfs 1970, p. 99). This colony's relatively favorable social and geographical environment for wheat growing contrasted with the eastern staple-producing regions. South Australian conditions comprised these three:

1. Settlement under the principles of the Wakefield scheme as a nonpenal colony, with systematic land survey and tenure patterns encouraging freehold grain farming conducted by skilled farmers (and non-exconvict farmers as in New South Wales and Port Phillip) (see Peel 1974, p. 46; Coghlan 1969, vol. 1, p. 507). South Australian agriculture developed in complement to the pastoral economies of the eastern colonies.
2. The relative shortage of labor and more agricultural capital encouraged technical invention. Ridley's stripper, invented in 1843 and of world agricultural consequence, was adaptable to the large wheat fields of the Adelaide plains, which resulted in higher grain yields and more profitable grain production (Coghlan 1969, vol. 1, p. 508). [The stripper reduced the expenses of harvesting from £2 per acre to 2s. per acre for bagged wheat, according to a letter in the 1843 South Australian *Register* (cited in Dunsdorfs 1970, p. 102).]
3. South Australia, with areas of soils known as red-brown earths close to the Gulf ports, was able to cultivate grain for market more rapidly than the other states in this prerailway age, in spite of the existence of a pastoral industry begun by overlanders from the east (Wadham et al. 1957, p. 17).

TRANSITION IN THE PASTORAL ECONOMY

Given the dependence of the pastoral enterprise on the labor supply, the reduction in convict assignment in the 1840s was bound to

---

[39] See Burroughs (1967, p. 106). For example, between 1833 and 1842, there was a net grain deficiency equal to two years' consumption, and grain cultivation lagged behind population increase.

Year	Population increase	Cultivation increase (acres)
1831	50,000	29,442
1840	129,000	72,193
1850	200,000	66,450

generate alternatives to the preceding characterizations of the pastoral economy. In particular, a settled labor force emerged in the rural districts as tenant farming developed.

Within the settled districts there was a traditional antipathy by the gentry toward the small landholder. Such resistance to small holders and those originally referred to pejoratively as "squatters" reflected a heightened social prejudice given the relative size of the convict–exconvict populations in the 1830s.[40] The gentry translated their fear into legislation discriminating against the settler of small means, backed by the police powers of the magistracy (see Chapter 4).

In the mid-1840s, in the context of a diminishing emigrant (both free and bond) labor supply, pastoralist resistance to small farmers lessened considerably.[41] The value of a small farming and tenant population as a source of hired labor increased. Indeed, the *Sydney Morning Herald* noted this development in a statement entitled "Prospective Want of Labour" (November 5, 1844):

Circumstances have for some time past been inducing our large landholders to encourage the settlement upon their estates of working tenants or leaseholders. And the difficulty which has of late been experienced by considerable numbers of industrious men of the labouring classes, in obtaining employment, has so far favoured the wishes of the landlords in this respect that it has caused multitudes to resort to this means of gaining a livelihood.

Such a reversal of attitude by the gentry marked the decline of the exclusivist vision of a patriarchal estate system, precipitated by the sociopolitical changes associated with squatting; it also emphasized the fundamental dependence of agrarian capitalism on a labor supply. As the estates developed and found their source of bond labor drying up, small landholding became socially viable and economically necessary. Thus, a rural labor force emerged, either housed on

---

[40] The gentry feared "small specialist cultivation farms, believing such farmers to be stock thieves, sellers of bad liquor that undermined the discipline of their workforce, and trespassers on the grazing lands" (Jeans 1972, p. 115).
[41] See Dunsdorfs (1970, p. 93) and Buckley (1957, p. 94). See also the Report from the Select Committee on the Extension of Elective Franchise to Leaseholders and Squatters and on the Representation of the Colony, *V&P, NSW*, 1844, vol. 2. There are also various statements by colonial capitalists concerning the advantages of closer settlement, in terms of extending the division of labor, in 1846 editions of the *Sydney Morning Herald*.

the employer's property in a tenant relation or as a cottage holder or working as day labor subsisting as small owner-cultivators.[42]

Similarly, tenant farming developed on squatting runs (or portions thereof) purchased following the 1847 order-in-council that granted tenure security and the possibility of buying sections of occupied land. Successful squatters emulated the estate model after they secured the home station block as freehold and permanent construction and capital investment in the station were allowed.[43] As part of this move toward greater self-sufficiency, squatters encouraged tenants as a potential labor force. William Gardner (1854, vol. 1, p. 267) reported such trends in 1850:

A minor system of renting and letting has lately been introduced by many of the northern settlers in letting out their cultivation paddocks or enclosed fields to emigrants. Most of those who undertake engagements of this description being men of families, the cleared land for cultivation on some stations being from twenty-five to thirty and on some stations forty acres and upwards – The arrangement with one individual being for leave to cultivate within the fences, using his own ploughs, oxen and every other implement . . .

At another station . . . the emigrant can draw on the stores of the lessee for his supplies of tea, sugar, beef, flour, tobacco, etc., in anticipation of his future crop . . . The whole produce of wheat with the exception of what is required for the use of his family to be delivered to the lessee of the station. Ploughing, reaping, threshing and every other expense to be performed or paid for by the Emigrant.

In both settled and squatting districts, then, an incipient small-farming population produced a greater diversity of goods for consumption and materials for pastoral enterprise. In the settled districts, this development supplemented production on the pastoral

---

[42] Small owner-cultivators (petty commodity producers) do not survive socially as viable commodity-producing units themselves, as Kautsky wrote.

The real basis of their survival is the fact that they cease to compete with the large capitalist farms which develop by their side. Far from selling the same commodities as the larger farms, these small holdings are often buyers of these commodities. The one commodity which they do possess in abundance, and which the bigger holdings need, is their labour power. [Banaji 1976, pp. 33–4]

[43] Thus, the Learmonths' Buninyong station in Port Phillip in 1851 consisted of:

A Dwelling with six rooms, Garden well-stocked with fruit trees in full bearing; four three-roomed cottages, eight one-roomed ditto. Blacksmith's shop; Cooper's ditto; Sheep Wash very complete with spouts and hot water apparatus . . . a boiling down establishment annexed, a two story mill-house with a four horse flour mill, threshing and winnowing machines, a 400 acre horse paddock, 50 acre grass ditto, 10 acre grass ditto (the greatest portion of which can be irrigated) and a pig paddock of 160 acres. [quoted in Kiddle 1967, p. 172]

estates, whereas in the squatting districts, it represented a self-sufficient tendency. In either case such a growing division of labor constituted the beginnings of a rural market.

CONCLUSION

The forms of expansion in pastoral enterprise in settled and squatting districts were intensive and extensive capital accumulation, respectively. Although the pastoral gentry profited from squatting, they directed capital investment into development and diversification of production on their estates. Squatters simply expanded their flocks to increase their wool clip, given their greater dependence on the merchant-financier.

The squatting run was an enclave, striving for self-sufficiency in food production and exchanging wool for supplies from the coast. Thus, no rural market developed in the squatting districts. The symbiotic relation between expanding hinterland and port cities as commercial bases stimulated the growth of domestic manufacturing in the urban centers. A good deal of this was financed by colonial merchants.[44]

The estates of the settled districts were more independent of the mercantile relation and therefore were a different kind of enclave in the coastal hinterlands. Their diversity of production allowed a general self-sufficiency such that Alexander Berry described Shoalhaven estate as "a colony in miniature" (quoted in Roe 1965, p.148). By confining the division of labor to the estate itself, the growth of rural markets in the settled districts lagged.

The 1840s proved to be a period of transition in colonial development. The constraint on pastoral accumulation of a limited labor supply following abolition of convict transportation dramatized the need for a small-farming population as a source of labor. At the same time it dramatized the barriers that squatting placed on colonial social and economic development. Around this theme developed an oppositional movement founding part of its case on the reemergence of small farming in the settled districts, which contrasted with the dearth of agriculture in the squatting regions.

[44] See *Returns of Mills, Manufactories, etc., 1831–41*, for details on individual merchant enterprise; for example, (1840) Hughes and Hoskins, Robert Cooper, A. B. Sparke, Aspinall, Brown & Co., Cooper and Levy, and A. Berry (NSWSA 4/ 7267).

7

THE CONSERVATIVE CHARACTER
OF PASTORALISM

INTRODUCTION

In Chapter 6 we examined the character of pastoral enterprise in the squatting period and its contribution to the division of labor within the colonial economy. Here we shall consider pastoralism from a different angle, in order to understand the pastoral ideology. Rather than focusing on the individual unit of production, an analysis of the social environment of pastoralism may show how pastoralists perceived themselves. As wool growers, they confronted a particular set of economic conditions, and their attempt to control these conditions necessitated political solutions. The goal here of connecting conditions and solutions is to discover the social origins of the ideology expressed by the dominant growers.

Pastoral ideology in colonial Australia altered with the impact of squatting. The pioneering gentry (landowning graziers) saw themselves as the patriarchs of a stable social hierarchy, with the possibility of creating a colonial aristocracy sustained by the British state. Once squatting took hold, however, a more materialist ideology displaced the traditional conception. Squatters, whose self-justification arose from their *productive* occupation of imperial wastelands, emphasized their economic value to colony and empire alike. In the attempt to forge a political hegemony in the colony against the Wakefieldian influence in imperial legislation, for example, the large landowning squatters' Pastoralist Association resolved in 1844 "that the Commercial and Trading classes of the community are most intimately connected with, and dependent upon the prosperity of the great Pastoral interests of the colony."[1] The squatting

---

[1] *Sydney Morning Herald*, April 10, 1844. In this chapter, particularly, "pastoralism" refers to the squatting system as anchored in the landowner–squatter nexus.

ideology was a neomercantilist view of the colonial economy as a staple producer supported by British government policy. Some elements of this view were a general aggression toward aborigines as marauders and obstacles to land occupation, a preference for bonded labor, little interest in colonial lands except as unimproved pastures for speculative wool growing, and an identification of pastoral prosperity with world market conditions at the expense of local economic diversification. The source of these attitudes was the particular *form* of accumulation of pastoral capital during the squatting period.

THE SOCIAL ENVIRONMENT OF PASTORALISM

Aside from imperial trusteeship of colonial lands, the most basic requirements of capital accumulation in colonial pastoralism were a continuing supply of labor and a market for wool. Each was essential to expanding commodity production and thereby attracting capital for further growth and profit. At the same time, the way these requirements were met gave colonial pastoralism its particular social character.

To begin with, pastoralists grew wool specifically as a world market commodity. As an industrial raw material, colonial wool supported a marketing apparatus created by merchants who used the wool trade to obtain foreign exchange and enhance their trading profits. Merchants did not advance credit to traditional growers to divert their product from household or domestic consumption to the marketplace; rather, they set up growers in the first place as commodity producers who were dependent on their marketing organization. The squatting system in particular epitomized the mercantile origins of colonial wool growing – origins at odds with the local horizons of colonial farmers and artisans, whose production was domestically oriented and whose interests lay in the development of a colonial market.

The origins of Australian wool growing in world-economic relationships made it a specific social form. Traditionally, colonial staples appeared because they met large-scale (consumption or raw material) needs that were unsatisfied by inflexible or limited metropolitan social production. Similarly, Australian wool competed successfully against metropolitan wools because it was a staple commodity produced in a thoroughly commercial environment. Unlike in the European rural economy, in the colony landholder and capitalist were one,[2] thus abolishing the traditional restraints of landed property (e.g., rent and, generally, moral economy) on rural commodity production. Accordingly, wool growing was more profitable and commercially precocious because profits were not shared with a landed rentier class. Although they were shared with merchants, the latter provided the funds that expanded the wool trade anyway.

The other basic requirement of pastoralism was a labor force, and this was largely supplied by the colonial state. The pastoral labor supply came from two sources: assignment of convict labor and regulation of land sales to create a wage labor force. Pastoral production often combined convict and free labor, although assigned convict labor tended to be the chief form in the squatting regions.

The source and conditions of pastoral labor had fundamental implications for the character of the settler economy and society. Whatever the type of labor, squatting was not suited to labor market conditions, given the physical expanse of the frontier and the un-

---

[2] Compare Marx's (1968, pp. 302–3) characterization of "planter capitalism":

In the second type of colonies – plantations – where commercial speculations figure from the start and production is intended for the world market, the capitalist mode of production exists, although only in a formal sense, since the slavery of Negroes precludes free wage-labour, which is the basis of capitalist production. But the business in which slaves are used is conducted by *capitalists*. The method of production which they introduce has not arisen out of slavery but is grafted on to it. And the *elemental* [profusion] existence of the land confronting capital and labour does not offer any resistance to capital investment, hence none of the competition between capitals. Neither does a class of farmers as distinct from landlords develop here. So long as these conditions endure, nothing will stand in the way of cost-price regulating market-value.

This last clause is especially significant because it refers to the operation of the law of value in the staple economy. That is, the law of value was uninhibited in its operation where the market price of wool ("market value") reflected not the actual value of the wool commodity, but the modified price of production, composed of production cost plus the average rate of profit. (Actually, the viability of colonial wool growing was based also on *surplus* profits derived from the differential between colonial pastures and inferior European land, which accordingly allowed colonial producers *differential rent*.) The average rate of profit is formed as a result of redistributing surplus value among the branches of capitalist production with differential organic composition of capital (the equilibrating function of the law of value). Where there exists modern landed property, "the monopoly of private property in land, however, prevents this surplus from passing wholly into the process of equalising profits, and absolute rent is taken from this surplus" (Lenin 1961, p. 117). Under colonial conditions such as existed in Australian pastoral economy, where there was no precapitalist landed class, there was no barrier to the participation of pastoral capital in the equalization of the rate of profit. Thus the relation between production cost and market price was reserved.

attractive nature of shepherding (the major form of pastoral labor). Accordingly, where squatters employed free labor, the wage relation was not a mature capitalist social relation. First, pastoral labor was dull and isolating, geared to constant flock supervision, and therefore incomparable with alternative forms of social labor in the colony. Second, the difficulty of attracting free labor from urban centers to the frontier circumscribed labor market conditions, leading to expensive labor contracting alongside assigned convict labor. Although state policy regulated the occupation of land to create a labor market – which it did in the urban and coastal regions – the peculiar conditions of squatting severely qualified this market. It was for this reason that convict labor was so important to pastoral capital accumulation. This drew attention to the conservative social relations of the pastoral economy – relations that stood in the way of liberal and progressive elements of settler society.

Although pastoral social relations were evidently precapitalist, convict labor was not slave labor just because it was not free labor. This distinction had immediate political significance and, of course, long-term cultural significance. To begin with, whereas slave labor is a privately regulated relation, the state administered convict labor for the Crown. This preempted an integrated private settler society imbued with the kind of antibourgeois ideology associated with slave societies.[3] Pastoralists may have been paternalistic, but their lack of control over the labor supply necessitated a political pragmatism when disruption of the labor supply threatened their capital. This meant that ultimately pastoralists could not stand aloof from political alliances and reforming currents, however much they aspired to.

Initially, the bulk of colonial labor was convict labor supplied by the state on assignment. It was a loan for a time period determined by the particular sentence and/or eligibility for a "ticket of leave."[4] Unlike the system of transportation in colonial America, where convict labor was sold by English authorities to private contractors

---

[3]Compare Genovese (1961, p. 23): "The essential features of Southern particularity as well as of Southern backwardness, can be traced to the relationship of master to slave."

[4] Coghlan (1969, vol. 1, p. 34) describes the assignees: "Their labour was not a chattel which could be sold by one employer to another; it remained the property of the Governor, and to him it would revert on the completion of the period of assignment, or previously if the conditions were not carried out."

for the term of the convicts' sentences (Coghlan 1969, vol. 1, p. 33), which resembled a limited form of slavery, an assignment arrangement between the employer and the state was revocable. Accordingly, assigned labor in the Australian colonies could in no sense be considered slavery.[5] Not only was the labor market the origin and future expectation of convicts,[6] but also the assignee was not (as in slavery) part of the producer's capital (Tomich 1976, p. 154). The producer could, at the termination of the contract period, end his responsibility for maintaining the assignee. This allowed the producer a certain flexibility to vary his labor force in response to market conditions – a feature of the wage system. In this sense the difference between bond and free labor was merely the length of the labor contract.

Despite pastoralists' indiscriminate demand for labor, the social differentiation between bond and free labor had political ramifications. This became clear in the 1840s, when the demands of growers for a revival of convict transportation increasingly conflicted with other settler interests in the development of a free and representative society.

THE CHARACTER OF PASTORAL CAPITAL ACCUMULATION

In 1847, after unshorn wool was considered legal collateral for commercial advances, Edward Curr wrote to Niel Black concerning squatting conditions in Port Phillip:[7]

As long as we have room to expand our flocks, never entertain any opportunities that (we) shall be short of capital to employ any reasonable amount of imported labour. The increase of sheep is capital, just as available to employ labour as money in the bank would be, and the wool of that increased capital can at any moment be either shorn or mortgaged to pay the cost of labor.

This expresses the accumulation dynamic of squatting. Given an open land frontier and the framework of the wool trade, the natural

[5] See, for contrary views, Dunn (1975), Shaw (1970, p. 105), and Forsyth (1970).
[6] David Levine (Economics Department, University of Denver) suggested the importance of this point to me. It assumes discrimination against the emancipist small landholder.
[7] *Niel Black Papers* (LaTrobe Library, Melbourne), Inward Correspondence: Edward Curr to Black, 7 July 1847. Parentheses are used where the writing is difficult to decipher.

increase of wool-bearing flocks (under shepherd supervision) constituted capital accumulation. There was nothing modern about the
growth of shepherded flocks. What transformed it into capital accumulation was its commercial dimension, linking it to metropolitan industrial capital. In other words, the mercantile organization
transformed an age-old industry into a branch of the modern capitalist economy.

In spite of the world-economic context of pastoralism, its pro-
ducion technique was elementary. Shepherding was a traditional
activity, and the insecurity of tenure prohibited capital investment
in labor-saving permanent structures. Consequently, the accumulation of flocks necessitated a parallel increase in the labor supply.
Organized within the metropolitan mercantile system, wool growing in this period could be called a form of "primitive accumulation"
of capital.[8] Such conceptualization helps to characterize the *combination* of social relations in wool growing, linking a precapitalist
mode of production and the wool trade.

The commercial context of pastoralism was critical to its survival.
It depended on a continuous supply of metropolitan capital (through
colonial bank discounting) and the mercantile mediation of wool
markets to grower. Precisely because of this framework, as alluded
to by Edward Curr, merchants speculated on future wool markets
through their credit relations with growers. In turn, the latter sought
to maximize the size of their flocks (through purchase and breeding)
to profit through their wool bill and through the sales of surplus
sheep to newcomers. Under these conditions, then, the pastoral
enterprise was essentially a center of commercial speculation within
the world market.[9] Accordingly, not only was pastoral capital accumulation limited primarily to the increase of flocks, but also the
colonial economy tended toward a pastoral specialization, so that
accumulation patterns were limited by the undeveloped social division of labor.

---

[8] Thus, the primitive accumulation of pastoral capital designates commodity production lacking the full technical (fixed capital and the application of scientific
technique to production) and social (wage labour market) relations most adequate
to "capitalist" accumulation of capital. (I am using the term here also to signify
the world-historical process of politically guaranteeing a bonded labor force for
capital in the periphery of the capitalist world economy.) See McMichael (1977).
[9] See the quotation from Marx in footnote 2.

LABOR REQUIREMENTS IN WOOL PRODUCTION

Shepherds supervised the year-long process of wool growing. Because this was an entirely natural process, increased productivity measures (such as certain breeding patterns and new pastures) did not alter the labor relationship. Wool growing was not technically dynamic in its organization of labor. However, the maintenance of an acceptable quality and level of fleece yield required a certain ratio of sheep to shepherd, and the scarcity of labor from the late 1830s threatened this balance.

The deleterious effects on wool production of raising the sheep/shepherd ratio (increasing the flock size) are described in the 1837 minutes of evidence taken before the Committee on Immigration, Indian and British, into New South Wales.[10] Thomas Potter Macqueen stated:

I know that many flock-owners have been obliged, from want of a sufficient number of shepherds, to double the numbers of sheep in each flock under the charge of their shepherds; and I have refused to punish shepherds when brought before me, as a Magistrate, because I considered the flocks they were in charge of were larger than they could properly attend to. The losses occasioned from want of hands to preserve cleanliness, to repel the invasion of native dogs, and from the impossibility of effectually securing large flocks, are infinitely greater than the additional expense of able-bodied shepherds, capable of doing justice to smaller flocks, would amount to.

John Blaxland stated:

[10] *V&P*, NSW, 1837. The use of such evidence is at face value; it has been suggested (Sinclair 1971) that evidence of the loss of output with greater flock size is contradicted by the actual increase in flock sizes; however, it is also true that there is little empirical evidence concerning the resulting effects on wool output. I am inclined to agree with Abbott (1972, p. 184) that the socially desirable proportion of labor to capital reflected the prevailing social conditions (and these conditions involved the social development of frontier production, including relations among squatters with respect to flock transfers and general health conditions, levels of black resistance, supervisory experience, and the incidence of wild dogs). Compare Kiddle (1967, p. 135):

A few had advocated this practice (increased flock size) for some time, not to reduce labour costs, but to improve the health of sheep by giving them more rest. It was possible only when the flocks were clean, and not many were then without scab. But by 1842 the Glenormiston flocks were left unguarded at night, and after several months no losses from either wild dogs or blacks were reported, a significant indication of the removal of both these former dangers.

Besides, we are interested in the accumulation rate and its determinants under the given mode of production, not *potential* levels of output (Sinclair 1971).

The want of labour has now become so alarming, that we have not men to plant our crops, or gather in what little may be grown of hay or corn, and the decrease in the quantity of wool, will soon become as rapid as was its increase under different circumstances. The settler is now compelled to put from 600 to 1000 sheep into each of its flocks, which will greatly decrease the number of lambs, and be productive of scab, in consequence of the neglect and filth which must result from so many being crowded together.

Increasing the flock size per shepherd in response to the labor scarcity reflects the primitive character of pastoral capital accumulation. Because the labor supply was a fundamental constraint, the only way to maintain operations was to intensify supervision by enlarging flocks and thus risk deterioration of the product. This response, sometimes combined with the substitution of unpaid labor by squatter management,[11] risked problems with labor discipline. As Edward Curr (1883, pp. 353–4) found:

The reader is aware that, at the outset, my squatting had been a losing business. On getting settled at Tongala my brother and myself made great efforts to bring this unfortunate state of things to a close, and the property into a paying condition. As it was impossible for the time to increase the yield of wool, the change had to be brought about by lessening the expenditure. To effect this, the most important steps in our power were, after lambing and weaning to run the whole of our sheep in two flocks instead of four, and discharge two of the shepherds, a hut-keeper, and the two bushmen. But, though wages fell shortly from £45 to £18 a year, servants were as scarce as ever, so that we had a great deal of trouble in getting our shepherds to agree to have their flocks increased. For notwithstanding that there was no difficulty in shepherding larger flocks, as the event proved, the convict instincts of my men led them to make a point of their labour not being too profitable to their master... Subsequently I further raised the minimum of my flocks – weaners to two thousand, and grown sheep to between three and four thousand, and on one occasion had as many as ten thousand ewes and lambs in one flock ... Carrying on the station with this reduction of hands brought about two results, for it both made the undertaking a success financially, and gave my brother and myself a great deal to do.

Curr's statement is particularly interesting in his reference to "the convict instincts" of his men; this is perhaps the key to the relation

---

[11] Or, indeed, the substitution of women in the labor force. In the Port Phillip district, for instance, wives were considered acceptable as hutkeepers by the 1840s, and Niel Black calculated that with male wages £40 a year, a woman's rations (no wage) cost him £20 (Kiddle 1967, p. 135).

between labor scarcity and flock size (as referred to in footnote 10). The resistance by assignees to more work is consistent with the fact that given a fixed (legally prescribed) level of wages in kind, the convict-shepherd did not have the inducement of higher wages that a free laborer expected. *This was an extremely vulnerable aspect of pastoral capital accumulation; it had no recourse to technical change to raise the productivity of its labor.*

Whether bond or free labor was used, the *quantitative* character of pastoral capital accumulation – flock aggregation requiring fresh pasture and parallel increases in supervisory labor – was always constrained by the labor supply in the colony. This limitation took either a physical or a value form. It is, therefore, reasonable to suppose that although *empirically* the rising sheep/shepherd ratio through the 1830s (with sustained output levels) may deny a labor scarcity, it may actually conceal the progressive transformation in the type of labor from convict to free. With increasing wages resulting, this would not negate the phenomenon of a labor constraint.[12] In this sense,[13] capital accumulation required sufficient and regular supplies of labor to maintain a viable level of wages where a rudimentary labor market existed. This appears to be the implication of Edward Curr's comments in the letter to Niel Black.

I agree ... that the minimum price of land is far too high, and that (most) costs arise from labour coming upon us in large and (uncertain masses ...) exceeded by still greater (dearths). This latter cost I always think will be best assisted by borrowing on immigration funds on (ten percent) of the lands, and the instalments of the fund so borrowed would be called for and expanded in immigration in amounts proportional to our *average* requirements, and not to the chance sales of any one year. [Black Papers, corresp. 7 July 1847]

LABOR SUPPLY AND PASTORAL CAPITAL ACCUMULATION

The supply of labor constrained the accumulation of pastoral capital both individually and collectively. This constraint was expressed in the Wakefieldian principle of combining immigration with the sale

[12] In the mid-1830s, for example, shepherds were offered an additional £10 a year if they could dispense with a watchman (*V&P, NSW*, 1835; C. D. Riddell's evidence to the Committee on Immigration, 21 May, 1835).
[13] Sinclair (1971) and Abbott (1972) ignore this sense in their discussion of the issue of labor supply.

of land, which itself was an indication of general prosperity in the pastoral economy. In the squatting regions, where pastoralists profited by the sale of surplus sheep to newcomers, the supply of labor to supervise such flock expansion affected individual enterprise. Hence, Lawrence Dalhunty's evidence before the 1842 Committee on Immigration:[14]

Q: To what cause do you principally attribute the noninvestment of capital in the purchase of stock?
Dalhunty: Principally to the want of labor, the rate of wages being still too high to induce capitalists to invest their money in stock.

Squatting outstripped the supply of labor, particularly after convict transportation ceased. Indeed, the strategic significance of convict labor to the industry was noted in the 1838 report of the Committee on Immigration (*V&P, NSW,* 1839):

The sudden discontinuance of transportation and assignment, by depriving the colonists of convict labour, must necessarily curtail their means of purchasing Crown lands, and consequently the supply of funds for the purpose of immigration.

This was not surprising because proportionally, the total number of convicts assigned to private capital in the 1830s exceeded two-thirds of the pastoral labor force.[15]

Additionally, the relationship of the labor supply to the colonial economy became the subject of intense lobbying of the Colonial Office by influential graziers. William Macarthur drafted a letter in 1839 to request that colonial authorities no longer restrict the emigration of labor to land revenue:

Indeed now that instructions have been given to raise the minimum price of land, in that Colony, it seems but politic to increase the supply of labor, without which the land can be of no value.

He continued, citing the following statistics:

---

[14] *V&P, NSW,* 1842, Committee on Immigration, Minutes of Evidence, 10 June 1842.
[15] See, for example, Fitzpatrick (1969, p. 56 fn.) (1834: 67 percent), and Coghlan (1969, vol. 1, p. 181) (1835: 73 percent). Following are figures from Dunsdorfs (1970, p. 87) on the number of convicts assigned:

1833	17,722	1836	20,934	1839	25,322
1834	18,304	1837	23,431	1840	25,299
1835	19,247	1838	25,929	1841	19,570

	Number of emigrants to Australian colonies	Value of land sold in Australian colonies
1832	3,733	£ 6,513.11.6
1833	4,093	14,133.16.4
1834	2,800	36,814. 9.1
1835	1,860	87,097. 9.1
1836	3,124	58,079. 6.9
1837	5,054	—

This falling off in the Land revenue was preceded by so great a deficiency in Labor, and increase in Wages, as to make it evident that if the Land Sales had been less productive it arose not from any deficiency of Capital, but because they had absorbed all available Labor in the Colony. It is known that this difficulty in procuring labor had driven capital into other Channels, and had been productive to extreme loss and inconvenience to many who had invested it in the purchase of land. [Macarthur Papers, vol. 22, pp. 223–4]

Macarthur further proposed that funds for emigration costs be advanced against future land sales to resolve the scarce labor problem. Such representations constituted an ongoing struggle by large growers against the rigidities of the Wakefieldian policy of the Colonial Office – a struggle that fueled the growth of demands for responsible government in the 1840s.

Labor scarcity is a persistent theme during this period, reflected in the continuing annual reports of Colonial Immigration Committees. Particularly striking in the minutes of evidence from these committee reports is the large number of landholders who were willing to give immediate employment to immigrant labor.[16] Estimates of the labor force that the colony could absorb indicate the collective awareness of the labor problem.

In 1835 Sir John Jamison estimated an immediate deficiency of "two to three thousand agricultural labourers."[17] Thomas Potter Macqueen estimated that 2,000 laborers would find immediate em-

[16] *V&P, NSW*, 1839, Committee on Immigration, Minutes of Evidence, 30 May 1835.
[17] *V&P, NSW*, 1837, Minutes of Evidence taken before the Committee on Immigration . . . , 23 June 1837.

ployment in 1837 in the Hunter District alone. In the same year, William Wentworth stated:[18]

I think ten thousand immigrants, including mechanics, farm servants, shepherds, cowherds, laborers, and household servants, would not be too great a number to import as soon as they can be procured, and, afterwards, about five or six thousand yearly ... Allowing two shepherds and one hutkeeper to each one thousand sheep, and two hundred supplementary hands, the next year's increase of sheep will require two thousand additional persons to attend them.

Finally, Henry O'Brien attempted to calculate labor requirements for 1838 in relation to the natural expansion of sheep numbers.[19]

The number of bales of wool shipped during the year 1836, was:	22,000
And suppose that on 18th January 1837, there remained to be shipped:	1,000
And that there were manufactured in the colony:	1,000
The aggregate produce of 1836, would thus amount to:	24,000
Again suppose that each bale contained 100 fleeces, the number of sheep clipped that year would be:	2,400,000
To which are to be added the September lambs not shorn; say to each 10,000 sheep, 1,200 lambs; making the total number of lambs:	288,000
To which add the next March lambing, say:	300,000
Making the total number of sheep in the colony, in the present year:	2,988,000
For each 1,200 sheep, 3 men are required as shepherds and hutkeepers, which would give:	7,470
And for every 100 men thus employed, 10 labouring men would be required as farm servants, labourers and bullock drivers, which would give for these purposes:	747
Making the number employed on sheep establishments:	8,217
To which add the number employed on cattle establishments, say:	1,200
Which would give as the total number of men employed in 1837, on the several sheep and cattle stations in the Colony:	9,417
For every 10,000 sheep, 10 extra men will be required in May, 1838, and taking for granted that the flocks will at that time amount to 3,000,000, there would then be new employment in tending the flocks alone, for:	3,000
And there would be required for the cattle establishments about:	500
Making the number of immigrants that would be required for the increased flocks and herds alone of 1838:	3,500

---

[18] *Ibid.*, 24 June 1837.
[19] *Ibid.*, 28 June 1837.

To attract immigrant labor, pastoralists resorted to inducement such as offering considerable wage differentials between agricultural England and the colony and provisions to settle laborers as tenants on their land.[20] Thus, Sir John Jamison reported having settled many "thriving" tenants,[21] and contracts such as the following between emigrant laborers and Messrs. James, William, and Edward Macarthur were common:

That we will give you during good behaviour for three years, that you may be in our service, Fifteen pounds per annum, a cottage rent free, a plot of ground for a garden, seven pounds of meat, also, the privilege of keeping a cow with Pigs and poultry on condition of their getting into no mischief, and being solely for your own use, and after five years should you continue that time in our service, we will establish each of you as a tenant on fertile land taking the rent either in labour or in produce and during the first six months in our service to give your wife one half of the above allowance of provisions. [Macarthur Papers, vol. 22, p. 118]

Such tenancy arrangements were confined to the settled districts where there was freehold land. In contrast, in the squatting regions, the concentration of sheep and the extreme difficulty of attracting a secure labor force exacerbated the general labor constraint on pastoral capital in the 1830s, giving rise to such schemes as importing coolie labor. Robert Scott argued for the "introduction of Indian labourers as a temporary measure only,"[22] and in 1840 the chairman of the Committee on Immigration, W. G. Australia, reported:[23]

Under the pressure of severe necessity, and every other resource having failed, it would be advisable to reverse the prohibition which is now in

---

[20] For example, in *V&P, NSW*, 1835, John Blaxland (30 May 1835) remarked:

When I left England in 1807, the wages of farm servants were in the following ratio:

Bailiffs, about	£15–20
First Waggoner	£12
Second Ditto	£10 etc.

But I understand that now men of that description get much lower wages in England. The rates of wages in this colony may be stated as follows:

A Bailiff from	£30–70 according to qualifications
A first waggoner	£20–25
Second ditto	£16–20 etc.

In all cases rations and lodgings were allowed.

[21] *V&P, NSW*, 1835, Evidence to Committee on Immigration, 30 May 1835.
[22] *V&P, NSW*, 1837, Minutes of Evidence taken before the Committee on Immigration, Indian and British, into New South Wales, 9 June 1837.
[23] *V&P, NSW*, 1840, Report, Committee on Immigration.

force against the employment of the Coolies, for a limited period, by Colonists, who might be willing to introduce them at their own charge, and who would give security for their return to their native country, at the expiration of their covenanted terms of service.

Ad hoc solutions such as these to the labor shortage reinforced the neomercantilist propensities of colonial wool growers. The need to maintain their capital, and therefore their viability as staple commodity producers, resulted from the world-market origins of their enterprise and encouraged demands for nonmarket mechanisms to remain competitive. This kind of particularism led them to embrace social relations that contradicted progressive tendencies within the settler society.

SOURCES OF PASTORAL EXPANSION

It has been traditionally held that the basis of pastoral profits was not the sale of wool but of stock. Thus, the source of expansion in the pastoral economy was production of surplus livestock for the local market.[24] This is a methodological issue, however, requiring the clarification of the concept of profitability. The traditional approach is neoclassical insofar as it extrapolates from the individual unit of production. An alternative approach is to consider the social context of pastoralism, since we are not examining a timeless form of pastoral production. Rather we are examining a particular form of pastoralism derived from specific world-historical processes and with specific social and political consequences within settler Australia. A neoclassical concept of profitability obscures this context.

If, for example, we examine the profitability of the individual production unit to derive a theory of economic expansion of pas-

---

[24] For example, in his attempt to understand the role of wool in the development, or growth process, of the New South Wales economy, Abbott (1971, p. 202) reaches the rather impotent conclusion that "the *recognition* of the potential future income from wool exports ... was the key factor, rather than the income realised from wool exports" based on the weight of contemporary evidence suggesting "that pastoralists' profits depended to an inordinate degree on the sale of sheep." Unfortunately, the study ends there. The most recent reference to this issue is that of Sinclair (1976, p. 70), who disagrees with Abbott's conclusion, arguing that "the separation of wool growing from sheep raising is an unreal one." Although Sinclair is correct in stressing the integral nature of the several operations of the pastoral unit in determining costs and profits, his understanding of the sources of expansion in pastoral economy is no less vague, basing it on new settlers' expectations.

toralism, then stock sales to newcomers can be the only precise answer. Growth accordingly depends entirely on the expectation of the continued productive occupation of the frontier. At the same time, the dynamic of mercantile credit is ignored, since the theory proceeds from the operations of the discrete unit of enterprise. It does not explain, for instance, why the squatter Henry Marsh should say that the possible 10–13 percent profit on sheep farming "is not obtained in one case out of twenty," and why therefore, although different levels of profitability existed among pastoral capitals, the small producing unit was reproduced on an extending frontier (especially during the years of cyclical upturn).[25] This can be understood only from a social analysis, within the marketing context of pastoralism.[26]

As suggested in Chapter 5, the driving force of pastoralism was the competition among merchants and financiers for the wool trade. In effect, merchant capital reproduced pastoral units as centers of commercial speculation. This predominance of credit, in conjunction with the state support of squatting, gave colonial producers sufficient commercial advantage in the world wool market. Profitability in pastoralism was not simply a local phenomenon. It is for this reason that the methodological individualist concept of profitability is contradictory.

Evidence for the profitability of the pastoral unit of production is sufficient and diverse enough to form some conclusions about the financial operations of pastoral capital.[27] Appendix 5 gives two statements about profitability by Edward Hamilton and Henry Marsh, the former a landowner (evidenced by his surplus stock supplying the meat market) and the latter a squatter from New England. All the evidence available on profitability combines the revenues from wool and surplus stock on the total financial calculations. However, the usual presentation of his finances by the pastoralist provides the clue to the *mode* of operation of pastoral capital. For instance, Lawrence Dalhunty gave evidence to the 1842 Immigration Committee thus:[28]

---

[25] *V&P, NSW*, 1843, Committee on Immigration: Minutes of Evidence, 20 July, 1842.
[26] For a theoretical elaboration of this point, see Banaji (1977).
[27] See Abbott (1971, ch. 5) for a summary of statements of profitability.
[28] *V&P, NSW*, 1842, Committee on Immigration, Minutes of Evidence, 10 June 1842.

Q: Do you think the clip of wool at present pays for the management of the sheep?

A: It depends wholly upon the management; with good management the wool at its present price (in 1842, average price was 15*s*. 1*d*. per lb. – before the trough of 11/5 in 1844) would pay all expenses attendant on sheep farming, but would not pay for luxuries ... we only require to get rid of our surplus stock to make our business profitable.

The implication, often explicit, is that the returns from wool cover current expenses and stock sales provide the profit. We know, however, that in most cases (see Appendix 5, for example) city merchants handled the returns from wool and, furthermore, that the returns to the pastoralist appeared as credit *advancing* the value of the wool before its realization. Now these advances to the wool grower entailed accounting operations centralized in the port city, mainly settling expenses on the debit side of the grower's account. In this system, then, where the current solvency of the wool grower depended on the link between credit and wool clip, it is easy to see how profits appeared to be related to occasional stock sales. The wool grower's finances depended on mercantile advances, which were geared to fluctuating London wool market prices, and the producer was locked into dependence on merchant capital. In other words, the domestic market for surplus stock assumed an *extraordinary* role in the wool grower's calculations, because it was through sales of surplus stock that the grower could realize immediate and tangible income. For the pastoralist this represented a transitory glimpse of financial independence, which was denied in his structural relation with the factor.

This raises the other aspect of stock sales in a pastoral economy: the relation between the emphasis on maximum breeding (manifested in the quantitative expansion of flocks) and supplying the means of production for new settlers through the sale of surplus stock. This was the speculative activity of the pastoralist himself in conditions of prosperity. Wakefield (from Pritchard 1968, pp. 29–30) drew attention to this.

Our rich sheep farmers owe their fortunes, not so much to the high price, in proportion to the cost of production, which they have hitherto obtained from wool, as to the monopoly which they have had of an article still more in demand than wool itself – namely, fine-fleeced sheep. Mr. Macarthur, for instance, who was the first to perceive how admirably this country is suited to sheep farming made more money by the sale of sheep to his fellow colonists than by the sale of fleeces to the wool-staplers of London

... But the advantage that he, and others who followed his example, enjoyed for some time, has already exhausted itself. The supply of sheep *for stock* is already equal to the demand; a great fall in price has ensued, and as sheep increase much faster than people, there is no chance of an alteration favourable to the flock-owner.

Speculation in flock expansion to maximize profits was, however, a derivative practice. It depended on boom conditions, which in turn required an expanding labor supply and, most important, an expansion of commercial credit. In other words, mercantile speculation (with wool as the ultimate object of interest) fueled speculation by pastoralists.

The pastoral unit of production was truly a center of commercial speculation. Benjamin Boyd expressed this most cogently when discussing boom and slump in the pastoral economy.[29]

This plethora of money, and the facilities of accommodation, had the effect of raising stock to absurd prices; and also the settler was indifferent what wages he paid, so long as his increase brought him from 50*s.* to 60*s.* a head, and instead of looking on his wool as the sole source of profit, it was considered quite of minor importance, and in most cases barely sufficient for wages; whereas now it is by concentrating the energies of the population upon the production of wool alone that we can look for relief.

Individual pastoral capital accumulation was uneven, showing concentration at one pole and continual proliferation of small enterprises at the other. The actual extent and course of accumulation of large pastoral capital are illustrated in Table 7.1 for Niel Black and Company's Glenormiston station.[30]

In spite of the differentiation among pastoral enterprises, the actual rate of return on wool growing itself may not have been all that uneven because production techniques were universally unchanged. Henry Marsh suggests this in his statement concerning profitability (see Appendix 5).

The profit I have spoken of ... may perhaps be obtained with a very small number of sheep as well as on a large scale, as although, in the latter case the proportion of expenses is less, in the former instance the squatter's own personal labour and exertions will be proportionately more.

[29] *V&P, NSW,* 1843, Select Committee on Immigration, Minutes of Evidence, 27 September 1843.
[30] *Niel Black Papers,* Box 38/44. For the unevenness of pastoralism generally, see Roberts (1970, pp. 362–3).

Table 7.1: *Half-yearly returns of the number of persons employed or residing at and of the number and description of the livestock on the licensed station (Glenormiston), 1841–7*

Date	Estimated acres of run	Acres in cultivation	Persons	Stock Horses	Cattle	Sheep	No. of licenses
July 1, 1841	16,000	25	21	4	312	3,500	
1842	16,000	20	28	19	463	6,601	1
1843	40,000	25	31	35	707	11,790	1
1844	60 sq. mi.	30	30	41	950	15,947	
Jan. 1, 1845	55 sq. mi.	26	38	42	960	18,660	1
July 1, 1845	85 sq. mi.	24	46	51	1,066	20,193	
Jan. 1, 1846	85 sq. mi.	24	60	52	1,204	17,273	1
July 1, 1846	85 sq. mi.	24	54	47	1,301	19,582	79
July 1, 1847	85 sq. mi.	24	88	56	1,525	20,245	39

Where net profitability did show considerable differentiation in relation to economies of scale (as suggested by Edward Hamilton's statement), the difference was in the mercantile relation. Large pastoralists could reduce their relative marketing expenses (merchant's commission, interest charges, and the like) by the sheer size of their clip.

The mercantile connection was determinate in the profitability of pastoralism in general. Not only did mercantile intervention sustain pastoral production over its year-long term, but also competition among merchants expanded the industry. Pastoral expansion was, in this period, a function of merchant capital accumulation. Merchants valorized colonial production because of their special connection to the world market and sources of commercial credit.

The convenience of merchant capital intervention in the form of credit is illustrated in the following statement by Alexander Mollison in a letter to his father on July 18, 1846: "My wool goes to London on my own account. The merchant advances 14*d*. and I could easily sell out at 16½*d*. or 17*d*., but I see no reason for doing so, expecting that it is not in such good condition as usual and of this of course I could not take advantage."[31] The normal interest on loans to merchants from banks was 10 percent, but interest rates on loans

---

[31] *Alexander Mollison* – Letters 1825–59. See also Appendix 6.

from merchants to pastoralists were often considerably higher (Roberts 1970, p. 202). This reflected the general practice of colonial banks refusing to make loans to producers on the grounds that they had nothing (either fixed or liquid assets) to secure such loans. The fact that most bank directors were also merchants, alluded to by the 1843 Committee on Monetary Confusion,[32] meant that they obtained interest charges twice on the single transaction. It also supported the system whereby the merchant gained the factoring agency of the pastoralists' operations through accommodation. In short, the mercantile community had a direct stake in the prosperity of the pastoral industry, since intervention facilitated the appropriation of profit in the wool trade.

CONCLUSION

The aim of this chapter has been to analyze pastoral capital accumulation during the squatting period as a way of understanding the specific social relations of pastoralism and the source of its conservative political ideology. This necessitated spelling out the institutional arrangements behind the supply of labor and capital to the pastoral industry and thereby giving them a particular world-historical content. The emphasis has been on the overwhelming commercial context of colonial pastoralism, where wool growing developed as a branch of production within the nineteenth-century world division of labor. It is from this world market context that we can see the primitive form of capital accumulation in pastoralism. Perhaps the most significant characteristics were the speculative nature of the industry and its dependence on a labor supply equivalent to its expansion of flocks of sheep.

According to this characterization, not only did large pastoralists espouse a socially conservative ideology appropriate to a precapitalist landed environment, but also this ideology included a reactionary theme. It was reactionary because of the tenuous nature of their economy; they had no control over their labor supply, and they did not own the land they occupied in the squatting regions. They were therefore compelled to argue for maintaining their monopoly of the landed economy. In so doing they brought their

---

[32] *V&P, NSW,* 1843, Committee on Monetary Confusion; see, for example, Samuel Lyons's evidence (21 September).

neomercantilist pretensions to the political arena of the settler state, generating opposition to the privilege and social consequences of squatting. These opposing settler ideologies symbolized the transitions under way in the capitalist world economy under British hegemony.

Part III

CONFRONTING THE AGRARIAN QUESTION (1840–1900)

8

THE 1840S CRISIS AND SOCIAL TRANSITION

INTRODUCTION

The colonial depression in the early 1840s was primarily due to a crisis in the pastoral industry and its relations with the world market. Existing accounts of the depression extensively document its cyclical characteristics[1] but pay little attention to its historical impact on capitalist development in Australia. In this chapter I will analyze the depression as a crystallization of the barriers to capital accumulation in the colony imposed by pastoralism. Whereas this is the focus of the chapter, there is a further implication to be drawn; that concerns the contradictory political responses (consolidation versus subordination of the squatter economy) to the external vulnerability of the pastoral economy revealed in the depression. These responses structured subsequent political debate in colonial Australia. The argument here is that the 1840s depression was a significant threshold in colonial political and economic development.

In the imperial context, there was a close correlation between the trade cycles in Britain and colonial Australia (Hartwell 1954b). More particularly, there was a steady downward trend in wool prices in London (where most Australian wool was sold) during the late 1830s, culminating in a depression in the English textile industry in the early 1840s. Two primary forces affected the reproductive circuit of industrial capital in textile manufacture.[2] On the one hand,

---

[1] See, for example, Butlin (1968), Coghlan (1969, vol. 1), Fitzpatrick (1969), Roberts (1970), and Shann (1930).
[2] The "circuit of industrial capital" refers to the purchase by textile manufacturers of wool (raw material), its subsequent fabrication in the labor process (with machinery), and its sale on markets as cloth. In this way the wool grower is linked to the final consumer, and the economy of the wool grower and the manufacturer, as well as mediating merchants, is dependent on the sale to the final consumer. The sale marks the realization of the value produced in the whole circuit.

British capitalism entered a cyclical downturn in which demand decreases in woolen export markets exacerbated the excess capacity of the textile industry (following industrialization). Wool prices in London dipped sharply. On the other hand, on a long-term basis, the shift in the source of wool supplies – that is, less from Germany and more from Australia[3] – represented an increase in the level of *world* pasture productivity and therefore a secular fall in wool production costs. Downward price trends were accordingly transmitted through the circuit of capital in the woolen textile industry, thus affecting industrial as well as pastoral capital accumulation.

The constraints on pastoral capital accumulation derived from its primitive character. At the most immediate level, its accumulation was limited by the supply of labor (and its cost), especially with the abolition of assigned convict labor in 1840. At a second level, the speculative relation with merchant capital also imposed constraints – most important, the preclusion of a supply of small-farmer labor on the frontier, which contributed to rising food prices (and therefore wages) as the pastoral economy imported grain. This inflationary tendency was exacerbated by the dominance of merchant capital and its monopolization of colonial trade. Increasing production costs for pastoralists, in addition to rising interest charges on loans, completed the profit squeeze experienced with falling wool prices.

TRENDS IN TEXTILE PRODUCTION

The 1830s and early 1840s were a transitional period for British industrial capitalism because it represented the denouement of the early phase of industrialization based on textiles. The next phase would be geared to the production of capital goods, stimulated by industrialization elsewhere in the world economy. As Hobsbawm (1969, p. 109) put it, "The age of crisis for textile industrialism was the age of breakthrough for coal and iron, the age of railway construction."

Early British industrialization, led by cotton textiles, depended on commercial strength and an imperial division of labor providing

---

[3] Percentage volumes of wool imported into England from Australia and Germany were, respectively, 7.9 and 70.7 in 1831, and 28.4 and 34.2 in 1843. See Burroughs (1967, p. 383).

Table 8.1: *Commodity structure of Britain's
export trade, 1830s*

Commodity	£ (millions)	% (rounded)
Cotton piece goods	16.7	34
Cotton yarn	7.4	15
Woolens	5.8	12
Linens	3.6	7
Iron and steel	1.5	5
Hardware	12.2	3
All others	12.2	24

access to raw materials and European and colonial markets. British commercial hegemony was the cutting edge of world economic development at this time, a period characterized by Schumpeter (1939, pp. 170, 252) as the "industrial revolution Kondratieff" – the long cycle of world-capitalist economy between roughly 1790 and 1850. In the quarter-century following the Napoleonic Wars, the production of cotton textiles increased at a rate of 6–7 percent per year (Hobsbawm 1969, p. 69), including an expansion of industrial production unsurpassed in the rest of the nineteenth century (Rostow 1961, p. 8). The financing of technical innovations in the new industrial sectors of textile manufacture, transportation, and coal and iron was aided by the emergence of the London discount market, which, through the practice of billbroking, channeled funds from country banks with surpluses to banks in industrial districts (King 1972; Scammell 1968).

The increasing importance of Lombard Street also stood behind the commercial expansion in this period. Trade with the United States, Britain's principal customer, developed through merchant banking agencies in London and Liverpool, with cotton leading the way (Jenks 1973, p. 67; Hidy 1941).[4] Following cotton exports was the category "woolens" in the commodity structure of Britain's export trade, as Table 8.1 shows (Matthews 1954, p. 43).

The woolen textile industry (composed of woolen and worsted

---

[4] For example, "in the post-Napoleonic decades something like one half of all British exports consisted of cotton products, and at their peak (in the middle of the 1830s) raw cotton made up twenty percent of total new imports" (Hobsbawm 1969, p. 69).

manufacture) expanded in the shadow of cotton manufacture but nevertheless adopting its revolutionary methods of factory production after high-speed machinery was adapted to work with wool fibers. Worsted manufacture (using long staple wools) led woolen manufacture (using shorter, more easily matted wools) in this development because it was less inhibited by centuries of tradition in the woolen trades (Checkland 1964, p. 119). It was not until the 1830s that both cotton and wool textile industries adopted the power loom, causing a 50 percent reduction in the wages of hand-loom weavers almost overnight (James 1857). The resulting expansion in the production of woolen textiles was approximately 30 percent in woolen mills in West Riding and 65 percent in worsted.[5]

The relation of the Australian pastoral industry to the secular expansion in the production of English woolen textiles depended largely on worsted manufacture. John James (1857) commented: "The rapid rise in the value of South Down and Australian wool may be attributed, in the main, to its being now [1830], from the improvements in machinery, adapted to the worsted manufacture."

A further development in worsted manufacture after 1837 was the introduction of cotton warps in the weaving of worsted stuffs. This arose in response to initial demands by American merchants for a suitable type of luxury cloth ("orleans cloth"). James (1857) remarked:

Of all the eras which have marked the history of this manufacture none exceeds in importance . . . It has imparted a new character to the worsted industry, enabled the manufacturer to suit the requirements of the age by producing light and elegant stuff goods, rivalling in the cheapness articles from cotton, and in brilliancy and delicacy those from silk. Henceforward the trade assumes a new and broader aspect, and exhibits a power of adaptation for all classes of goods, and a capability of expansion which, a few years previous to this period, could not be conceived.

In Schumpeter's schema, this expansion in the 1830s represented the working-out of the process of technical advance in consumer goods production through the downward phase of the Kondratieff cycle. The latter would trough before consolidating a new technical basis for expansion in the producer-goods industry – the foundation

[5] "Such growth was extraordinary. It showed a burst of confidence in the industry that was almost unlimited" (Checkland 1964, p. 125).

of the next long cycle of world capitalism. Schumpeter identified railroads as the compelling new technology.[6]

Superimposed on this emerging technical barrier to capital accumulation in textile industrialism was the particular trade cycle (in Schumpeter's terms, "Juglar cycle") of English capitalism in the early 1830s boom and the late 1830s crisis. This cycle was closely woven, through commerce built around the cotton trade, with a similar cycle in American capitalism, whereby the voracious U.S. importing of British manufacturers (consumer goods and railway iron) created a growing debt with London.[7] The severe drain on the Bank of England's reserves triggered an increase in the discount rate and a subsequent crisis in the accommodation of American merchants, beginning in the cotton trade (see Jenks 1973, pp. 57–8; Matthews 1954, pp. 57–8). The cycle of expansion was reversed, leading to a sharp decline in British exports to America.

Although the 1837 crisis in the cotton trade did not induce a general commercial depression in Britain, it certainly affected the stability of the British textile industry. The state of the U.S. market largely governed the fluctuations in exports of woolens at this time (Matthews 1954, p. 43); indeed, about 30 percent of all British woolen exports were accounted for by the U.S. market (Heaton 1929–30, p. 147). Table 8.2 shows the trade cycle in woolen exports associated with the fluctuations in the U.S. economy, with a downturn after the mid-1830s.[8]

The downturn in the British woolen textile industry resulting from the uncertainties of the American market was described in

---

[6] Hobsbawm (1969, pp. 69, 72) agreed, stressing that an ongoing process of industrialization required the stimulation of "heavy capital goods industries of coal, iron and steel," and arguing that industrialization on the basis of one sector of the textile industry was "limited" and "neither stable nor secure."

[7] As Jenks (1973, p. 84) writes:

The increased sale of American cotton was more than matched by the purchases of British implements and cutlery, silks and cloths, and some railway iron. Between 1830 and 1836 the volume of Anglo-American trade doubled, and in the year ending September 30, 1836, the imports from Great Britain exceeded the exports to that country by more than twenty million dollars. On her entire trade the United States was debtor for the year to the extent of sixty million dollars. And she was debtor besides for interest upon previous borrowings. The export of British capital had created a relation which only still larger capital exports could sustain.

[8] Data from Matthews (1954, p. 153) and James (1857).

Table 8.2: *Exports of British woolen and worsted goods, 1832–42*

Year	Pieces exported to the United States (rounded)	Value of woolen and worsted exports (in £ millions)
1832	337,000	5.2
1833	512,000	6.3
1834	342,000	5.7
1835	560,000	6.8
1836	461,000	7.6
1837	127,000	4.7
1838	316,000	5.8
1839	498,000	6.3
1840	273,000	5.3
1841	498,000	5.7
1842	285,000	5.2

letters to colonial merchants and growers from the English wool-importing firm, Robert Brooks and Co. Ltd.[9]

To Messrs. R. Campbell Jnr & Co., London, 8th May, 1841

. . . I enclose you particulars of the 15 Bales Wool shipped by you to my consignment on the Jane – I regret to report that the Public Sales are going off more heavily than usual. I really wish I could hold out to you any fair and reasonable prospect of an improvement in prices; we cannot look to the United States of America for customers for our manufactures to any extent as nothing can be more gloomy than the monetary affairs of America.

To W. J. Macmichael Esq., Cornhill, 27th Sept., 1841

. . .Although the monetary affairs of the United States are yet in an unsatisfactory position yet there becomes a little growing demand for our manufactures and I am led to believe that the demand will be considerably increased next spring, hence we may look forward to better prices for wool.

The instability of the export market for woolens partially accounted for a decline in the price of wool after a peak in 1836. Wool prices remained low until the 1850s (Abbott 1971, p. 64; Imlah 1950). This price decline reflected both demand and supply trends; the demand trend was a short-term cyclical phenomenon, exacerbating the longer-term secular trend in supply conditions.

[9] Robert Brooks & Co., London, *Papers 1822–1890*, Mitchell Library.

This secular trend was not independent of the demand for wool, however. The latter was changing with industrialization, involving changes in the type of wools required both in production and as a result of competition with cottons in the cloth trade. The rise in demand for long-stapled colonial wools was one component of the long-term displacement in the London wool market of Saxon and Spanish supplies, which had been developed as short wools for the cloth trade (Ker 1962, p. 27).

A shift in the social conditions of world wool production accompanied this relocation of wool growing for the London market. There was a link between the emergence of specialized wool growing on the periphery of the world economy (e.g., Australia) and the development of the German home market for industrial capital. Social transformation in the German economy led to declining wool exports as German textile industrial production developed around midcentury and to rising costs of wool production, giving Australian supplies the edge in London. Following early nineteenth-century land reform, which undermined manorial and estate systems of land tenure, agricultural capitalism (commercial landlords and farmers) began to emerge. This included the engrossment of common lands (enclosure), the extension of land areas for cash cropping, and the expropriation of small cottagers who became agricultural laborers. The consequences for wool growing (particularly in eastern Germany) were rising rents on pasture land, as arable farming expanded to supply growing urban markets, and a secular decline in green fodder crops (Clapham 1966, pp. 292–3; Conze 1969; Heaton 1948, ch. XIX; Milward and Saul 1973, p. 393).

German attempts to increase wool-growing productivity scientifically tipped production costs in favor of Antipodean wools (Roberts 1931, p. 352). This worked in two ways. On the one hand, colonial squatters paid nominal "rents" to the state as landed proprietor so that the profits of the colonial wool trade were retained among merchants and growers, thereby enhancing the competitive position of colonial wools. On the other hand, German producers increasingly specialized in very fine wool, such that John McLaren remarked in 1843 to his colonial agents, Frew Bros & Co.,[10] that "the demand for Australian was much aggrandised by the discovery

---

[10] John McLaren (London) to Messrs. Frew Bros. & Co. (Adelaide), 19 September 1843, *Frew Papers* (ML A738), p. 137.

that has been made that the German fairs cannot supply us with middling quality wool ... on nearly so good terms as the Colonies can." Hence the displacement, between 1830 and 1850, of German by Australian wools on the London wool market involved a secular fall in wool prices. This trend combined both the reduced production costs in open pastures in a settler colony that lacked a landed property class to inflate rents and the secular decline in circulation costs, as Australian wool freight costs dropped from 4½d. per pound in the 1810s to 1d. per pound in 1850 (see Broeze 1975, p. 587).

Returning to the *demand* conditions affecting wool prices, by 1839, according to James, not only were there large accumulated stocks of wool (thereby aggravating the price decline into the 1840s), but also declining profitability was reflected in the textile mills. Furthermore, it was "estimated that in the month of October there were no fewer than three hundred spinning frames in the Bradford district alone unemployed, owing to the insolvency of their owners" (James 1857).[11] The excess capacity of the textile industries at the end of the 1830s revealed the limits of further industrialization on the basis of textiles. The series of practical applications of technical processes in an age-old industry in response to widening urban markets, had run its course. The maturity of this process (and therefore its limit) ended in a speculative boom financed by the large merchant-financier interests. This was the transition from mercantile to industrial capitalism.

A new phase, or cycle, of capitalist development required a revision of investment opportunities to shift capitalist production to a more advanced technical base while the textile industry concentrated its capital resources under crisis conditions. The opportunity came through the stimulus that foreign industrialization gave to British capital-goods production, including the railway, which ad-

---

[11] Mann (1971, p. 176) cites a Yorkshire manufacturer's lament in 1840 that "in the woolen industry it was extremely difficult, even in good times, to make the average profits of the country." Matthews (1954, pp. 154–5) summarizes the depression in the woolen industry thus (emphasis added):

In the trough of the slump, wool and worsted were even harder hit than cotton. Unemployment in Leeds in 1842 was worse than in Manchester. Halifax – after Bradford the most important centre of the worsted industry – showed a greater proportional decline in brick production between 1836 and 1843 than anywhere else in England, although until 1839 the level maintained was quite high. *The burden of the extra capacity created during the boom was very widely complained of.* Woolen and worsted manufacturers did not have the same facilities for dumping their wares abroad as were enjoyed by cotton manufacturers.

vanced via the destruction of preindustrial domestic production. In the meantime, the crisis in the early phase of textile industrialism revealed itself in both declining profitability in textile production with falling prices and a general economic crisis in the early 1840s. In the colonial branch of the British textile industry, the accumulation of pastoral capital also suffered under the joint pressures of a wool price decline and the restriction of British capital imports. The importance of Britain's reexport business in her world trade relations thus highlights the world-economic context of Australian wool growing in this period (Brown 1976, p. 122).

THE 1840s CRISIS IN COLONIAL CAPITALISM

Interpretations of the 1840s depression in Australia are divided between emphasizing the role of external and internal factors. Current conventional wisdom gives precedence to the latter interpretation (Sinclair 1976, p. 73). I shall outline the arguments of the protagonists in this debate, primarily to identify how this awkward dichotomy arose.

Traditional interpretations of the slump assigned primary causality to the interruption of capital flow from Britain following the tightening of the London market in 1839 when the Bank of England raised the discount rate.[12] The effect of this financial stringency, according to Fitzpatrick, was to undermine the colonial land boom and hence the stability of pastoral expansion. Wakefield's beneficent cycle – land purchase, immigration financed from land sale receipts, increased production, increased land purchase (Fitzpatrick 1969, p. 73) – had been checked by an external factor, "English capital shyness," which was also due to falling wool prices. Intervention by the colonial government to finance immigration from bank reserves exacerbated the local capital shortage, thus undermining the land and stock markets.

Butlin's (1968, p. 318) reinterpretation, the basis of current conventional wisdom, set out to replace "the Australian tradition of explaining every slump as caused by overseas events." He posits a "natural limit" to physical expansion of the pastoral industry, which resulted in decreasing returns with rising costs of production. The industry suffered "apparent exhaustion of opportunities for prof-

---

[12] For example, Fitzpatrick (1969, pp. 71–2) and Shann (1930, p. 105).

itable expansion into new areas after a decade in which its profits and its technique of growth had been reckoned in terms of geographical spread," leading to a general contraction in credit, land sales, prices, and incomes (Butlin 1968, p. 318).[13] The notion of geographical limits, however, is contradicted by rising export figures for wool throughout this period (see Appendix 4) and evidence for the expansion of squatting regions at this time, which appears later in this chapter.

Because of the explicit thrust of Butlin's argument for internal causality, subsequent representations of the historiography of the 1840s depression fall into the trap of viewing it as a controversy involving a *dichotomous* explanation of the primacy of internal or external causality (see Sinclair 1976, p. 73). Actually the difference between Fitzpatrick's and Butlin's interpretations is methodological. Whereas Butlin considers the Australian colonies as his unit of analysis and focuses on the sequence of events, Fitzpatrick considers the Australian colonial economy as an integral part of the British Empire, and so considers the relationship between depressions in metropole and colony and how the former was transmitted to the latter.

Thus, Butlin contests Fitzpatrick's identification of 1839 as marking the reduction of British capital export to Australia, arguing that the available statistics (actually import trade figures) demonstrate that this reduction did not occur until 1841. He remarks (Butlin 1968, p. 318): "The truth is rather that the sharp fall in British investment was initiated by bad news of returns in the colonies, and that its role is in greatly accentuating a slump already begun and so producing the dire disasters of 1842–43." Fitzpatrick's point, however, was that whereas capital inflow continued into New South Wales through 1840, land speculation in South Australia was halted following the Bank of England's action. This "deprived New South Wales stockowners of an important market" and, in conjunction with falling wool prices, dampened new capital investment in Australia, thereby disrupting capital accumulation in pastoral production (Fitzpatrick 1969, p. 72).

The capital inflow issue is certainly not clear, because the data

[13] A variant of this interpretation is expressed in Peel's (1974, p. 31) study of Port Phillip, where she argues that sheep prices fell as land became less available, thereby undermining the value of the pastoral enterprise.

Butlin uses are distorted by incorporating the great speculative importations of goods in 1840–1 to which he refers in his study of the Australia and New Zealand Bank (1961, p. 90). Fitzpatrick cites only circumstantial evidence. Hence the dispute is reduced to the determination of limits to expansion of the pastoral industry. Fitzpatrick's limit is essentially profitability (a squeeze), and Butlin's limit is a natural one, producing a cost squeeze through the impact of declining marginal productivity. If indeed crisis in the pastoral industry is a question of limits to expansion, it follows that, to avoid the pitfalls of arguments based on the sequence of events, attention should be directed to the method of analysis of the sources and/or conditions (and therefore limits) of expansion. This would avoid the geographical determinism of Butlin and the one-dimensional tendency of Fitzpatrick's argument.

It has been argued that the conditions of expansion of the pastoral industry were: (1) the system of relationships whereby wool was grown to meet the needs of the English textile industry and the reproduction of pastoral capital depended on a continuous supply of commercial credit; and (2) a determinate supply of labor in the absence of a viable local labor market to match the expansion of colonial flocks qua capital. These conditions will now be investigated to establish the constraints on pastoral capital accumulation.

CIRCULATION CONSTRAINTS ON PASTORAL CAPITAL ACCUMULATION

Fitzpatrick's analysis is basic to an understanding of the boom and slump of the pastoral industry. In a general sense, its significance is affirmed by Hartwell (1954b, p. 83) who, noting Herbert Heaton's study of the fluctuating fortunes of the English woolen industry between 1835 and 1843, remarked: "This chronology of events in the woollen industry, with a year time-lag, almost exactly parallels events in Australia."

This time lag corresponds to the time of circulation of money capital (qua circulation credit). This is the time lapse between the realization of revenue at London wool sales and the communication of price trends through the accommodation policy of English importers. In this way, the law of value was mediated (with considerable delay) from the metropolitan economy to the raw material producer.[14] Thus, the declining wool prices in London would, along with the tight London money market following 1839, raise the price of circulation credit (increased discount rate), and this would in turn lower the aggregate profits of grower and merchant-factor in the colonial economy. A useful illustration of this mechanism of communication of loan-capital price rises is an 1837 letter received by George Russell of Geelong from his agents, Eddie, Walsh and Co., of Launceston.

We think you must be aware ere now of the serious fall which has taken place in the Wool Market at home, and the consequent large losses here. At this moment our best Wools are worth no more than 1/6, & the general run of Wools 1/ - p. lb. Port Phillip Wools will not bear this value, unless very clean & strong in the staple, which none of them were last year; and the same fault will apply we fear, to all sheep sent over during last season, as the sea voyage rots the first clip completely.

We are amongst the largest buyers of & advancers on Wool in V.D. Land, but without inspection we would not venture on giving even 1/ - p. lb. for any of the P.P. Clip; we shall, however, be happy to give you an advance on your Wool of 9d. p. lb., which we are confident is more than any one else would do. [quoted in Brown 1952, pp. 112–13]

This mechanism of restricting credit by raising the price of discounting highlights an aspect of capital inflow that is confused and misrepresented. This is the actual concept of capital inflow, which is incomplete and therefore distorting – particularly where debate seeks to identify the turning point in capital inflow and its effects on pastoral expansion. Those positing internal causality base their arguments on trade statistics, which register only the capital on trading accounts.

There were three forms of capital inflow from Britain: the import of specie, the sale and issue of bills of exchange on London, and imported goods accompanied by a bill of trade drawn by the British exporter of goods on the colonial importer. The latter bill would normally be a three-month bill settled in London through the colonial mercantile or banking firm's London agency.[15] The acceptance of bills of exchange and bills of trade in the London money market represented the credit system established between metropole

[14] The Marxist law of value refers to that determinate process whereby, in a system of commodity production and exchange, the competitive position of individual commodity producers is mediated through market phenomena such as price and profit. It constitutes an impersonal allocation of social labor.
[15] See Butlin (1968, pp. 237, 263) for a discussion of the London agency.

and colony. Financial stringency – either in the London money market or in the accounts of the wool-importing agent, given the declining wool price – would necessarily be expressed in a higher rate of discount, thereby checking the flow of credit. It would therefore be normal to expect that the interruption of capital inflow from metropole to colony would be triggered initially by a rising metropolitan discount rate. For the colonial merchant, the restriction of credit would appear accordingly in discounting advances to wool growers, as illustrated in the foregoing letter to George Russell. Thus, the rate of accumulation of both merchant and pastoral capital would be slowed, as the realization of value declined and was communicated back through the chain of credit. Because of the integral relation between grower and the London money market, the dampening effect of declining prices and rising discount rates was bound to check pastoral expansion, even if there was a time lapse of up to one year.[16] It stands to reason that Fitzpatrick's inclination to date the beginnings of the economic downturn in the pastoral economy with the combination of falling wool prices and the Bank of England's action in 1839 is valid. The effects, of course, would be lagged for a sound structural reason, given the circulation time in the wool trade.

This does not resolve the issue of capital inflow, however. What also requires attention is the import surpluses on which Butlin and Sinclair focus. The relevant trade statistics were as shown in Table 8.3 (Butlin 1968, pp. 275, 325). Butlin's (1968, p. 318) comment, unguarded as it is, was: "Recorded trade figures, for what guidance they give, show the great drop in capital transfer as occurring in 1842 with 1840 as the great peak. *These facts hardly point to stringency in the English capital market as a major circumstance.*" [Emphasis added.]

A strong case can indeed be made to the contrary, because the large import surplus in 1840 and 1841 most likely represented a redirection of commodity stocks from depressed markets in both England (with high food prices in addition, due to poor harvests in 1838–9 and high grain imports) and the United States (Checkland 1964, p. 17). With the difficulties of sales in these two markets, English exporters turned with imperial impunity to the Australian

---

[16] Barnard (1958, p. 96) gives delay estimates of nine to ten months.

Table 8.3: *New South Wales (including Port of Phillip) trade statistics, 1836–45*

Year	Imports	Exports	Surplus Imports	Surplus Exports
1836	1,237,406	784,624	488,782	
1837	1,297,491	760,054	537,437	
1838	1,579,277	802,768	757,509	
1839	2,236,371	948,776	1,287,595	
1840	3,014,189	1,399,692	1,614,497	
1841	2,527,988	1,023,397	1,504,591	
1842	1,455,059	1,067,411	387,648	
1843	1,550,544	1,172,320	378,244	
1844	931,260	1,128,115		196,855
1845	1,233,854	1,555,986		322,132

colonies to unload their unsold stocks.[17] Butlin (1961, p. 90) himself writes in his history of the imperial banks (the Bank of Australasia and the Union Bank of Australia Ltd):

A general fall in import prices, the result of excessive speculative shipments from Britain, produced a liquidity crisis in the last months of 1840 and early 1841. Sales by auction of a wide range of goods were recorded because they were subject to duty; those of 1840 were two and a half times those of 1839, and those of 1841 nearly as great.

(See also Holder 1970, vol. I, p. 112.)

Contemporary evidence of the dumping of British goods is provided by a statement of Sydney merchants in a January 10, 1842 edition of the *Sydney Morning Herald*, entitled "Custom of Merchants":

Our attention has been drawn to a practice, which is anything but honourable, although we have reason to believe that it has been extensively acted upon by many honourable men. We allude to parties in London who receive orders for goods drawn up so as to suit this market, from persons resident here, sending out at the same time similar goods on their own account, thus availing themselves of the judgements of their con-

---

[17] Compare Phillips (1977, p. 13): "In the pre-planning days of capitalism, the peripheries could play a crucial part in counter-acting cyclical crisis – by providing markets for the excess consumer goods which the perennial imbalance between production and consumption has created in the centres."

stituents to meet them in their own market. A shopkeeper who called upon us on Saturday stated, that he had just seen an exact duplicate of the invoices sent from the same house that he had employed to send him a particular description of articles, and the trade being a peculiar one, he considered that his goods were rendered almost valueless by the competition likely to be induced. Some time more the same person assured us that the goods sent out in accordance with his orders were lost by the wreck of the Ocean Queen in Bass Straits, and that shortly afterwards he ascertained that by another ship which left England about the same time, an exact copy of the goods was forwarded to Sydney and sold to a shopkeeper in town, who thus in fact reaped the benefit of another's tact and industry. We have no reason to believe that our Sydney merchants are implicated in this fraud, for such it really is, but they might do a good deal towards stopping its continuance, were they to write stringent letters to their London friends. Such breaches of faith are positively repugnant to the character of a British merchant, and we are surprised to find that men standing high in the professional world should be guilty of such conduct. But apart from the interest of the party sending for the goods the trade of the Colony is affected by this practice. If every person who receives an order for goods sends out as many on his own account as he sends to his constituents, it must disarrange the proceedings of the merchants here, and tend to being about that great commercial evil – an overstocked market.

Evidently, the dumping of British commodity stocks was a response to stringency in the London money market, and English merchants tried to gain liquidity by drawing bills on their colonial counterparts, relying on the time lag of shipments. The liquidity needs of imperial merchants in a tight money market were thus transmitted, again with a time lag, to the colonies in the form of excess commodities, thus touching off the colonial liquidity crisis of 1840.

The point, then, is that because of the structural relations of the wool trade, forged by merchant capital between metropole and colony, the depression in British capitalism was inevitably communicated to the pastoral economy. Not only did the import surplus reflect illiquidity in London, but also its contribution to a colonial liquidity crisis (manifested in the slump in land sales in 1841) was bound to affect further the wool growers' supply of credit. Where pressure for settling accounts and generally for ready cash increased with the glut on the import market, mercantile capacity to make advances to pastoralists declined. Credit to the producer came with higher interest charges, reaching up to a discount rate of 40 percent.[18] The burden of increasing interest charges was an inherent problem for pastoral capital where production conditions were impermanent (lack of tenure security and fixed capital), thereby raising the risk premium on mercantile advances. The further the crisis developed, the more untenable became the security of pastoral capital to the merchant, especially with declining wool prices.

PRODUCTION CONSTRAINTS ON PASTORAL CAPITAL ACCUMULATION

We have argued that pastoral capital fundamentally depended on a labor supply to match its accumulation of sheep. Contemporary evidence indicates that the scarcity and high price of labor impeded pastoral capital accumulation to such an extent that the labor constraint appeared to some colonists as a primary cause of the depression.[19] A glance at the minutes of evidence in the various committees of inquiry in the New South Wales Legislative Council during these years attests to this. In the 1842 Committee on Immigration, for instance, Robert Scott was questioned about the effect of the scarcity of labor and its high price on the pastoral economy. His reply was:

Certainly, we are now suffering from that cause; the high rate of wages running away with all profits, no man would enter into pastoral pursuits, and in consequence there has been no sale for our surplus stock. This has, as a natural consequence, deteriorated the price of land, as the less the surplus derived from land, of the less value that land becomes, whereas, in the face of this, the Government have increased the price of their land from 5s. to 12s. an acre, and thereby, I am of opinion, disorganised the agricultural system, and the relation between land and produce. The squatting system also, has materially contributed to the effects, as it has deteriorated the price of land, and prevented its sale; I may say I am an extensive squatter myself.[20]

Scott went on to say that the squatters, by employing labor without contributing to the land fund, were responsible for raising the price of labor. What is significant is his articulation of the link between

---

[18] For example, in a letter to Henry Dangar from his agents, R. Campbell Jnr & Co., Sydney, in 1840, it is stated that the rate of discount was as high as 40 percent in some areas (M393 Australian Joint Copying Project, misc.). See Appendix 6 for a full statement.

[19] See, for example, Alexander Mollison, *Letters 1825–59*, LaTrobe Library, Melbourne (M 57956656/A114).

[20] *V&P, NSW*, 1842, Committee on Immigration, Minutes of Evidence, 10 June 1842.

land and labor – a nexus that was fundamental to capital accumulation in the pastoral economy. A breakdown in the entry of labor into the pastoral economy threatened the self-expansion of capital. Labor itself was basic to the system of accumulation.

Contemporary statements regarding the cause of the depression often included a variety, or arbitrary cataloging, of influences. However, in establishing the cause of the crisis in the accumulation of pastoral capital, the supply of labor becomes the key. Arguments that connected depression and the high price, or scarcity, of labor with the government's land price rise and the depletion of the emigration fund were, in assigning causality to institutional interference or breakdown in the supply of labor, merely expressing its fundamental importance. This is reminiscent of the difficulty Wakefield had in stressing the distinction between the theoretical requirement of guaranteeing wage labor for settler capital by pricing land and the practical system of using revenue from land sales to finance the emigration of labor. He wrote (from Pritchard 1968, p. 954): "As the only object of selling instead of giving is one totally distinct from that of producing revenue – namely, to prevent labourers from turning into landowners too soon – the pecuniary result would be unintended, one might almost say unexpected." The point was that settler capitalism was nothing without a labor supply.

As far as timing and the proximate causes of the labor scarcity are concerned, witnesses at the Committee on Monetary Confusion of 1843 made pertinent comment. Thomas Stubbs, auctioneer, attributed primary causality to the "sudden stoppage of transportation, at a time, when the landed interest, spent immense sums of money in the extension of their estates, under promise of assigned labour."[21] Charles Roemer, an emigré from Leipzig by way of London, colonial merchant, and one-time director of the Commercial Banking Company of Sydney (*Australian Dictionary* 1967, vol. 1, p. 392), argued his particular international perspective.

The distress has arisen from the failure of speculations on prices which were too high to be maintained; the value of wool in the Colony, had been regulated by prices which were obtained in England previously to the failure of the large American houses in about 1837; and the prices of Colonial produce were then notoriously driven up by the assistance of newly created Joint Stock Banks, in England, as well as in America. It

[21] *V&P, NSW*, 1843, Committee on Monetary Confusion, 21 September 1843.

must be remarked, that almost at the same time when persons flattered themselves with the continuance of high prices of wool, they also calculated on the continuance of prison labour, which has since been withdrawn; and under this impression, they made purchases on land, at prices which appear now quite preposterous.[22]

The point was that the end of assignment was the end of the supply of cheap labor and, for the squatting districts particularly, the end of a reliable supply of labor.

With respect to the price of labor, bond labor was considerably cheaper than free labor; Wentworth estimated the difference at £14 a year between the employment of a convict for £22 and wages of £36 for a free laborer.[23] This margin increased with rising wages in a scarce labor market, where the convict's wages in kind were a legally specified quantity of provisions. The conversion to free labor, in a mode of production where the technical adjustment of labor in relation to capital was limited, necessarily became a formidable barrier to pastoral capital accumulation. Rural wages rose with the cessation of assignment, being highest at the perimeter of the squatting frontier (Coghlan 1969, vol. 1, pp. 427, 430). The impact of this conversion was not confined to small and medium pastoral capitals, as the Australian Agricultural Company found:

Much to their dismay the directors learned that the assignment of convicts to private individuals was soon to cease and that they would, therefore, be faced with greatly increased costs ... Captain King found his most difficult task in the change from convict to free labor, and whereas this was of no moment in the coal trade, where the company controlled prices, it was serious in the Stock Department, particularly as the necessarily increased expenditure was coincident with a drop in wool values. [Wilson, *ML* MSS 1581]

The cessation of assignment affected wool growers particularly because they were compelled to seek labor on the open market and they offered unattractive employment.[24] According to Coghlan (1969, vol. 1, p. 424), "when assignment was abolished in 1839 there were 25,322 convicts in assigned service in New South Wales, and these were reduced by the expiry of sentences at the rate of about 5000 a year." In the New South Wales squatting districts,

---

[22] *V&P, NSW,* 1843, Committee on Monetary Confusion, 22 September 1843.
[23] Cited in Jeans (1972, p. 148). See also Appendix 3.
[24] See, for example, Roe (1965, p. 71) and Coghlan (1969, vol. 1, p. 431) for a discussion of rural employment conditions.

Table 8.4: *Pastoral statistics of New South Wales unsettled districts, 1839–43*

Year	No. of stations	Population		Cattle	Sheep
		Free	Bond		
December 1839	694	4,143	3,144	371,699	1,334,593
December 1843	939	6,277	1,296	501,541	1,804,046

Table 8.4 indicates the extent of the conversion from bond to free labor.[25] It is clear from the table (which, incidentally, contradicts Butlin's physical limits to squatting) that labor requirements overall did not match the stock increases on squatting runs, even where many of the runs were small and some labor was provided by the squatters themselves (included in the "free population" category).

Because of the labor constraint, exacerbated by the reliance on an undeveloped free labor market, the wool growers developed the bounty system. This involved private contracting of immigrant labor, and the government paid a bonus, or bounty, out of the land fund for approved immigrants. This system initially resembled government-assisted immigration. Though begun in the latter half of the 1830s and operated irregularly for the next twenty years, the bounty system's most significant period was in 1840 and 1841, when it supplied 6,675 and 20,103 immigrants, respectively (Coghlan 1969, vol. 1, p. 360). During this time, government immigration was suspended under pressure from the wool growers through their influential representatives on the New South Wales Legislative Council. In spite of arguments about the superiority of the bounty system in terms of less cost, greater selectivity, proportionately more single persons, and so forth, the motive behind the Legislative Council's decision to rely primarily on the private bounty system was economic.[26] To sustain their enterprise, pastoralists had to regulate directly their labor supply. By concentrating on the bounty

[25] Compiled from "Abstract of the Returns of the Commissioners of Crown Lands for the half year from 1st July to 31st December, 1839 ..." (NSWSA, 2/2366, Treasury: Record of Boundary License Fees); and Enclosure no. 1 to Sir George Gipps's *Despatch*, no. 75, Sydney, 3 April 1844 (ML A1639).
[26] See Chairman Pinnock's Report in the Committee on Immigration, *V&P*, *NSW*, 1838; and Coghlan (1969, vol. 1, p. 358).

system, they attempted to minimize the competitive forces of the labor market; that is, by seeking to contract for immigrant labor, they could bypass the urban labor market and hold down wage costs as well as effect some control over the quantity and regularity of labor. This move to avoid the competitive forces of an open labor market constituted a rearguard action.

The prominence of the bounty system as a method of controlling the supply of labor by pastoral capital did not last. Its private character generated increased power on the part of recruiting agents and/or shipowners, causing an unpredictable supply; its increasingly speculative operation transgressed the principles of imperial land and emigration policy (Madgwick 1969, ch. 9; Coghlan 1969, vol. 1, pp. 359–61). In 1843, following intervention by the British authorities, government-assisted immigration was resumed on a limited basis.

In spite of the short life of the bounty system as an attempt to control the supply of pastoral labor, its introduction was significant because it substituted quasi-indentured labor for a lapsed system of assignment of bonded labor. It was a logical response by pastoralists to an intensification of the labor constraint on pastoral capital accumulation with the ending of assigned convict labor.

SOCIAL CONSTRAINTS ON PASTORAL CAPITAL ACCUMULATION

The concept of social constraints on pastoral capital accumulation refers to the system of relationships within which pastoral capital was reproduced: the system of pastoral economy. The primary relationships were those of merchant capital to the production unit and the nexus among land, labor, and capital. The discussion so far, in focusing on the credit nexus and the labor supply as the proximate vehicles of crisis, has implicitly assumed the *social context* of reproduction of pastoral capital. It was in and through this particular social context that the character of the crisis in the pastoral economy emerged.

The nexus among land, labor, and capital was essentially a way to establish the social relations of settler capitalism. Colonial state policy (as an arm of the imperial state) guaranteed a labor force for pastoral capital by discriminating against small farming and assigning bonded labor to private capitalists. The Wakefield principle of pricing land to generate land to generate a labor force formalized this policy.

The constraint in this social nexus was the assurance of a productive expansion of wool growing to stimulate "Wakefield's beneficent cycle" in order to maintain value in the pastoral economy. Many observers proceed from considering land, labor, and capital as factors of production, and therefore they pose the problem of crisis in colonial pastoralism as a breakdown in the supply of, or in the particular proportions among, these factors. Thus, the increasing price of land becomes a cause of the depression, or the cessation of convict assignment or the physical exhaustion of the frontier is singled out to explain crisis. These can, at the most, be only partial explanations because they ignore the fundamental social relation among these categories, through which the law of value operates. That is, capital accumulation, or the self-expansion of value, does not proceed because of the empirical presence of these (discrete) factors, but because of their *relational* quality in the reproduction of the social environment for capital.

The land component of this nexus was socially determined through an artificially imposed price and became the practical instrument of financing, and guaranteeing, a supply of labor for capital. Reproduction of the capital relation broke down only when the cycle was checked by the decline in the profitability of wool-growing to a level at which insufficient new pastoralists were attracted to the industry. The profitability crisis meant not only the insolvency of pastoral capital in relation to merchant capital, but also a rising cost of credit. The number of newcomers trailed off, causing a slump in the stock market; whereas sheep prices in 1838–9 ranged between 30s. and 60s. a head, in 1843 they had fallen to between 6s. and 7s. a head.[27] The result was devaluation of pastoral capital and a corresponding crisis in merchant capital accumulation.

With regard to the labor constraint on profitability, where pastoral expansion was checked, Benjamin Boyd's evidence to the Select Committee on Immigration of 1843 is instructive. (It also directly contradicts Butlin's notion of the geographical limits to pastoral expansion.)

---

[27] See Alexander Mollison, *Letters 1825–59*, 31 January 1843; LaTrobe Library, Melbourne; and Roberts (1970, p. 203).

It is well-known that nearly one-third of the ewes last year did not get the ram, not for want of room for increase, for plenty of runs in the back country were still open for new stations; but from scarcity of labour, and the consequent high prices demanded for it, which completely checked any inducement to increase. Stations far in the interior, but often most calculated for sheep, are almost considered valueless from distance, and difficulties attendant on getting up supplies, and forwarding wool; but this also proceeds from the same cause, namely, the want of labour in the interior, so much indeed, that I have found it cheaper to purchase wheat in Van Dieman's Land, and to forward it two or three hundred miles into the interior, instead of growing it upon the stations, nor have I, at this moment, a single acre in cultivation. Had there been a supply of labour, however, every necessary might have been raised on the stations, and the only supplies for the return wool drays to bring back, would have been a few slops, tea, and sugar.[28]

Boyd's remarks about the grain importing forced upon him by the scarcity of labor draws attention to the contingent nature of the staple-producing economy. The issue of a cheap supply of grain is clearly relative to the social conditions in the economy. The scarcity of frontier labor discriminated against the local provision of subsistence needs in favor of wool growing, thus dictating grain importing. The pastoral economy generally was never self-sufficient in grain in this period, however.[29]

A severe drought in eastern Australia during 1838–40 exacerbated the drain in foreign exchange due to grain importing, which, of course, added to inflationary trends in the colonial economy. The price of wheat in New South Wales, which fluctuated around 7s. per bushel in the 1830s, rose to between 20s. and 30s. in 1839, and 18s. in May 1840 (although by the end of the year the price fell to 5s. 6d. per bushel with restored harvests) (Coghlan 1969, vol. 1, pp. 281, 460–1). Such price inflation of basic foods contributed to increasing wages at the turn of the 1840s, thus checking the profitability of wool growing. (Remember, the grain component of the squatter's payment of wages in kind to his labor force was an increasing market item according to Boyd's evidence.) Also, the colonial merchants engineered a price inflation. Being in a special credit relation with the banks, they were in command of the market and

---

[28] V & P, NSW, 1843, Select Committee on Immigration, Minutes of Evidence, 27 October 1843.
[29] See Coghlan (1969, vol. 1, p. 251); and V&P, NSW, 1849, Statistics of New South Wales, 1837–1849.

able to demand double prices from the settler. This they allegedly achieved by establishing trade monopolies for buying commodity cargoes and raising prices, since many settlers did not have ready cash and access to the market.[30]

The point is that the limits to pastoral capital accumulation revealed by the 1840s crisis were not simply scarcity of labor and declining wool prices. The limits were inherent in the character of accumulation itself, which indeed dramatized the scarcity of labor precisely because of the particular labor constraint. The latter in turn was a barrier to subsistence production on the sheep run, which would have held costs down. Grain import requirements resulted from the specialized character of the staple-producing economy. Here, mercantile promotion of staple commodity production and pastoralism's tendency toward a monopoly of the landed economy retarded the settlement of a small-farming sector in the countryside. The lack of a small-farming population exacerbated the problem of labor supply in the wool-growing regions.

Thus, the character of accumulation in pastoral economy was limited in a twofold sense: in terms of specialization in staple commodity production and in the primitive form of accumulation (quantitative, rather than qualitative, expansion of value) – crystallized in the phenomenon of scarcity of labor, which became most acute when convict transportation ended.

CONCLUSION

This discussion of the 1840s depression has attempted to explain the particular crisis in the colonial economy by examining the relationship between contradictions within the pastoral industry and the cyclical downturn within the metropolitan economy. The approach has been to emphasize the analytic framework of the world division of labor, of which the pastoral economy was an integral branch. This allows us to see the source of crisis in the contradictions of the particular forms of capital accumulation in the metropole and the colony.

In Britain, textile industrialism had run its course as the first phase of industrial capitalism, and the downturn in textiles production

---

[30] *V&P*, NSW, 1843, Committee on Monetary Confusion, Minutes of Evidence, William Bradley, 21 October 1843.

followed an overproduction based primarily on speculation in the American market. Falling wool prices resulted, strengthening the decline of prices caused by social change in the conditions of world wool production, as the latter shifted to the Southern Hemisphere. This, in conjunction with the straitened London money market in 1839, checked and suspended the flow of mercantile credit to the colonial economy.

The dependence of pastoral capital accumulation on mercantile advances reflected the speculative character of wool growing. This, added to the lack of tenure security, placed pastoral capital accumulation on a primitive basis, where technical change was not integral to expansion, and labor was the fundamental constraint on accumulation. This constraint asserted itself decisively following the cessation of transportation; labor was sufficiently scarce and expensive to discourage further investment in wool growing and threaten the value of pastoral capital. A crisis of profitability was the outcome and the foundation of the 1840s economic depression.

9

FOUNDATIONS OF THE
AGRARIAN QUESTION

INTRODUCTION

The 1840s crisis in the pastoral economy precipitated the colonial agrarian question – an extended social conflict over land settlement patterns that reshaped colonial society during the second half of the nineteenth century. Although the formal solution to the agrarian question was the land legislation of the 1860s (and beyond), the social divisions over the character of the landed economy emerged during the recovery from the crisis. During the 1840s there were three main developments concerning the role of landed property in the colonial economy and society.

1. Political maneuvering by the large squatters to consolidate their form of economy and their political power in colonial Australia.
2. A growing perception, following the crisis, of the vulnerability of the staple economy and the emergence of an alternative concept of development involving economic diversification.
3. An expanding social base for the groups that held this concept as a consequence of the rationalization of the colonial economy following the crisis. (This rationalization was in fact a turning point in the form of capital accumulation in the colonial economy.)

These economic and political developments anticipated the flowering of the agrarian question in the gold rushes of the 1850s, when gold-immigrant radicalism accelerated the opposition to squatting.

Alongside these developments, and very much informed by them, was the gathering political momentum toward colonial self-government. From the settlers' viewpoint, the control of the disposal of Crown land and revenues from sales underlay the demand for political independence. However, the question of who should benefit shaped the course and tenor of agitation for self-government.

191

From the increasingly liberal perspective of the British state, a consolidated colonial middle class checking the squatters' pretensions, as well as growing popular forces during the gold-mining period, enabled responsible government to be established in colonial Australia.

ECONOMIC RECOVERY AND RATIONALIZATION

The political debates concerning the origins of the crisis and recovery measures demonstrated the contradictory character of the pastoral economy.[1] General opinion was that, on the one hand, the pastoral industry needed to be placed on a more secure footing, and on the other that the colonial economy needed to reduce its dependence on the wool trade. Although these emerged as the dominant themes of recovery, the immediate concern was the colonial economy's position in the world market.

In the early 1840s, during the contraction (1842–3), colonial politicians attributed the crisis to speculative capital inflow. Additional causes were the reduction of labor supplies following the ending of convict transportation, the fall in wool prices, and the drain of capital to finance immigration and unnecessary imports. There was nothing unusual about links to the international economy, but the specific form of that connection gave cause for concern. The Committee on Monetary Confusion had the following to report:

In a new Colony remote from the focus of the commercial world, and where the majority of transactions are carried on upon credit, the consequences are necessarily more disastrous. An undue contraction of the circulating medium, and the absence of all confidence and credit, forces on, in New South Wales, the ruin of the most solvent.[2]

Under these circumstances, the colonial state introduced practical financial measures to preserve property generally and to secure pastoral capital specifically. The first measure was the Insolvency Act of February 1842, designed to stay the execution of debt and generally preserve property. Debtors who were confident of regaining solvency with their very real assets were enabled to declare bank-

---

[1] See, for example, the Report of the Committee on Monetary Confusion, *V&P, NSW*, 1843; and MacMillan (1960), Irving (1963, 1967), and Dyster (1967).
[2] Report of the Committee for Monetary Confusion, *V&P, NSW*, 1843.

Table 9.1: *Insolvent estates, 1842–9*

Year	Sequestered estates
1842	629
1843	539
1844	192
1845	137
1846	110
1847	115
1848	145
1849	56
Total	1,923

Estates not proceeded with 42

ruptcy in order to sequester their estates as a way of satisfying creditors. Table 9.1 shows the significance of the Insolvency Act in the colonial economy.[3]

The group most in need of relief in 1842 was the colonial merchants, who comprised approximately one-quarter of all insolvencies in that year. Merchants were the first to feel the liquidity squeeze, from both British houses calling in their debts and insolvent rural producers – pastoralists and agriculturists. Colonial merchants were caught with excess cargoes in a depressed market. Given the extent of credit within the colonial economy, legislators considered it important to preserve, rather than dismantle, colonial property as a means of stabilizing the economy.[4]

Among the 1843 insolvents was the Bank of Australia, the original banking company of the exclusives. Its failure symbolized the difficulties of the colonial banks, difficulties exacerbated by their previous reluctance to develop foreign exchange facilities – an activity that the Anglo-Australian banks monopolized from the 1830s. Consequently, one result of the crisis was the greater dominance of the imperial banks in colonial banking (Holder 1970, vol. 1, pp.

[3] Abstract of the Returns in Insolvency Proceedings, ordered to be laid before the Legislative Council of New South Wales, June 1849, *V&P, NSW*, 1849.
[4] See, on the situation of the merchants, Butlin (1968, p. 323 fn.). For examples of the interdependence of merchants and landed capital, see *Insolvency Files* (NSWSA 2/8821).

130, 143; Butlin 1968, ch. 10). The imperial banks (the Bank of Australasia and the Union Bank), by mediating between colonial merchants and the London money market, profited from the increase in wool exports.[5] Their access to London funds allowed them to undermine the early dominance in the wool trade of the colonial merchants, whose capital resources were inadequate to purchase the increased supplies of wool at the coast.

Also, local banks were unable to give growing cash discount accounts to merchants during the long period of circulation of wool and realization of revenues.[6] Consequently, consignment marketing mushroomed as the imperial banks entered colonial commercial financing, alongside private squatting partnerships with British commercial connections.

The 1840s crisis consolidated this trend, compelling colonial merchants who were interested in remaining in the wool trade to become consignment agencies for British mercantile houses. In addition, colonial banks entered the foreign exchange business in 1845 in competition with the Anglo banks (Butlin 1968, p. 508; Holder 1970, p. 143). With access to a London agency, colonial banks now purchased export bills secured by the bills of lading of the commodity in circulation. Not only did this extend consignment marketing, but it also allowed colonial banks to survive; as the Bank of New South Wales directors argued, it was necessary to retain "in our own hands all the transactions of the large mercantile accounts which the Bank already possesses" (quoted in Holder 1970, p. 144).

The consignment system of wool marketing, consolidated in the 1840s, symbolized the engrossment of the wool trade by British capital. By the 1860s, 80 percent of colonial wool was consigned

---

[5] Butlin (1961, p. 78) thus characterized the exchange activity hitherto of the Anglo banks, the Union and the Australasia:

Following the lead of the Bank of Australasia, the Union Bank made agency arrangements for remittance of funds to Australia, whether for migrants or stay-at-home investors with the National Bank of Scotland, National Provincial Bank of England, Bank of Liverpool, Devon and Cornwall Bank, and Bank of Ireland. On the other side of the world, the rapid rise of wool exports meant a constant flow of exporters' bills to buy, to enlarge still further the available London funds. The other side of these transactions was an increase in Australian imports predominantly from Britain, to pay for which merchants were buyers of bank bills on London. So far as other banks went, the Union had to share this business only with the Australasia.

[6] For discussion of this, see Barnard (1958, p. 137).

(Barnard 1958, p. 47). This system established regular exchange between metropolis and colony and encouraged the development of specialized consigning agencies – those that had access to London funds (Barnard 1961, p. 165). Within this system of exchange, competition for the wool trade intensified between imperial and colonial merchant banking capitals. This struggle continued over the next half-century; its significance, by providing more finances to the grower on a longer-term basis, will be discussed later. The point is that a rationalization of the conditions of capital accumulation in the pastoral industry grew out of the 1840s crisis.

The maintenance of wool growing was clearly perceived to be the basis of economic recovery. Pastoralism was the productive anchor of the colonial economy, and the solvency of pastoral capital was, in turn, vital to the solvency of the colony at large. The data for the volume and value of wool exports during the 1840s indicate the continuing significance of wool production (see Appendix 4). Although the rate of expansion decreased owing to a relative shortage of capital and labor, wool growing showed a definite secular increase.

By focusing on the difficulties of pastoralists in obtaining loans, the crisis drew attention to the unsecured nature of wool growing. Wentworth (the parliamentary leader of the squatters) proposed a bill to establish a lien on wool and mortgages on livestock. English law did not recognize the principles of the bill, as Colonial Secretary Stanley communicated to Governor Gipps.

The Act number 3 dated the 15th of September 1843, and entitled "An Act to give a preferable lien on wools from season to season and to make Mortgages" is a measure ... so irreconcilably opposed to the principles of legislation ... recognised in this Country respecting the alienation or pledging of things moveable, that, under any other circumstance than those in which the Colony has unhappily been involved, it would not have been in my power to decline the unwelcome duty of advising Her Majesty to disallow it.[7]

Stanley's dispatch, though ambivalent about the use of pastoral commodities as security for loans, demonstrates the acknowledged need to secure squatting financially as the productive basis of colonial economic recovery. Roger Therry (1863) commented appropriately on the function of the lien on wool.

---

[7] *Despatches*, Stanley to Gipps, 28 October, 1844, pp. 253–5 (*ML* A1295).

A settler, by giving a guarantee to a merchant in the early part of the year that he would deliver his wool at the end of it, when at the wool-season it was deliverable, obtained an advance usually of 8*d*. per lb., on the wool. . . . This innovation on the strict principle of English law may be vindicated on the ground that pastoral land is only valuable for the wool it yields, and the stock it feeds. There is no money-rental from the greater part of the land, as in England, where rents are applied to the payment of mortgage-debts. Wool and stock may, therefore, be considered in Australia as an equivalent for rent. In New South Wales, as well as in other British Colonies, it has been found necessary to mould the laws of England agreeably to the nature and peculiarities of property there.

In effect, the liens on wool legally secured a practice that existed already in relations between merchants and pastoral capital. Whereas merchants had advanced credit as a device to obtain the wool clip (and hence access to foreign exchange), wool growers were now able to seek loans actively on their particular form of capital, and, in turn, the loan gained legal security. Squatting capital could now anticipate its returns on a systematic basis.

Liens and mortgages immediately helped revive pastoral capital in the latter 1840s as a secure form of credit expansion. They also served a vital function in the transition to capitalist methods of wool production. Until the 1870s when pastoralists were securing long-term loans on mortgages of freehold land, leaseholding pastoral capital was able to obtain the bulk of its finances on the basis of wool and stock collateral. As before, loans secured in this way were the preserve of mercantile finance, banks being confined mainly to commercial financing (exchange bills and export bills, as discussed). Following the 1847 granting of long-term squatting leases, mortgage financing on leasehold land emerged (Butlin 1964b, p. 127).

The phenomenon of mortgage financing of pastoral production was matched by a general reorientation toward mortgage financing in the economy. The practice of bill discounting as the characteristic form of credit in a basically mercantile economy was beginning to give way to mortgage loans (Butlin 1961, p. 91). These were preconditions of industrial capital, where mortgage financing encouraged longer-term investments,[8] most notably in railway development and capitalization of existing industries.

---

[8] Compare Pentland (1950). Mortgage financing is a form of "investment credit," as opposed to "circulation credit," as stated in Mandel's (1971, p. 223) distinction:

Circulation credit is intended to realise in advance the value of commodities already produced: investment credit has for its purpose to increase the capital of an enterprise. In both cases the amount of surplus-value increases, either by reduction in the rotation-time or by growth in the amount of capital.

This reorientation began with the arrival of the new British mortgage companies in the colony during the contraction period. Although it has been argued that the lending of British shareholding capital to illiquid colonial capitalists slowed the impact of the depression (Butlin 1968, p. 309),[9] of more significance was their perceived role as imperial usurers in a depression. Inevitably, the transfer of the surplus capital of small British shareholders (especially Scottish) in staying bankruptcy among property-holding colonists became usurious as these companies absorbed insolvent property at low prices. The colonial outrage at these foreign companies, led by Wentworth in the Legislative Council, took the traditional antisemitic and conspiratorial position against these "Jews and Companies of Usurers" responsible for "the immense influx of foreign capital . . . which encouraged the vile and reckless spirit of speculation" (quoted in MacMillan 1960, p. 3). In the face of colonial protest, such companies switched from loan financing to investing in property and industry (such as pastoralism and mining) (MacMillan 1960, p. 62). Thus the measures for financial rationalization during the economic recovery in the 1840s promoted a long-term transition in the colonial economy from commercial to industrial capitalism.

CONSOLIDATION OF URBAN CAPITAL

Railway development in colonial Australia began in the mid-1840s, signaling the mobilization of urban capital for colonial economic development. Faced with the threat of English investors establishing colonial railway-building companies, colonial merchant-capitalists and landowners considered the viability of financing railways. The terms were very much circumscribed by the depression, so the criterion became that of a nonspeculative colonial project (Abbott 1966, p. 34). Accordingly, colonists identified the railway as a public resource for development and therefore eligible for state assistance.[10] A meeting in 1848 of colonial capitalists resolved the following:

. . . that from the consideration that it is the duty of the Government to make and maintain the public roads and bridges of the colony, and that the cost of constructing and maintaining economical railways would not, in this country, equal that of macadamized roads . . . private enterprise

---

[9] The companies were British Colonial Bank and Loan Company (1839), Australian Trust Company (1841), and Scottish Australian Investment Company (1840).
[10] See Dyster's (1967, p. 72) discussion of this "philosophy of development."

Table 9.2: *Value of New South Wales*
imports and exports, 1840–9

Year	Imports	Exports
1840	£3,014,189	£1,399,692
1841	2,527,988	1,023,397
1842	1,455,059	1,067,411
1843	1,550,544	1,172,320
1844	931,260	1,128,115
1845	1,233,854	1,555,986
1849	1,739,420	1,891,270

Source: V&P, NSW, 1850.

ought to be extensively assisted out of the public revenue. [*Sydney Morning Herald*, Jan. 28, 1848]

This notion of a joint venture between state and private capital, which characterizes the subsequent history of capitalist development in Australia, marked the emergence of an alternative ideology of colonial development to that of the graziers.[11]

The crisis in pastoral accumulation itself produced this alternative. On one hand, rationalization of the wool trade displaced colonial merchants from this sphere of commerce. The consignment of wool was increasingly concentrated in the hands of specialized mercantile agencies, thus freeing financially uncompetitive merchants for alternative fields of finance (Barnard 1961, p. 165).[12] At the time when new commercial horizons appeared feasible, and indeed necessary, pastoralism drew criticism for its singular interest in production for foreign markets and its monopoly of the landed economy. The emerging urban mercantile class thus found its interest in domestic commercial development in conflict with the squat-

---

[11] Connell and Irving (1980, p. 115) refer to

the conflict between the plantation style of social order favoured by the squatters – an attempt to revive the set of relationships surrounding the assignment system, which had established the leadership of the gentry in the earlier period – and an urban bourgeois social order. This was clearly understood. Just as the squatters had justified their programme in terms of the good of the colony, so now the urban merchants and manufacturers associated a "free" labour market with a free society, and profits with prosperity for all. A liberal individualism was easily inserted into these arguments. There was even a tinge of nationalism.

[12] See details on merchant investors in Kolson (1961, pp. 18–21). See also Birch (1965).

ters' interest in the legal consolidation of their form of economy.[13] This marked the beginnings of the agrarian question in colonial Australia.

On the other hand, the 1840s crisis revealed the shortcomings of pastoralism – vulnerability to the outside world and a basic lack of self-sufficiency in foodstuffs. At the same time, the disruption of foreign trade and the temporary introversion of British capital to fuel railway speculation boosted the fortunes of local commodity production (Jenks 1973, pp. 99, 126). Coghlan (1969, vol. 1, p. 513) refers to the decline in deep-sea shipping entering Australian ports after 1841: "In that year 251 British ships were entered inwards; from 1843 to 1847 the numbers declined to between eighty and ninety, and did not rise again until the gold discoveries." The consequent, and consequential, decline in imported commodities is clear from Table 9.2, which highlights the uncharacteristic change in the balance of trade in the 1840s.

The decrease in imported goods and a general deflated cost structure stimulated local manufacturing – the processing of rural products and the production of building and construction materials (Coghlan 1969, vol. 1, p. 462; Hartwell 1954a, p. 147). In conjunction with diverting vessels from the declining whaling industry to a growing coastal trade, internal commerce continued to expand.

Sydney became the centre of a very active coastal trade, and there is almost daily mention in the newspapers of small vessels going to or arriving from Wollongong, Port Macquarie, Morpeth, the Hawkesbury, Brisbane Water, the Hunter, the Paterson, Port Aitken, Kima, the Clarence, Broulee (Moruya), Boyd Town, and Jervis Bay . . . By this means were carried grain, meat, tallow, hides, butter and cheese, tobacco, timber, coal, lime and, in fact, all sorts of colonial produce. [Coghlan 1969, vol. 1, p. 513]

Even while colonial commodity production expanded, the east coast pastoral colonial settlements were unable to develop agriculture to match their population increase.[14] Grain imports remained high throughout the 1840s, much supplied by the systematic colony, South Australia.

Urban manufacturing expanded with the encouragement of artisans and mechanics from English manufacturing districts to migrate to the colonies. For example, the system of bounty

[13] For further discussion of this, see Dyster (1978).
[14] See table on p. 200.

immigration, organized by Britain in conjunction with private colonial interests, included skilled tradesmen.[15] It was this growing
urban petit bourgeoisie that added weight to the emerging interest
in the development of a home market, the touchstone of which was
the ideal of a bourgeois agrarianism.[16] The ideal had an insignificant
social base, which highlights its specific *ideological* function in gal-
vanizing attitudes against the squatters in an emerging *political* challenge to their dominance.[17]

Return of the Quantity and Value of Grain, &c., Imported into the Colony
of New South Wales (including the District of Port Phillip)
From the Year 1839 to 1848, inclusive

Year	Wheat (Bushels)	Maize (Bushels)	Barley, Oats & Pease (Bushels)	Flour & Bread (Pounds)	Rice (Pounds)
1839	171,207	30,862	64,093	3,579,076	1,414,747
1840	290,843	19,185	63,363	7,108,663	6,849,896
1841	239,224	12,773	41,610	14,929,603	3,603,076
1842	163,224	1,120	37,798	7,247,076	2,260,046
1843	395,374	583	61,361	6,941,760	1,678,208
1844	265,704	17	35,194	4,370,240 & 250 casks of Biscuit	260,288
1845	109,355	—	46,399	3,327,632	450,000
1846	237,717	536	46,454	3,367,936	1,283,968
1847	224,720	—	37,469	5,335,680	1,044,288
1848	143,235	—	49,163	3,131,744	932,582

Source: *V&P, NSW,* 1850.

[15] See, for example, "Return of the Trades or Callings to which the Bounty
Immigrants who Arrived between the 1st of July, 1841, and the 30th June, 1842,
Professed to Belong," New South Wales Colonial Secretary, *Returns of the Colony,
1842* (NSWSA 4/274).
[16] See Irving (1963, p. 21). For an extended study of the development of this
conception of colonial society, see Irving (1967).
[17] Irving's work on "the corn question" has revealed the extent of the ideological
challenge to the squatters. As Connell and Irving (1980, p. 115) write:

The liberal rhetoric of the British anti-Corn Law movement was used to justify a campaign
on behalf of the farmers. Although its supporters argued that they were only trying to defend
the farmers as they had earlier defended the squatters against imperial discrimination, the
campaign implicitly challenged the pastoral ideology by asserting that agriculture, too, could
be a productive interest. As for the composition of the movement, there were not many
farmers, but there were liberal landowners, radical newspaper editors and urban businessmen.

LIMITS OF SQUATTER HEGEMONY

As discussed in Chapter 4, the conflict between exclusive and emancipist capitalists ended when the cessation of convict transportation threatened their common interest in squatting. As the large landowning squatters closed ranks, opposition to their privileges grew. Colonial laborers and men of small means suffering from the economic crisis opposed the apparent favoritism toward the landed class in the colonial land regulations, especially in the context of a further increase in the fixed price. Alexander Harris recorded this dissatisfaction thus:

That they suit pretty well the highest class, those who legislate in the colony, those from whom the legislators of the colony are drawn, those from whom emanate the representations which by one means and another are rendered so influential in the Imperial legislature, may be true. But they suit nobody else. . . They entirely prevent persons of small property from becoming landholders and agriculturists; by which again they coercively construct an immensely larger labouring class than otherwise would exist in the colony. Consequently the rich landholder both keeps the produce market to himself, and again procures labourers at a vastly lower rate of wages . . . (causing) a very bitter and continually deepening feeling of disaffection to the British Government and its Australian employés in the minds of colonial youth. There is a settled sense among them, they are debarred of their rights.

Harris (1964, pp. 224–5) speculated:

I am persuaded that unless this feeling be looked after and allayed, it will eventually result in the separation of the colony from British jurisdiction: for, when it comes to the point to save their possessions, the rich will go with the poor. At present, and nothing can be more certain, the whole rising and mature race of Australians of the middle and lower class look on our dominion as an usurpation, and as one of the most selfish character.

Harris was referring to the link colonists were making between land disposal and political sovereignty. This connection was the touchstone of the squatters' bid for hegemony, as they challenged Britain's land policy by demanding self-government. Such a strategy arose out of frustration with the 1842 Australian Constitutions Act (granting colonial representative government), following the rapprochement between the exclusives and the emancipists (Ward 1976,

p. 168). The act established a blended Legislative Council composed of an elected majority of two-thirds (based on a property-owning electorate, including emancipists and weighted in favor of country districts) and a one-third nominated minority. The fundamental contradiction in the eyes of the colonial capitalists was that, whereas the new council represented them, it still reserved power to administer land and revenues for the British government (the details were set out in the Land Sales Act of 1842). This contradiction was the catalyst for political mobilization by the landowning squatters.

The issue of the disposal of Crown land in the colonies arose from the conflict of interest between the imperial state and colonial producers. Whereas Whig policy regarded unalienated land in the colonies as an imperial asset, colonial capitalists advanced an appropriate parochial view (1843).

The Waste Lands of the Territory cannot be considered a source of profit to the Community, until they fall into the occupation of private individuals. If, by the application of private means and industry, they become sources of profit to individuals, they will benefit the Community at large. The Country at large therefore, and even the Empire itself, is interested in bringing all its Territory under the management of private industry; and that can only be done by allowing a *certain facility* in obtaining it to private individuals. So far, however, as Australia is concerned, there is no such facility; on the contrary there is a prohibitory price on the soil, and, until it is withdrawn, the Australian Colonies cannot prosper.[18]

What the landowning squatters were demanding was an alternative framework of land policy to the continuing Wakefieldian principles, which contradicted their extensive land requirements. They demanded leases on their occupied land longer than an annual licensing, with preemptive rights to ownership. Their form of capital accumulation was premised on unlimited access to land, and, contrary to their declaration, squatting was very profitable.[19] In fact, the landowner-squatters were beginning to assert their economic power and to secure a hegemony by demanding a legal

[18] Quoted in *Despatch* from Gipps to Stanley (Extracts), 17 January 1844, reproduced in *Select Documents on British Colonial Policy 1830-1860*, Bell and Morell, eds. (1928, p. 229).
[19] Gipps makes this point in *ibid.*, p. 231.

monopoly of the colonial landed economy. Governor Gipps, opposed to their social pretensions, nevertheless recognized their claims (and limitations) when he commented:

It seems to me premature to pronounce that land in Australia is valuable only with reference to its capacity for feeding sheep...

It is undoubtedly very much to be denied that the Colonists, and even the Squatters, should possess a fixed interest in some portion of the lands they occupy, for otherwise they will have no inducement to improve them; but it is, in my opinion, by no means desirable for them to become the proprietors of extensive tracts of land, which they have no means whatever of improving.[20]

Governor Gipps's attitude materialized in a set of squatting regulations designed to check squatting though not pastoralism. They provided some security in allowing the limited purchase of occupied land. At the same time, lagging immigration levels would be bolstered by the resulting land revenues. These regulations, published in 1844, had two parts:

1. occupation regulations, which defined a squatting run (an area not more than 20 square miles) for purposes of annual license payments; and
2. purchase regulations, which allowed the squatter first option to purchase a homestead section of his run; otherwise it could be sold in the open market.

To secure his run for eight years, and for eight yearly intervals afterward, the squatter was compelled to buy at least 320 acres. Two proximate motives of Gipps were to encourage improvements and some fixed capital investment on squatting runs to upgrade squatting material existence, and to challenge the inequality of large and small squatters both paying the single license fee.

To the squatters, and particularly the large landowning squatters, these regulations threatened to exacerbate the depressed financial situation resulting from the crisis.[21] Not only would license fees

---

[20] Gipps makes this point in *ibid*.
[21] See Buckley (1956, p. 181). Many squatters were in debt from the preceding boom, and others – particularly landowner-squatters – had lost capital through the slump in urban commercial and banking capital during the depression.

increase, but also they would be committed to large purchase requirements as the legal number of their runs was increased.[22]

In response, the squatters formed the Pastoral Association, an extraparliamentary organization supplementing the formal activities of the Legislative Council. The membership overlapped (eighteen members of the council belonged to the Pastoral Association), but the association was responsible for mobilizing colonial opinion. Meanwhile, the council was proceeding with committees of inquiry into land administration and formulating its own political opposition to the imperial monopoly of land disposal and revenue. Through its recently acquired power of veto over the governor's bills, it rejected Gipps's occupation regulations on the grounds that taxation without rights of appropriation contradicted the constitutional obligations of an elected council (see Melbourne 1963, pp. 295, 303).

The demand for self-government that the Pastoral Association took up as a public demand in support of the conclusions of the council was tactical.[23] Behind the formal conclusions lay the informal interests of the wool growers in tenure security.[24] The squatters ultimately wanted long leases and preemptive rights to purchase the land they occupied at locally determined prices. (The minimum upset price of £1 was established in 1842.) The political tactic of demanding self-government (in particular, local control over land administration and revenues), however, readily tapped dissatisfaction with imperial land policy in the colony among the land-hungry. In this way, the squatters were able to mobilize colonial opinion behind their cause and thus build a temporary hegemony. The material foundations of squatter hegemony lay in the clear predom-

---

[22] The largest squatter, Benjamin Boyd, "held at least sixty stations under the terms of Gipps occupation regulations, and would have been charged £600 annually in license fees. To secure these stations he would have needed an outlay of £19,200 each eight years (under the purchase regulations)" (Morrissey 1976, pp. 94–5).

[23] See Irving's (1964, pp. 196–7) discussion of the fusion of the idea of *self-government* with that of *responsible* government – a logical development because the proponents of self-government wanted to replace the governor with an executive composed of ministers responsible to the legislature.

[24] This is the emphasis in Buckley (1955). See also Irving's (1964, p. 197) discussion; radicals stated that the demand for self-government was a pretense.

inance of pastoralism in the colonial economy.[25] The empirical reality of the Pastoral Association's resolution was therefore quite apparent: "That the Commercial and Trading classes of the community are most intimately connected with, and dependent upon the prosperity of the great Pastoral interests of the colony."[26] The kind of hegemony obtained by the Pastoral Association was expressed in the April 9, 1844 edition of the *Sydney Morning Herald* (by no means the special mouthpiece of the Pastoral Association of squatters generally, Dyster 1965, pp. 47–9):

> The interests of the graziers are the interests of the whole community . . . to injure them is to injure all ranks and conditions of the people. We are all therefore, to a man, bound to stand by them, and to exert ourselves, to the utmost limit of constitutional resistance, to protect them from the cruel oppression with which they are menaced.

On April 19, 1844, the *Sydney Morning Herald* sharpened the hegemonic assertion: "This is no *political* controversy – no *party* warfare. There is here no collision of rival interests – no strife of class pretensions. The cause is pre-eminently THE CAUSE OF THE COLONY."

Implicitly, influential colonial opinion legitimized the neomercantilist assumptions of the squatters, who sought control of the state to install their mode of staple commodity production as the basis of the colonial economy.[27] Urban radicals and landowners disapproved of squatting as a form of economy,[28] and the radicals also feared self-government in the absence of a wider franchise to ensure that the colonial government would be responsible to interests other than those of the squatters (Irving 1964, p. 197).

Given the climate of liberalism in British politics in the 1840s, the Colonial Office also wished to avoid granting responsible government where a squatter oligarchy would rule. This contradicted

[25] Dyster (1965) has convincingly documented this "mutual interdependence" of colonial society. For a discussion of the land-hungry's dissatisfaction with British land policy, see McQueen (1970, pp. 147–50).
[26] Reported in the *Sydney Morning Herald*, April 10, 1844.
[27] This position had been advocated as early as 1840 by James Macarthur, who was now involved in squatting and "wanted men of wealth and standing to decide in N.S.W., not in Britain, the great questions of land policy, land revenue and immigration on which colonial development depended" (Ward 1976, p. 164).
[28] Irving (1963) discusses the opposition of the urban radicals to squatter monopoly of the colonial political economy.

the emerging concept of independent colonies embodying the liberal political and civil culture of England (Ward 1976, ch. 7) – a concept that has been called "the positive theory of empire" (Pares 1937). Nonetheless, the neomercantilist view of the colonies as an agrarian periphery was part of this concept.[29] Consequently, the British government recognized the squatters' informal demands in the presence of a powerful lobby of squatters' business connections and British manufacturers. They reminded the authorities of the competitive value of colonial wool growing for British capitalism (see Appendix 8). Britain acceded to the squatters' demands, thereby securing the source of almost 50 percent of its imported wool. By the Privy Council's 1847 order in council, squatters obtained renewable leasehold tenure of as long as fourteen years. During this time they alone might purchase the land, and at the end of the period they had preemptive rights to the land, as well as the alternative of compensation for improvements should they waive that right.[30]

For the other settlers this imperial concession to the squatters was tantamount to "locking up the lands," and it confirmed the hollowness of the antiimperial united front set up by the squatters.[31] An antisquatter alliance sprang up among urban commercial, professional and working groups, landowners, and small farmers, evidenced in the decline of squatter representation in the 1848 elections (see Roe 1976, p. 95). To this alliance, political independence with an extended franchise would ensure a more democratic administration of colonial land settlement. In addition, the alliance was fighting new demands by many squatters for renewed convict transportation

---

[29] See Chapter 1 of this book for a discussion.

[30] The order in council "also contained the seeds of all future legislation on pastoral lands. It recognised, however crudely, the variable quality of the Australian land. . . It was a step towards the acceptance of the fact that there was a low yield per unit acre of land in the arid and semi-arid parts of the country" (Williams 1975, pp. 68–9).

[31] See Reeves (1969, p. 227), for example:

At one stroke the flock owners of the wide interior were to be turned into leaseholders. In a moment a vested interest was created. . . Up to the moment of the receipt of Earl Grey's Order-in-Council, the squatters with Wentworth at their head, had fought against the high upset, denouncing the £1 an acre as loudly as the Radicals. The instant the leases were secured they dropped the mask.

to secure their economy (Kiddle 1967, p. 158).[32] (This struggle had already been kindled by an imperial state policy compromise of sending "exiles" – convicts on parole – during the 1840s to swell the labor market.) To the progressives, the revival of an unfree labor force would retard home market development as well as the establishment of democratic institutions (see Irving 1976, Dyster 1965). Initially urban workers organized the Anti-Transportation Association, but increasingly it became the vehicle of urban middle classes, who attached it to the issue of responsible self-government (Blackton 1955, p. 125; Irving 1976, p. 199; Ward 1976, p. 300). This movement framed the politics of the 1850s.

GOLD AND SELF-GOVERNMENT

It is customary to view the 1850s gold-rush decade as a turning point in nineteenth-century Australian history. It was, but only to the extent that the social and demographic impact of gold mining crystallized existing political themes of constitutional change and land use. In fact, gold provided the solution to the political impasse in the Australian colonies, where squatters and their economy constituted a powerful brake on the development of effective government. This much the 1850 Australian Colonies Government Act reflected, insofar as it created a new state legislature in Victoria and modified those of South Australia, Tasmania, and New South Wales, granting the power to transform their blended legislatures into bicameral ones (with Royal assent). Nevertheless, it still withheld control over land and land revenues. Implicit in this gradual move toward self-government was continued British opposition to oligarchical rule by the squatters (Ward 1976, pp. 294–6). Imperial retention of control of the land was in fact recognition of the inability of colonial Australia to present a viable political opposition to the squatter interests.

---

[32] For accounts of this phenomenon, see, for New South Wales, Coghlan (1969, vol. 1, pp. 333–50), and for Port Phillip, Kiddle (1967, pp. 152–61). The labor shortage for pastoral capital – particularly in the squatting regions – was not resolved in the 1840s despite unemployment in the coastal towns. Immigration was tied to land sales still, and the slackened demand for land in most of the decade added to the unpredictable and faltering supply of pastoral labor (Coghlan 1969, vol. 1, pp. 361–3).

In this sense the agrarian question was central to colonial political development. It is for this reason that the social impact of gold within colonial politics resolved the constitutional task put to the colonial legislatures by the imperial state. What were the components of this social impact?

Populism: the settler variant of democracy

In the first place, new concentrations of miners in the fields and wealth seekers in the towns introduced a democratic and radical tenor to colonial politics, especially in Victoria. The ideas promulgated in the midcentury European popular uprisings obtained a second wind in the colonies. As one contemporary of 1850s Melbourne observed:

The years I speak of were years of political excitement and turbulence. Among the new-comers were combative Chartists . . . brim-full of schemes for the reformation of mankind in general and of the people of Victoria in particular. . . . Many of them had been . . . in the revolutionary movements which had agitated Europe in 1848. You met men who had fought in the streets of Paris; political refugees from Frankfort, Berlin, Vienna, and Buda Pesth, and Carbonari from Italy. Mostly young, ardent, enthusiastic, and animated by more or less Utopian visions of reconstructing the political and social institutions of civilised mankind so as to bring about an era of universal peace and prosperity, these heterogenous exiles flung themselves heartily into the popular movements of the day.[33]

In Europe these social movements combined demands for political reforms of government with programs, such as Chartism, for recovering expropriated land for the resettlement of the laboring poor. Such demands resonated in the colonies where squatters monopolized the land. They gained increasing urgency through the 1850s as gold miners lost their means of subsistence on the fields when alluvial gold disappeared and mining became capital-intensive.

Agitation for land reform against the squatter monopoly was not simply a materialist demand for the redistribution of land. It included a politicoideological theme (Kiddle 1967, p. 221), beginning in the cities and proceeding from the image of bourgeois agrarianism that hitherto governed imperial land settlement policy. With the changed social environment, however, the agrarian ideal

[33] J. Smith, "Melbourne in the Fifties," *Centennial Magazine*, December 1889, quoted in Ebbels (1960, p. 49).

assumed a more populist character – inextricably linked to the constitutional reform of the newly self-governing colonial states.[34] The bourgeois designs of Wakefieldian imperial policy that so patently discriminated against small landholders were to be superseded by the democratic implementation of a petit-bourgeois ideal. Hence the linking of manhood suffrage to the homesteading movement in the demand of an 1860 public demonstration of the Land Convention: "Every man a vote, a rifle, and a farm." The popular arcadian view of Australia circulating in England at this time ("Where every striving man ... may sit under the shadow of his own vine ... – not without work, but with little care – living on his own land"),[35] and animating the desires of artisans and working men in the gold fields and the towns, fashioned the colonial democratic movement into a distinct petit-bourgeois mold.

Extension of the franchise was not simply an issue of political rights (and was generally not viewed as part of working-class mobilization as in England).[36] It was indeed considered integral to the political regulation of squatting in creating a productive society founded on the agrarian producer. The metamorphosis, or tempering, of foreign democratic impulses in the colonies (see also McQueen 1970, p. 156) was aptly described in an article (1857) in the then-radical Melbourne newspaper, the *Argus*, comparing Australian society to that of European countries

in which a dangerous class has been created, not merely, as in England, through the want of wise laws devised to effect a just distribution of national wealth, but also by the tyranny of their rulers. In these old countries arguments are not wanting in favour of a gradual and cautious extension of equal political rights to all citizens. But the social condition of this colony is, thank Heaven! widely different. There, we have no "dangerous class." The number of paupers bears an insignificant proportion to the mass of the community. Every Australian citizen is interested in defending the just rights of property, and the smallest freeholder will as earnestly maintain those rights as the large capitalist who has invested tens of thousands in the soil. The wealthy classes have nothing to fear from manhood suffrage. It will prevent them from abusing their power, but

[34]Compare the treatment of populism in Connell and Irving (1980, p. 120).
[35]From S. Sidney, *The Three Colonies of Australia: N.S.W., Victoria, S.A.*, 1852, quoted in Lansbury (1970, p. 75).
[36]Except perhaps in South Australia, where the land-administration favored farming and working men formed an Elective Franchise Association and then a Complete Suffrage League in 1850 on publication of the government act. See Pike (1967, p. 417).

there is no danger of its encroaching upon their rights. [quoted in Ebbels 1960, pp. 39–40]

The strengthening of the urban bourgeoisie

Whereas gold immigration profoundly altered the balance of social forces in the eastern colonies in favor of small producers and working men, it consolidated the political and economic power of urban capital. Gold accelerated colonial commerce, serving a population that trebled during the decade and strengthening the colonial banking system (Cotter 1976, p. 130). Colonial merchants suddenly had new markets in which to trade, as imported British goods flooded the newly liquid urban economies, and rural markets expanded with the growth of commercial agriculture – first in South Australia to supply the new Victorian market and then in the vicinity of the gold fields (Powell 1970, p. 67; Pike 1967, p. 452).

The commercial liberalism in the colonies, underwritten by gold, was indeed a local manifestation of trends within the world-capitalist economy. Gold mining in Australia and California fueled an international trade expansion in this age of capital through its inflationary effect and the provision of an adequate bullion base for sterling as an international currency (Hobsbawm 1975, p. 35). In the colonial state legislatures, merchants combined with pastoralists to establish uniform laissez-faire commercial policy in 1852 – before that of Britain.[37]

Adherence to the principles of commercial liberalism by the colonial administrations was important in confirming the informal relationship that the British state was conferring upon colonial Australia in the expectation of retaining its commercial hegemony. Colonial merchants were at this stage independent of industrial capital in the domestic economy; their commercial interests were in the development of a home market by expanding commodity production (including wool) and circulation (especially by the development of transportation). It was the new vitality of the urban bourgeoisie, however, as a check to the politically conservative squatters, that

---

[37]Thus, "the Australian colonies (as their citizens were characteristically aware) led a world entering upon a new era of free and mutually beneficial commercial intercourse ... in the application of the principles of commercial freedom the Australian colonies were in advance of Britain herself" (LaNauze 1955, pp. 78, 89).

convinced the British authorities of the political maturity of the colonies in their accession to self-government in the mid-1850s.

The conservative mobilization circumscribed

The flourishing democratic movement in the 1850s put the squatters on the defensive. Suddenly, with the leveling tendencies of gold wealth, the £10 franchise qualification of the 1850 act gave rise to a democratic mass alongside the newly enfranchised squatters (other than landowning squatters). When in 1852 the Victorian squatters agitated for what they considered to be their rights in the 1847 order in council (implementation of which was delayed by survey requirements) (see Kiddle 1967, pp. 222–3), the new social forces crystallized in opposition. Cognizant of the altered political balance (including the *temporary* character of gold mining) and confronted with the mobilization of miners, farmers, and the urban bourgeoisie, Governor LaTrobe deferred to the democratic forces, arguing: "The pastoral interest, great as it undeniably is, cannot be opposed to the forward and irresistible movement of regular settlement in any direction...The pastoral interests must become more restricted, as the agricultural may be presumed to acquire strength by every sale of land" (quoted in Powell 1970, p. 27).

A subsequent colonial royal commission, encouraged by the British government, upheld community interests against those of the squatters by licensing them rather than granting the leases they wanted (Gollan 1966, pp. 34–7). In New South Wales the squatters gained some leasehold rights, but throughout the colonies the local resolution of the agrarian question awaited responsible self-government.

The squatters' other defensive tactic was to attempt to transform themselves into a quasi-colonial aristocracy by constitutional means. They established upper houses to safeguard the special interests of landed property against the more broadly representative lower houses, although the British authorities disallowed their attempt to subvert responsible government by blocking the possibilities of constitutional reform (Ward 1976, pp. 327–8). Wentworth's proposal for a hereditary upper house, ridiculed as it was, represented an extreme version of the conservative mobilization against the popular forces. The popular forces, as noted before, however, were not singularly motivated by the principle of popular sovereignty. The historic social polarity feared by conservatives since Edmund Burke was inappropriate to the colonies (see Loveday 1956). Besides, the urban bourgeoisie had considerable interests to protect from popular excesses, and they accepted the bicameral principle of an upper house of review (Irving 1976, p. 199).[38] Although there were pockets of radicalism (such as the miners' Ballarat Reform League and the Victorian Land Convention's explicit combining of small landholder demands with notions of popular sovereignty), the specificity of the democratic challenge produced a moderate political outcome.

The specificity of the democratic challenge lay in its *immanent* character. This was no attempt to recover a prior small landholding tradition in the colonies. There was a *displacement* of metropolitan experiences of expropriation and political repression, but within the colonies there was no exploitative social relation between squatters and their democratic opponents. Hitherto the social organization of the squatting system had been shaped by imperial relations. What was now in contention was the structuring of power in the newly independent colonial states and how this could affect the reorganization of social relations in the colonies at large to eliminate the landed monopoly. The democratic movement was concerned with both the social and the economic consequences of the squatters' irregular, wasteful, and discriminatory occupation of the land. It was a question of establishing a political modus vivendi respecting interests (actual and potential) other than those of the squatters.

It is not surprising, then, that the antisquatter movement conceded to the political hegemony of the colonial bourgeoisie. The latter led the constitutional struggle against the squatters, linking agrarian ideals to political reform in a classic populist formula. Since the petit bourgeois interest was in formation and therefore tenuously in the balance of political forces, it readily accepted the liberal framework imposed by the merchants, professionals, and landowners. Accordingly, the electoral basis of the legislative assemblies rested on the principle of interest, rather than popular representation (Main 1957, pp. 378, 384). This emphasis on interest, essentially securing political rights to property in general, would produce a liberal resolution of the agrarian question (i.e., toothless land

---

[38]In New South Wales, where squatters had greater social power than their counterparts in the newer and more fluid "gold society" of Victoria, a nominated upper house was installed. See Main (1957), and compare LaNauze (1967).

reform) to be analyzed in Chapter 10. In this age of British hegemony, it was fitting that utilitarianism should dominate constitutional reform in the passage to self-government in colonial Australia.[39]

CONCLUSION

The agrarian question as a political struggle in colonial Australia originated in the aftermath of the 1840s crisis in the pastoral economy. Not only did the crisis reveal the exigencies of staple commodity production, but also the economic rationalization that followed produced a more coherent colonial urban bourgeoisie. Mortgage financing and international trade contraction encouraged mercantile investment of fixed capital in primary production and transportation. This represented the early stages of long-term transition to an agroindustrial complex, heralding twentieth-century industrial capitalist development. Meanwhile, these new commercial horizons fostered an alternative concept of economic development, including the development of a rural market. This concept, which viewed squatting as a barrier to commercial agriculture and to the general development of landed property, underlay the bourgeois (businessmen and landowners) political challenge to the squatters.

The challenge to pastoral dominance began at the end of the 1840s. This was when British concessions to squatters' demands for tenure security (and possibly their bid to revive bonded labor) unraveled squatter hegemony, which had been constructed around a demand for independence, especially in land administration. The resulting antisquatter alliance represented an incipient counterforce to squatting interests. At this stage, it lacked the solidity and breadth of vision to convince the imperial authorities to institute responsible self-government immediately. The 1850 Australian Colonies Government Act was designed to encourage the colonists to forge this emerging pluralism into a constitutional framework.

Gold discoveries in the eastern colonies resolved the constitutional issue as they dramatically altered the balance of social forces. Gold strengthened the urban bourgeoisie financially and politically,

---

[39]McNaughton (1977, p. 108) has aptly commented: "Because Australian institutions were shaped in a Benthamite age, the very predominance of grazing in the economy foreshadowed the political decline of the landholders."

providing them with an immigrant constituency espousing petit-bourgeois agrarian ideals. The urban bourgeoisie challenged the political pretensions of the squatters by mobilizing the popular forces around the ideology of political rights to landed property. Since the land-hungry gold immigrants identified squatters as social enemies, the liberal formula of responsible government and land reform articulated by the colonial middle classes secured a popular constituency against the conservatives. This newly consolidated pluralism encouraged the transfer of state power to the colonies by 1856. At the same time, urban capital began to subordinate pastoral capital in the colonial economy.

10

STATE FORMATION AND TRANSFORMATION OF THE LANDED ECONOMY

INTRODUCTION

The colonial governments addressed the agrarian question in the last four decades of the nineteenth century, setting the framework for twentieth-century Australian political and economic development. Land reforms reshaped colonial society largely by the way they transformed the pastoral economy. The shift of pastoral production to a capitalist basis (through fixed capital investment) at the same time promoted urban development. Urban financial penetration of pastoralism allowed the city to exert its control over the countryside, thereby achieving a more stable, integrated domestic market. Behind this developing agrocommercial complex was active government involvement in social capital formation.

The politics of the land question not only dominated social and economic development, but also largely governed colonial state formation. The whole question of land settlement arose in the urban centers and was a primary concern of politicians and administrators. Consequently, the politics of the conflict with the squatters overshadowed the productive settlement of the land. Whereas exploitation of the land was properly a concern of the rural settlers, exploitation of the land *issue* took precedence and largely established the framework of rural production.

State building itself was integral to the regulation of landed relations. Revenue from land sales was a critical source of public finance, just as land legislation facilitated the subordination of rural economy to urban capital. This interrelation of state formation, resettlement of the land, and shifting patterns of landed and urban capital accumulation depended on a sustained inflow of British capital and labor. When the boom ended in the early 1890s, so did the

215

hegemony of the mercantile bourgeoisie. New social forces comprising working-class (urban and rural) and farmer movements buttressed an emerging social democratic nationalism, which replicated trends in the metropolitan states as British hegemony waned.

PASTORALISM IN TRANSITION

Wealthy squatters began the long process of transforming their runs into freehold land following the 1847 order in council, which allowed the preemptive purchase of one square mile of their runs for £1 per acre. Where possible (in terms of available finance as well as rural district classification), squatters purchased additional land following the process of survey; because rental land had to be assessed for grazing quality, this favored the current occupants (Powell 1970, pp. 26–7). Given sustained favorable wool prices, the more systematic method of short-term mortgage financing established in the 1840s, and the greater security of tenure, squatters moved to secure what in their minds was a moral right to the land they grazed (and would potentially graze). Such preemptive purchasing was increasingly a response to the threatening gaze of the towns – as the first encroachment of town on the squatting country (Kiddle 1967, p. 219). Indeed, although freehold land purchase was largely defensive, it anticipated the subjection of the landed economy to the requirements of urban finance capital.

Fencing accompanied the extension of pastoral freehold and was perhaps symbolic of the transformation of pastoralism in the latter half of the century. It was, in fact, the long-term solution to the pastoral labor problem because fencing eliminated the need for shepherding and thus transformed the nature of pastoral work. It encouraged a more settled laboring population of tenants and selectors (landowners who lived on the land made available by land reform legislation). At the same time, fencing initiated large-scale capital investment in the rural economy, encouraging the penetration of loan capital into pastoral production.

Although fencing had been adopted on a limited scale in landowning regions in the 1840s, the gold rushes were the proximate cause of extensive fence construction. Not only did dispossessed gold field labor constitute a ready labor force for fence construction, but also the presence of dispossessed miners acted as a political catalyst for land reform, which moved pastoralists to secure property.

The immediate impact of the gold rushes was labor absenteeism on pastoral stations. The ratio of sheep flocks to shepherds was increased (in the Riverina district, for instance, flocks grew to 3,000–4,000; Buxton 1967, p. 42), and pastoralists resorted to non-European labor, as contemporary William Gardner noted.

A considerable number of Chinamen are engaged as Shepherds, and even with this supply a deficiency of labour is still complained of by the Flock-masters, they have been compelled to accept of the services of the native blacks, who to give them their due praise, bring in the Sheep in good condition... Their services are attended with this disadvantage, they occasionally sneak a fat sheep or two for their tribe, while they are careless in keeping up the stragglers and weak sheep of the flock... With these disadvantages they are little to be depended upon in continuing with the flock, and suddenly disappear from the station upon the business of the tribe, without the slightest warning ... This conduct with the ration of clothing supplies to them, makes these savages as expensive to the flock-master for their labor, as that of the Chinese. [Gardner 1854, p. 89]

Gardner went on to outline the kinds of indentured contracts made in 1854 with Chinese and "Hill Coolies" from India, which involved board plus £7, 4s. wages per year (Gardner 1854, p. 196) – cheap for the time. Indian government policy thwarted the regular importing of Hill Coolies. The temporary nature of these arrangements and the general one-third rise in wages in the 1850s encouraged fencing.[1]

The construction of fences to enclose stock runs became a permanent economic activity throughout the next half-century, reducing the labor cost of flock supervision. According to Jesse Gregson in a memo on fencing (see Appendix 10), it allowed a new method of flock management that "revolutionised the pastoral industry." In terms of economy, Gregson estimated a 10 percent reduction in the number of employees on a sheep station. The Australian Agricultural Company's property, Warrah, showed the following cost reduction resulting from fencing.[2]

[1] The wage increase did not appear to affect cost estimates for fencing (Gardner 1854).
[2] Robertson (1964, p. 36) observed of Warrah: "The property's demand for labour now depended less on the number of sheep grazing on its pastures and more on the miles of fencing stretching across it," which is in effect a statement registering the basic change in the technical relations of production in pastoralism. The preindustrial labor of shepherding was replaced by a matching of wage labor to fixed capital.

Year	Wage bill	Sheep	Cattle
1868	£4,052	65,000	9,000
1875	4,951	103,000	13,000

Apart from economy in labor costs, the introduction of fencing transformed both the social and technical character of pastoral productive forces. Enclosed runs dispensed with twenty-four-hour supervision of flocks, and consequently the year-round labor force (boundary riders replacing shepherds) became more settled. As Gregson noted: "The stamp of man who is placed in the position of a boundary rider is very different from the shepherds of older times. He is generally a family man and on most stations is provided with a comfortable house and probably keeps a cow and poultry." Of course, this development gave greater social stability and coherence to the inland regions.

In addition to the boundary rider and all-purpose working hand who made up the regular pastoral workforce, there was what writer Anthony Trollope referred to as the "nomad tribe of pastoral labourers." This tribe comprised seasonal workers who washed and shore sheep in the late spring and early summer, and contract workers who labored as fencers, splitters, sawyers, and well sinkers. With an expanding pastoral industry, the number of laborers engaged in work for pastoral capital in these various categories expanded.[3] As the rural economy expanded, this migrant labor force increasingly settled in the countryside. Seasonal pastoral workers particularly, and no doubt some contract laborers, established small farms on lands made available by selection legislation. It has been estimated that by the 1860s in the western districts of Victoria, 90 percent of shearers were small farmers or bushmen (Kiddle 1967, p. 403). (Later on when pastoralists had secured their land, they encouraged reliable tenants and selector farmers.) With the mechanization of rural production, engineers and artisans settled in small country towns to service the surrounding economy with pumps, windmills,

---

[3] Some idea of the relative expansion of the rural and urban labor force is provided by Kiddle's (1967, p. 468) study of Victoria: "Between the years 1870 and 1880 the numbers of hands employed in manufactories increased from 18,600 to 39,000. During the same period the numbers employed on farms and stations increased from about 86,000 to about 118,000."

agricultural machinery, boilermaking, and blacksmithing (Kiddle 1967, p. 408).

Fencing had a profound effect on the quantity and quality of sheep grazed. Between 1861 and 1894, for example, the number of sheep grazed in New South Wales increased from 6 million to 57 million (Ward 1970, p. 185). Fencing raised lambing averages (Bailey 1966, p. 52), and it was acknowledged to increase the carrying capacity by as much as 50 percent (Robertson 1964, p. 31). As far as the sheep were concerned, Gregson's account speaks for itself.

The sheep have benefitted by the change of system no less than the employees of the station. Instead of being kept part and parcel of a flock moving in one and the same direction or camping in a dense mass as was formerly the case, every sheep is now an independent individual free to choose its own companions and to feed where and when it likes...Its bodily condition responds accordingly – the growth of the fleece, no longer impeded and packed by a constant cloud of dust, is more natural and weighs better – the wool fibre is cleaner and stronger – the fleece is not only heavier but is more valuable pound per pound...The quality of the sheep depastured in Australia has improved wonderfully within the last fifty years. In shepherding days 7 lbs. per fleece was a good average weight. Today the average may be as much as from 9 to 12 lbs. for merino breeds. [See Appendix 10.]

From this account, it is clear that the introduction of fencing raised the yield of wool, and the control it allowed over the spread of sheep diseases was clear to pastoralists. At the same time, given its capacity to isolate flocks, fencing was a precondition for scientific breeding to enhance the colonial wool yield.

Building fences was expensive, costing approximately £50 a mile. Loans did not appear very regularly in the accounts of finance companies, which suggests that fencing construction was financed from current accounts (revenues from wool and livestock sales) (Bailey 1966, p. 52). The point is that fencing was a labor-intensive activity that required liquid capital for the wages bill; consequently, unlike investment in land or livestock, it was likely to be financed from current revenue – an account normally kept with a city agent or bank. Thus, not only did fencing promote the (short-term) mortgage financing relation between urban capital and pastoralism begun in the aftermath of the 1840s crisis, but also it signaled the transition to free labor in the colonial economy, as preindustrial shepherding by contract gave way to a rural labor market.

LAND REFORM AND THE TRANSFORMATION OF THE LANDED ECONOMY

The series of land reforms introduced in the 1860s in the individual colonies were ostensibly designed to open colonial wastelands to selection by small farmers. Under the progressive mantle of universal rights to landed property, the reforms created land markets in regions that squatters considered to be in their productive possession. The abiding liberalism of the market principle, reflecting urban bourgeois dominance in colonial legislatures,[4] was expressed by the author of the New South Wales Act, the landowner John Robertson.

All I want to see is this branch of business (i.e. agriculture) in common with all others have fair play, leaving people to take up whatever business they please. I have no desire that agriculture should have any special privileges or advantages, but I want to see that no restrictions are put upon it that are not put upon other branches of business, that the privilege extended to pastoral people may be extended to agricultural people. [quoted in Baker 1958]

The flaw in these sentiments, other than the lack of government discrimination in favor of the intending farmer (especially in capital assistance), was the inability of the land market as such to distinguish "pastoral" from "agricultural people." Whereas urban politicians sponsored such reforms in the interests of a *social* ideal of an industrious yeomanry, ignorant of the practical *economic* measures necessary for its realization, squatters easily found loopholes to engross the best of the land for themselves (Kiddle 1967, ch. 12). At the same time they used their wealth and political influence to subvert the formulation and operation of the land laws (Kiddle

---

[4] For example, according to Martin (1956–7, p. 54), the percentage representations of occupations (aggregated) in the Legislative Assembly of New South Wales were as follows:

	1856	1860	1875	1889
Pastoral	42.6	26.4	23.6	14.1
Commercial	24.1	14.0	28.6	34.2
Manufacturing	1.9	4.2	6.9	5.9
Professional	14.9	23.0	22.2	29.3

A similar pattern emerged in the Victorian assembly, but with even greater representation of the urban bourgeoisie. See, for example, Mills (1942).

1967, pp. 259–62). In the competitive struggle for land, the market naturally favored the squatter, who, in the face of widespread speculation and the fixed upset price of £1 an acre, could obtain bank credit and mercantile mortgage finance to secure freehold land. Finally, squatters accumulated land forfeited by bona fide selectors[5] who were unable to surmount the problems of lack of viable markets, cheap transportation and adequate capital free of high interest on loans from money lenders and storekeepers (Kiddle 1967, p. 265).

The details of the acts, their amendments, and operation have been well documented elsewhere;[6] what is significant for this study is the impact of land reform on the landed economy of the colonies. As suggested, the creation of a land market consolidated pastoralism, preserving its land monopoly in certain regions while farming generations struggled onto the land. At the same time, settling farmers transformed pastoralism because freeholding altered the social and technical relations of wool production. Necessarily, the developments in each sector were *relational* insofar as the pastoral industry provided wage work for small selectors, and family farms in turn provided a source of regular and seasonal labor for pastoral capital.[7] The relationship was two-sided, as each form of rural production developed a stake in the reproduction of the other.

---

[5] Some selectors speculated on land markets as well (Powell 1970, p. 141).

[6] There are many studies of the fortunes of selector farming; for example, Karr (1974), Powell (1970), and Kiddle (1967). Whereas Buxton (1967, p. 189) argues that between 1861 and 1891 the area cultivated in the districts of Albury, Deniliquin, and Wagga increased from less than 8,000 acres to nearly 200,000 acres, Waterson (1968, pp. 99–101, 120, 125) details the failure of selection on the Darling Downs, arguing that agriculture succeeded only in a mixed farming arrangement. Fitzpatrick (1947, p. 8) claims that only 400,000 of the 23 million acres sold on conditional purchase terms in New South Wales were under cultivation in 1880. It is generally agreed that land reform hastened the indebtedness of squatters, because farming settlements required further technological and state assistance at the end of the century for successful consolidation. One other result of, and indeed assistance to, selector farming was the provision of seasonal labor to pastoral capitalists; indeed it has been argued that the difference between a conservative coastal shearer and the radical western shearers in the 1880s was related to the selector (petit bourgeois) status of the shearing labor force in the east. See Waterson (1968, p. 21).

[7] See, for example, Powell (1970, pp. 140–1) and Kiddle (1967, p. 423). Mixed farming also was common.

Creation of an agricultural sector

The stabilization of agriculture involved the intergenerational accumulation of farming capital by selector families. The dynamic was generally twofold: (1) *expansion* of the scale of farming to survive in a market increasingly governed by world prices, and (2) the resulting *migration* of the agricultural frontier inland as initial selections were abandoned (Powell 1970). These developments involved manipulating kinship relations within extended families to exploit land and labor markets and so to accumulate land and income from land sales and wage labor. Although selectors faced considerable competition from squatters and speculators in the marketplace, those selector families that survived used the marketplace to accumulate farming capital.[8]

This process began two decades earlier in South Australia, which differed from the eastern colonies in its settlement history. Its distinctiveness derived from its Wakefieldian tradition of encouraging cultivation from its inception with a consistent policy of survey before selection in central and coastal regions, thus different from the grazing districts in the hinterland (Meinig 1976, p. 25). Already supplying grain to the eastern economy in the 1840s, South Australia sustained a considerable number of farmers whose presence was further favored by the absence of preemptive rights to occupied land in the squatting districts. This did not prevent squatters from purchasing land in the settled regions (75 percent of alienated land in the 1860s), but it did result in considerably more practical measures to aid selection than those in eastern land reforms. Disregarding the opposition of Adelaide commercial financial interests to public controls on the investment of capital in the land, the South Australian government passed its Waste Lands Amendment Act in 1869, providing credit to selectors in areas reserved for cultivation (Hirst 1973, pp. 10–14, 79–81). The intent of this land reform was to stem the exodus of some (mainly German) farmers to Victoria, where new land acts made the Wimmera region attractive (Hirst 1973, p. 82; Meinig 1976, p. 23). Additionally, it aimed to consolidate South Australian agriculture's export potential against Victorian and Californian competition (Meinig 1976, p. 24). The latter reveals the relative maturity of the farming sector in South Australia.

---

[8] See Friedmann (1978a) for a theoretical statement concerning this process.

(By 1873 Britain was the largest buyer of its wheat; Hirst 1973, p. 24.) The credit provisions promoted a speculative and migratory use of wheat lands on an extensive and specialized scale (encouraging machinery and scientific practices), which brought success in the export market. This also anticipated the patterns of farm settlement in the eastern colonies (Meinig 1976, pp. 118–21; Powell 1970, p. 156; Dunsdorfs 1970, ch. 4).

In the eastern colonies, the agricultural frontier was beginning to stabilize by the 1880s as selectors consolidated their hold on the land. In Victoria, with its more democratic environment (reflected in its radical populist land ministers, Duffy and Grant), land legislation had a systematic intent that was missing in New South Wales, where survey did not precede selection. Also Victorian selection in the 1860s benefited from the proximity of goldfield markets. By 1877 Victoria was exporting grain, and it had more cultivated acres than New South Wales (Powell 1970, pp. 110, 126, 228).[9] In spite of the large-scale evasion of the land laws by squatters, who in each colony retained their monopoly of the best land, agriculture did advance into the interior (Fitzpatrick 1947, p. 9; Reeves 1969, vol. 1, p. 248). Table 10.1 illustrates this process.

As a rule, the railway followed the agricultural frontier and consolidated it. The absence of the railway in the pioneering stages of agricultural settlement increased the importance of local markets in securing the selectors' farms (Powell 1970, pp. 170, 263). These markets played a dual role. First, they made possible early selection in the vicinity of towns and goldfields and second, they provided a context for expansion of individual family enterprises. Many enterprises began with mixed farming, and grew by manipulating the local land and labor markets in the rural economy (Kiddle 1967, p. 413; Powell 1970, pp. 93–4; Peel 1974, p. 20). A common pattern in the sequence of intergenerational selection by families was a form of land speculation whereby selectors sold their first allotments, sometimes having "dummied" them for local squatters.[10] This accumulation of money capital for farming often was undertaken on a familywide basis. At the same time, such speculative

---

[9] Compare Fitzpatrick's (1947, p. 10) comment: "The percentage of farmers and farmlands to all male breadwinners rose from 15.5 to 27.7% between 1861 and 1881, but in New South Wales the percentage actually fell from 24.5% to 21.5%."
[10] For New South Wales, see Karr (1974, p. 200), and for Victoria, see Powell (1970, pp. 150–264).

Table 10.1: *Internal migration of eastern agriculture (wheat area),*
1860–90

| | 1860 | | 1890 | | |
| | Acres | % of | Acres | % of | % |
Districts	(thousands)	total	(thousands)	total	increase
New South Wales					
Coastal divisions	73	56.6	2	0.6	
Tableland	44	34.1	95	28.5	
Farther inland	12	9.3	236	70.9	
Totals	129	100.0	333	100.0	258
Victoria					
Coastal (Gippsland,					
central, western)	107	66.5	20	1.7	
Inland counties	54	33.5	1,125	98.3	
Totals	161	100.0	1,145	100.0	712

Source: Dunsdorfs (1970, pp. 115–16, 119).

selection promoted inland migration. Selectors and their families engaged in dummying land for themselves also, and this encouraged economic differentiation among the farmers, giving rise to "boss cockies" who employed nonfamily labor on their larger capitalist farms (Powell 1970, pp. 178, 254–5).[11] The extent of economic differentiation, or land concentration, is shown in Table 10.2.

A further form of accumulation of money capital for farming by the small selector depended on the labor market in the rural economy. This was provided by the existence of landed capital, whether pastoral or agricultural (Walker 1957, p. 75; Powell 1970, pp. 140–1; Karr 1974, p. 202; Kiddle 1967, p. 423). The following remarks in an 1874 country town newspaper by a farmer illustrate the gen-

---

[11] In South Australia, for example, Charles Bonney (inspector and valuer of lands purchased on credit) confirmed the practice whereby "a number of farmers on the Border, between South Australia and Victoria, applied to be allowed to let their wives and families reside in South Australia whilst they went to take a selection in Victoria," in Minutes of Evidence, June 27th 1879, in the *Report of the Select Committee of the House of Assembly on Credit Selectors Under the Crown Lands Act* (SAPD #71), (South Australian Archives).

Table 10.2: *Land concentration in New South Wales and Victoria, 1857–96*

Size of holdings (acres)	New South Wales			
	1878–9		1895–6	
	Acres (thousands)	%	Acres (thousands)	%
1–5	3.4	0.59	6.0	0.45
6–15	8.7	1.29	15.4	1.61
16–30	23.8	3.67	36.4	2.74
31–50	54.3	8.53	59.3	4.47
51–100	94.5	14.66	108.0	8.14
101–200	116.1	18.88	160.1	12.07
201–500	158.8	25.88	298.0	22.49
501 and over	154.0	26.50	642.7	48.03
Totals	613.6	100.00	1,325.9	100.00

Size of holding (acres)	Victoria					
	1857–8		1879–80		1891 + [b]	
	Acres (thousands)	%	Acres (thousands)	%	Acres (thousands)	%
1–5	1.8	0.76	3.0	0.18	6.3	0.26
5–15	8.0	3.37	13.5	0.80	13.2	0.54
15–30	12.3	5.18	22.6	1.34	22.3	0.91
30–50	14.6	6.14	31.8	1.89	30.1	1.22
50–100	40.3	16.96	86.6	5.13	85.1	3.48
100–200	59.8	25.17	219.6	13.01	207.1	8.44
200–350			665.2	39.42		
350–500	61.4	25.84	146.3	8.67	899.7	36.62
500 and over	39.4	16.58	498.9	28.56	1,190.4	48.53
Totals	237.6	100.00	1,688.3[a]	100.00	2,454.2	100.00

[a]The difference is Crown land cultivated, the percentage calculated of 1,687,500 acres.
[b]The data for 1891 are not quite comparable with the rest of the table. For 1857–8 and 1879–80 the sizes of holdings are 1 acre to less than 5 acres, 5 acres to less than 15 acres, etc. For 1891 the scaling is 1–5 acres, 6–15 acres, etc.
Source: Dunsdorfs (1970, pp. 117–18).

eral preference for, and indeed reliance upon, local labor and commodity markets in the early stages of land selection.

> We find that we can make nothing out of the thirty two acres we are compelled annually to plough and cultivate. The time wasted by us in destroying the natural product of the soil [grass] would be more profitably employed in carting goods, splitting timber, or fencing for the large landowners. The sums we could thus earn would clothe our wives and little ones, and the thirty two acres, left in its natural state, would feed our cows and stock, enabling us to clear more by the sale of butter, cheese, etc., than we could raise from the land were it cropped. [quoted in Powell 1970, p. 263]

The consolidation of agriculture in this period succeeded not as a direct result of land reforms, but because of the coexistence of a capitalist environment with the rural economy. To be sure, the land legislation created a land market essential to the development of pastoral landed property, selector speculation, and the rise of capitalist agriculture, but the stabilization of farming on a family scale (simple commodity production), with an increasing proportion on a capitalist scale, depended to a great extent on the manipulation of both land and labor markets in addition to traditional forms of rural labor cooperation (Powell 1970, p. 254). The reproduction of farming on an expanding scale was not the product of a stubborn yeomanry (the reform ideal) but of a complex of social relations within the whole rural economy. It is for this reason that the relations between squatters and selectors switched from hostility to cooperation over time (Walker 1957, p. 78; Kiddle 1967, p. 423).

The consolidation of agriculture was not achieved simply through the development of social relations in the rural economy; it required government assistance.[12] Once colonial administrations recognized the complexities of land settlement under pressure from both a growing farming constituency and commission reports that revealed squatter monopoly of the public estate, they moved to secure the selection process. Tactical measures, such as altering residency requirements to allow selector participation in the rural labor market

---

[12] Compare Friedmann (1978a, pp. 96–7): "Simple commodity production can survive on a stable basis only in social formations with fully developed markets in labour power, and thus fully developed capitalist relations of production. While capitalist social relations make possible the reproduction of simple commodity production, however, *they by no means ensure it.*"

and making financial loans, aided farmers (Reeves 1969, p. 239; Powell 1970, pp. 179–82). As the agricultural frontier matured, government intervention changed from putting selectors on the land to creating rural development programs, aided by public agricultural colleges from the 1880s. (This was the case for Queensland sugar cultivation and New Zealand agriculture also; see, for example, Fitzpatrick 1969, pp. 249–53.)

The growing government commitment to reproducing farming on a more intensive and diversified basis stemmed from three forces (Reeves 1969, ch. VI). In the rural economy, farmers began to form cooperatives, or unions, to lobby for greater control over the circulation sphere (in such matters as lowering railway freight costs, enhancing marketing, and obtaining greater financial assistance in the face of the banks' traditional pastoral bias). They also demanded a more scientific approach to agriculture (Karr 1974). At the same time, in the last quarter of the century, the populist ideals associated with Californian Henry George resonated in the urban centers, especially within the emerging labor movement, which included shearers and miners in rural districts (Powell 1970, ch. 8; McQueen 1970, pp. 163–73). The former democratic theme of eliminating the land monopoly (including holding unused land), in combination with George's phsyiocratic notions of the primacy of land in creating wealth (the single tax base), exerted political pressure on governments to *administer*, rather than simply dispose of, land (Powell 1970, p. 221). Finally, these ideological developments obtained particular potency in the aftermath of the early 1890s depression, when emerging labor parties prescribed rural settlement as a remedy for unemployment. Subsequent public rural development programs responded not simply to the new social democratic climate in Australia, but also to the need to settle the financial debts of the preceding boom, which had precipitated the crisis (Boehm 1971). Government intervention (land grants, finance, transportation, and scientific programs) further consolidated Australia's rural economy and the range of primary exports.

In summary, by securing an environment for capital in the landed economy through land reform, the urban bourgeoisie indirectly encouraged agricultural development alongside the pastoral industry. As the century progressed, new social forces emerging in colonial politics pushed the colonial administrations toward a greater involvement with agricultural development. The result was to intensify the Australian economy's primary producing role in the world-capitalist economy.

The subordination of pastoral capital

The process of land selection transformed pastoral capital accumulation, which shifted to a capitalist mode as land became a commodity. Production methods intensified and increased wool yields, labor relations changed, and pastoral finance switched to a long-term basis. Indeed, the transformation of squatting runs into permanent, improved pastoral stations marked the subjection of pastoral production to urban capital.[13] Traditional wool-growing practices regulated by natural forces and makeshift methods of squatting submitted to the rationalizing forces of urban capital, oriented to unit productivity in a *qualitative*, rather than *quantitative*, sense. The impact of the penetration of urban capital into the pastoral economy was threefold.

1. The securing of pastoral landed property intensified pastoral capital's dependence on merchant loan capital.
2. The ensuing competition for pastoral agency (and mortgage loans) among merchant-financiers concentrated pastoral finance and banking capital, a competitive process of international dimension.
3. The growth of "grazing farm" selections, where agricultural specialization was unprofitable, enlarged the economic constituency of colonial wool merchants, who, by competing through local auctions with the London wool market, successfully relocated 50 percent of wool sales to Australia by 1900 (Barnard 1958, pp. 47–8; Bailey 1966, p. 154).[14]

The defensive purchases by squatters of strategic and homestead sites on their runs beginning in the 1850s restructured the relation of pastoral and merchant loan capital. Until the challenge of land

---

[13] Although some leasing still occurred in semiarid regions.

[14] This phenomenon was aided considerably by the establishment of telegraphic links with London. The story of Thomas Mort, who began wool auctioning in the 1840s, rationalized the wool-selling process in Sydney, and precociously entered pastoral financing in the 1860s, maintaining his firm in a competitive position vis-à-vis consignment agencies, is well told by Barnard (1961). The success of wool auctioneers, such as Mort, attested to the competitive abilities of colonial merchant capital in fashioning commercial organizations in Australia as part of the national trading strength in world commerce.

legislation, pastoral capital maintained seasonal liquidity by borrowing on wool liens and stock mortgages. Colonial wool merchants and consignment agencies (in their ascendant phase)   re the source of this *mercantile* finance, which was, in turn, sustai..ied by the discounting of wool bills at the banks. Long-term capital financing was not characteristic of this period leading up to the 1860s, even though squatters had begun the process of capital investment (homesteading and fencing) financed by short-term loans and current profits.

Passage of the 1860s land legislation directly challenged the squatters en masse to enter the land market to preserve their runs. The prosperity of wool growing in this decade was the immediate facility. The upswing in the world economy, combined with the specific boost to wool prices resulting from an interruption of the cotton trade by the American Civil War,[15] enhanced the squatters' capacity (through profits and loans) to consolidate their monopoly by buying land.

Merchant and banking interests, however, soon produced a more permanent facility in long-term mortgage financing because the challenge of selector farmers was as much a threat to merchant and banking capital as it was to the squatters. The profits on commissions and money lending to pastoral capital were already an integral part of the merchant and banking economy, and were potentially larger and more secure than those to be earned in financing agriculture. Accordingly, banks and mercantile houses encouraged squatters to buy land as a way of securing their interests (Bailey 1966, p. 53; Waterson 1968, pp. 25, 41). At the same time, squatters and financiers recognized their long-term benefit from the general inflation of the value of the land, resulting from its alienation via the land laws (Kiddle 1967, p. 254).

Land purchasing indebted squatters to their urban financiers; banks foreclosed on two-thirds of the squatting runs of the western districts in 1869 in Niel Black's estimation (Kiddle 1967, p. 274). The long-term results of this process are shown in Table 10.3 (Butlin 1964b, p. 135).[16]

---

[15] Fitzpatrick (1947, p. 12) claims that "during 1861–65 the export of Australian wool rose 71% above the export of the previous four years."
[16] Note that where the growers' assets consisted of leasehold, not freehold, properties, the lender took title to the lease in order to secure the loan.

Table 10.3: *Shares of total registered pastoral lessees in New South Wales, 1866–89/90*

	Banks	Other companies	Partners	Individuals
1866	0.2%	0.8%	22.5%	76.5%
1871	7.5	1.6	27.3	63.6
1879	13.4	3.6	25.8	57.2
1888/89	23.5	13.5	17.1	45.9
1889/90	22.9	15.2	17.5	44.4

The application of mortgage finance to pastoralism resulted in two significant trends. First, financial institutions became increasingly committed to accumulating pastoral capital, thus stimulating technical change in production methods. Second, as banks and finance companies competed for capital in the City of London, British capital shifted to Australia.

The entry of loan capital into production fostered both quantitative and qualitative expansion. Lands that were once uneconomical to stock (e.g., those without river frontage and those in the semiarid interior) became economically viable with capital to finance establishment and water conservation techniques. These measures, in addition to fencing, the construction of washing facilities, and the purchase of electric shearing equipment in the 1880s, expanded the yield of colonial wool growing. Whereas the number of sheep increased from 40 million to 106 million between 1871 and 1891, during the same period, the wool yield grew exponentially from 208 million pounds to 634 million pounds (Hall 1963, p. 130). The expansion of pastoral facilities, in fact, resulted from a positive correlation between mortgage financing and profitability (Butlin 1964b, p. 120). This relationship, undoubtedly compelled by the continual threat of selection, had the additional stimulus of the changed mode of competition in the pastoral industry. Indeed, even when indebtedness grew, the tendency was either to attempt to increase the yield of the property through increased capital investment (Buxton 1967, pp. 245–6), or for companies to foreclose and use their total control to increase efficiency (Bailey 1966, p. 41). In cases of foreclosure, companies purchased land defensively simply to maintain property value (Barnard 1961, pp. 40, 158). Thus, the entry of loan capital into the sphere of production compelled financiers to identify with the competitive position of the particular pastoral properties they financed. Optimal security of loans brought closer supervision of property management and in many cases outright intervention in expenditures and operations through the power of finance (Barnard 1961, p. 107).[17] Short of foreclosure and the assumption of company management, the ultimate development was the employment, by company lessees, of pastoral inspectors in the 1890s (Bailey 1966, p. 95).

Although the process of securing pastoral capital was founded upon the increasing penetration of loan capital, mercantile activity (marketing with short-term financing) lasted through the 1870s as a profitable form of pastoral agency. By the 1880s, wool marketing and pastoral financing had merged as colonial wool merchants (consignors and/or local wool sellers such as Mort in Sydney and Goldsborough in Melbourne) added regular mortgage financing to their agency, incorporating as public companies (Bailey 1966, p. 55). (Public British companies, such as the Australian Mercantile Land and Finance Company, added consignment to their original financier role, and banks entered the consignment trade themselves in the 1870s; Bailey 1966, pp. 43, 70; Barnard 1958, p. 59.) Banks took up consignment as an outcome of their increasingly direct financial relation to growers, and wool merchants in turn sought alternative sources of finance to retain their independence from banks and maintain their competitive position in the wool trade.[18] Following the lead of British finance companies, colonial banks and merchants registered on the London Stock Exchange, thereby enhancing their ability to raise finance capital independently (Bailey 1966, p. 55; Hall 1963, p. 110).

The competition to profit from the development of colonial pastoralism encouraged financial speculation (alongside an urban con-

[17] See the debate between Butlin (1950) and Fitzpatrick, attached "Note," p. 111. Fitzpatrick argues that pastoral capitals became increasingly subordinated to corporate enterprise (banking and agency companies), which owned the proceeds of sale by virtue of the agency relationship. Butlin challenges the idea of the decline of individual enterprise. This would seem to be a semantic debate, the point being that the relationship, characteristic of finance capital, was increasing integration of commercial and pastoral (qua industrial) capital, reflecting a certain phase of capitalist development under highly competitive conditions.
[18] Hall (1963, p. 108) claims that opposition by colonial banks in the 1870s prevented the entrance of additional Anglo-Australian banks into Australian finance.

struction boom in the 1880s) and an overproduction of wool. Each contributed to the severity of the early 1890s crisis, which was induced by British loan restrictions on apparently profligate borrowing by the colonies and exacerbated greatly by the Baring Crisis of 1890 (Jackson 1977, p. 73; compare Boehm 1971 and Butlin 1964b).

This discussion has suggested how, by the mid-1880s, the various mercantile and finance companies combined mercantile and banking capital in competing for the service of an increasingly productive pastoral industry. Essentially, this was a reintegration of the 1830s form of merchant banking (located in the metropole) at a higher stage of capital accumulation.[19] The penetration of the production sphere by urban capital (as pastoral finance capital) was the outcome of competition for pastoral agency by merchants and bankers, merging with pastoral capital as capital concentration and centralization proceeded. By 1888–9, almost 90 percent of company lessee arrangements (38 percent of total pastoral leases) were based in ten pastoral financiers: the Bank of New South Wales, the Commercial Banking Company of Sydney, the Australian Joint Stock Bank, the Australian Mortgage Land and Finance Company, the Union Bank of Australia, New Zealand Loan and Mercantile Agency Company, Australasian Mortgage and Agency Company, Goldsborough, Mort and Company, and the Bank of Australasia (Butlin 1950, p. 97). This is one measure of the extent of interpenetration of urban and pastoral capital.

It also indicates the subordination of pastoral production to capital which is another way of referring to the tendency in capitalist development to industrialize rural production. What is particularly interesting about this process is that it was undertaken within the context of competition between Australian and imperial capitalists. In this context, local urban capital increased its hold over the pastoral economy by using land reform to compel pastoralists to capitalize their operations, and by opening up and transforming the landed economy with selectors and railways.

STATE BUILDING AND THE WORLD ECONOMY

The British state granted self-government to the colonies with an understanding that the consolidation of a bourgeois democratic

[19] Hall (1963, p. 71) notes the general decline of merchant banking, which he associates with the growing financial maturity of peripheral regions as well as the redirection of British investment away from traditional commercial connections.

society would arrest the squatters' social conservatism. The balance of political forces that emerged within the gold-strengthened colonial economy was propitious, and the metropolitan-colonial division of labor favored liberal trade relations. Colonial Australia appeared to be an appropriate bastion of mid-Victorian British civilization. How indeed did the Australian colonial administrations interpret this responsibility?

The answer to this question is twofold.

1. It concerns the question of public policy, in particular toward resolving the agrarian question to enhance commercial opportunities.
2. It also concerns the particular role that Australian colonies played in the capitalist world economy as international depression and growing rivalry intensified Britain's relationship with its Empire.

These two components complemented each other, because colonial economic development was both cause and consequence of the diversion of capital from older spheres of British investment to newer spheres, such as the Australian Dominions. The colonial administrations secured this nexus.

This commercial nexus was the material framework of colonial state building. As economic diversification proceeded, it depended on an increasingly intensive development of export-commodity production, promoted by the colonial governments. They actively pursued fiscal policies to develop social capital on the one hand (Butlin 1959, p. 41), and on the other, social policies directed toward colonizing the hinterlands with agricultural producers, with a strong presumption of the social benefits of family farming.[20] Such policies generally sought to enhance the value of colonial landed property, while also establishing a source of public finance through land sales. Overall, these policies anticipated and promoted (however unevenly) the integration of the urban and rural social economy and, consequently, political centralization. This was achieved not only by the subordination of pastoralism to urban capital, but also by the recognition that political coherence depended on far more stable

---

[20] See the report in the *Sydney Morning Herald* (31 January 1861) of John Robertson's "Opinions" as expressed in the New South Wales Parliament, in Clark (1971, p. 344); and Powell (1970).

(geographically and demographically) land settlement than was hitherto the case.[21]

The colonial governments assumed the responsibility for territorial expansion and organization formerly undertaken by the imperial state. The particular way the social organization of rural hinterlands in each colony proceeded depended on the balance of social forces in each colony. The relative success of selector legislation was secondary to the actual process of centralizing land settlement policy by the creation and administration of the land market. If agricultural selectors were not readily settled in some regions, squatters at least were called to account through land purchasing. Centralized political regulation of the social conditions in the rural economy was the significant effect. Initially, of course, this assumed primarily an ideological form, where legislation challenged squatting in liberal terms, compelling the purchase of runs and thus greater dependence on urban finance. Subsequent revision of this laissez-faire approach – evidenced in new land settlement legislation, the establishment of commissions of inquiry, and government intervention in agriculture – enabled a more direct regulation of rural economy, as, on the heels of the railway, a farming interest emerged and governments sought to develop trade in agricultural products. Although squatter power initially subverted land reforms, the indirect effects of creating land markets and railways facilitated commercial agriculture. The resulting home market, to some extent *organized* by agricultural policy at the end of the century, was indeed a social consequence of the colonial governments' policies of territorial integration, which began with the land reforms.[22]

The creation of a land market by the colonial governments had obvious revenue considerations acknowledged by the authors of the legislation (see Lamb 1967, pp. 43–4). In particular, the sale of the colonies' greatest resource provided a source of funds other than direct taxation (MacGillivray 1982, p. 47). [At the same time, public officials raised revenue through land sales to reduce the competition for overseas funds from private capitalists, thus attesting to the

---

[21] As Reeves (1969, pp. 237–8) has written: "Indeed the history of the Land Question in Victoria from 1860 to 1884 may be summed up as a series of efforts to multiply small freeholds by a system of cheap land and easy purchase, coupled with more and more stringent conditions of residence and improvement."

[22] Friedmann (1978b) provides a useful conceptualization of the politics of territorial integration.

complementary role played by governments in colonial capitalist development (Butlin 1959, pp. 48–54).] The use of land sales to generate public finance was a primary method in New South Wales, where land reserves were sufficient, but in Victoria, where this was not the case, tariffs on manufactured imports supplemented public revenue (Jackson 1977, pp. 165–8; Patterson 1968). Such a steady source of revenue, in addition to the liquidity provided by gold production in the 1850s, encouraged early involvement by the colonial state in social capital formation (Butlin 1959, pp. 39–40).

Nevertheless, the long-term availability of revenues stemmed from the large-scale transfer of capital from London as the historic shift in British investment fields proceeded. The shift in British investment (recorded as a net disinvestment in Europe by the mid-1870s) reflected a decentralization of capital investment (Hall 1963, p. 10) as British capital sought more profitable areas than the contracting markets in the centers of world capitalism (cf. Arrighi 1978a; Luxemburg 1963, ch. 30). The initial attraction of London funds (in the third quarter of the century) resulted from the growing competition for urban and pastoral financing among companies operating in Australia. This, of course, stemmed from land purchasing.

Revenue from land sales was central to public infrastructure projects. This was especially important for *servicing* public loans on London for this purpose, and a large part of these loans financed railway construction. Government responsibility for mobilizing railway finances resulted from the historic preference of private capital for pastoral financing in Australia. Nevertheless, this was the railway age throughout the world, when governments raised public loans (especially in London) to finance railways for commercial reasons and/or to accomplish "national objects," leaving entrepreneurs free to accumulate local capital for industrial development (in Europe and the Dominions in particular) (Jenks 1973, p. 168).[23]

The Australian colonial governments perceived railway construction as enhancing land values and facilitating the wool trade (Lamb 1967, p. 47). Railway development quickly became symbolic of competition among the colonies for a common pastoral hinterland

---

[23] Mandel (1976, pp. 51–2) argues, in addition, that concentration by British, French, and Belgian capital on foreign railways (1848–60) gave breathing space to Italy, Russia, Japan, and Spain to undergo a local primitive accumulation of capital.

(Hall 1963, p. 7). In world-economic terms, railways intensified Australia's primary-producing contribution to the world division of labor, because the resulting national debt linked government policy to the encouragement of export commodity production. Public expenditure thus forged a nexus between the developing colonial landed economy and a London capital market that required alternative fields of investment from the traditional, and now saturated, fields in Europe.

The last quarter of the century, framed by the great depression, was a time of growing international loans as European capital sought higher rates of profit overseas. Loan capital secured spheres of influence. Companies strengthened by their international success, initiated the general shift toward monopoly capitalism, marked by growing protectionism and imperial rivalry (Arrighi 1978a). British capital was no exception in this decentralization process. Given the economic crisis and the emergence of European and U.S. neomercantalism, the reorientation of British foreign investment was clearly toward the Empire, although the lion's share went to the Dominions.[24] Table 10.4 shows a decline in investment in the industrial regions and an increase and relocation of capital investment to the Empire and South America.

This distinctive attraction of British capital to the Dominions during the world-economic contraction, in countercyclical fashion, marked the process of colonial state formation itself (Saul 1960; Cochrane 1980, ch. 2; Butlin 1959, pp. 61–2). Broadly, the colonial governments were implementing the initial urban bourgeois concept of reducing barriers to commercial expansion in the colonial economy by providing public loans. These actually underwrote the commercial link with the London capital market, where in 1890 Australia accounted for the largest proportion of colonial government securities sold (Hall 1963, p. 7). Railway construction was a prime example of how public loans financed exports of British materials and capital goods to Australia (as well as immigrant labor)[25]

---

[24] For example, Simon (1968, pp. 28–30) takes issue with Saul (1960) and Hall (1963) (who both qualify their argument to some extent) over their thesis of a clear trend of British investment toward the Empire in the last quarter of the century. Although Simon disagrees with this thesis, he agrees that with the export of capital to the Empire, there was a concentration in "regions of recent settlement."
[25] This was assisted with monies from loans, not general revenues (Butlin 1959, p. 66). Colonial governments encouraged "nominated immigration," whereby Australians could sponsor relatives or friends to emigrate. See Sherington (1980, p. 72).

Table 10.4: *Geographical distribution of British overseas trade and investment, 1860s through 1911–13*

Area	1860–70		1881–90		1901–10		1911–13	
	E[a]	I[a]	E	I	E	I	E	I
Total empire	32	36	34	47	34	47	36	46
Dominions	12	12	16	29	17	30	18	30
India	11	21	11	15	12	12	11.5	10.5
Africa[b]	1	—	1	0.5	2	2.5	2	2.5
Europe	39	25	36	8	36	5	36	6
S. America	12	10.5	11	20	10.5	21	12	22
United States	13	27	14	22	9	21	9	19
Other	4	3.5	5	3	10.5	6	7	7
Total	100	100	100	100	100	100	100	100
£ (thousands)	144	770	230	2,040	333	3,770	474	4,415

[a]E, exports (%), I, investment (%).
[b]Excluding South Africa.
Source: Brown (1970, p. 110).

to convert surplus capital in the metropolis into productive capital in the periphery of the world economy. In this way, colonial state formation was a process of political organization of an expanding capitalist world market (Luxemburg 1963, pp. 428–9).

State building involved more than the financial and material integration of colonial lands, however. A social policy was necessary to stabilize and secure market relations, but this took time in the Australian context, given the initial need to reclaim and resettle the squatting regions. It emerged naturally out of this process but not without conflict (given the confrontation of initially distinct interests) within the utilitarian context of liberal land legislation. A modus vivendi between government, farmer, and pastoralist formed only following a crisis in these relationships. Throughout the 1870s it was apparent that land reform policy was not effective in settling a farming population. In addition, it emerged that land sales policy outstripped the ability of pastoralism to remain profitable in the face of mounting debts and falling wool prices (Jackson 1977, p. 64). In the 1880s, the cost of railway construction outstripped productive returns, and therefore export earnings, from the pastoral industry, thus contributing to the early 1890s slump (Butlin 1964b).

Under these circumstances, the initially rather instrumental role of land sales policy in raising public revenues became increasingly apparent. In the late 1880s, then, further land reforms attempted to adjust the respective needs of pastoralism (for leasehold land safe from selection) and agriculture (for credit, leasehold land, and the ability to combine grazing with farming) (Lamb 1967, pp. 54, 64–5; Reeves 1969, pp. 245–6). Thus, government policy surrendered its orientation to revenue needs to the concrete needs of producers.

Policy shifts toward greater involvement in economic regulation represented a new balance of social forces in late-nineteenth-century Australia. These forces challenged the unregulated market consequences of the mercantile bourgeoisie's laissez-faire policies. The 1890s depression highlighted this conflict, particularly with the emergence of a politically organized labor movement espousing social democratic solutions to the ills of unemployment and landed and financial monopoly. Defeat in the great strikes of the early 1890s reoriented labor's strategy toward using the state as the vehicle of social reconstruction in securing local industry and stabilizing the landed economy for the small producer (Gollan 1966, ch. 9).

The success of the social democratic ideology depended on the support of a nascent manufacturing class for regulating a *national* economy. Manufacturing, however, was not yet a significant economic sector in Australia. It represented a mere 7.7 percent of gross private capital formation in the 1880s [compared with 37.7 percent for primary production (Butlin 1964b, pp. 20–1)], and in 1901 the labor force in primary production was twice that in manufacturing (Boehm 1971, p. 59). Hitherto, its stimulus came largely from population growth in an economy geographically protected from the metropolitan centers of the world market, and from servicing and processing the primary products.[26] [Nevertheless, the Victorian government did subsidize local manufacturing (Linge 1975, p. 160), in addition to the indirect encouragement from revenue tariffs.] Manufacturing was characteristically small scale and labor-intensive. As a consequence, the manufacturing class was too immature to be a powerful force for political unification of the national economy. However, the industrialists who operated across colonial borders and were dependent on intercolonial markets and labor

---

[26] For example, for New South Wales, see Linge (1975, p. 164).

migration understood the advantages of a national economy (Linge 1975, p. 178). The iron and emerging steel manufacturers particularly anticipated the benefits of national tariff protection against increasing imports of iron and iron products (Hughes 1964, p. 29). They organized pressure groups accordingly, such as the National Protection League and Chambers of Manufacturers. At the same time it was felt by manufacturers and politicians that a unified national state stood a better chance of restoring confidence among foreign investors in purchasing Australian securities (Hughes 1964, pp. 30, 36).

This set of social forces dovetailed with, and accelerated, earlier nationalist impulses derived from the changing international context. Australian nationalists (with a strong dose of racism) were increasingly alarmed in the 1880s by the growing rivalry of France and Germany with British and Australian expansion in the Pacific. Although Britain attempted unsuccessfully to delegate the responsibility for imperial defense to the Australian colonies (in the context of British decline), the nationalist movement presumed a British naval presence and sought an integrated defense policy in a federated state (see Fitzpatrick 1969, pp. 259–61; McQueen 1970, ch. 1–4).

The movement toward the creation of a federal state (1901) thus originated in the dual processes of social transformation within urban and rural Australia and the growing politicoeconomic rivalry in the interstate system. Domestic pressures for state regulation of a national economy (including more state involvement in rural development) echoed the protectionist impulses elsewhere in the interstate system (Polanyi 1957). Australia's international context was specific to its colonial role, however. Given the tenuous character of British world power during this period of increasing European imperial rivalry, the political and economic interdependence of Britain and the Australian colonies gave Australian nationhood a double significance. While the colonies unified to secure themselves politically, economically, and militarily as a modern capitalist state, they also shored up a consequential segment of an increasingly vulnerable British Empire.

CONCLUSION

This chapter has examined the way the politics of the agrarian question reshaped the colonial economy and society in the latter half of the nineteenth century. The urban challenge to the squatters, formalized in land legislation, transformed the pastoral economy as squatters moved to secure their runs through long-term mortgage loans. As a consequence, urban loan capital (some of it metropolitan) brought pastoralism within its domain, thereby both shifting pastoral capital accumulation to a capitalist basis and laying the foundations for an integrated home market.

The role of land legislation was not limited to forcing the squatters' hands because the land market thus created provided a commercial environment to assist new farmers onto the land. Land speculation, combined with waged labor for pastoral proprietors, enabled intending farmers to accumulate capital in lieu of government assistance to agriculture. (It was only the subsequent farming generations that began to agitate for the public regulation of farming conditions.) In addition, revenue from land sales was the source of government provision of social capital. While there was land to be sold, colonial governments managed to borrow funds in the London capital market to finance infrastructure projects. They thereby redistributed British capital from traditional and contracting spheres of investment to Australia.

Thus, under the political pressures of increasingly equal or superior commercial competition, British capital emulated the mercantilist trends of the age, despite political adherence to free trade in the British state – a consequence of the City's power. This movement strengthened the direct aspects of British hegemony, elevating the importance of Britain's political empire. In this context the metropolitan-colonial relation revealed two processes:

1. The recomposition of loan capital from London into private and social capital formation in the Australian economy underwrote state formation along national lines in Australia.
2. This same process of recomposition expanded colonial primary-commodity production, maintaining the multilateral payments system, which also sustained rivals to Britain, and thus helping to anchor British capitalism until World War I destroyed the unity of the world market.

CONCLUSION

When Kochachiro Takahashi (1978, p. 96) drew attention to the "deep inner relationship between the agrarian question and industrial capital, which determines the characteristic structures of capitalism in the various countries," he emphasized the role of political forces in the transition to capitalism. The agrarian question is necessarily political when the genesis of capital transforms landed property relations and produces social conflict between the traditional landed classes and an emergent commercial bourgeoisie. The latter's historical attempts to subordinate landed property as an instrument of production contributed to the rise and transformation of the modern nation-state (Marx 1965–7, vol. III, p. 618). Such conflict was a structural feature of the absolutist state, a power apparatus divided between securing traditional forms of landed property and promoting commerce for financial and military purposes (Anderson 1974; Moore 1968; Skocpol 1977). Military security was necessary to territorial sovereignty in the emerging European states system. This system was premised on the developing world market, within which states competed through mercantilist policy (Wallerstein 1974b; Arrighi 1978b). The commercial framework of state policy thus not only affected the domestic conflict between landed and mercantile classes, but also revealed the *international* origins and consequences of the agrarian question as an issue of social policy within states.

The purpose of this book has been to investigate the world-historical origins of the capitalist transition in nineteenth-century Australia. This investigation has been threefold in its intent:

1. To reconstruct Australian colonial history as the history of a settler society, by definition an extension of European capitalism,

241

and therefore decisively shaped by the forces of an expanding world-capitalist economy.

2. To give content to the concept of a world-capitalist economy in such historical analysis.

3. To consider the agrarian question in nineteenth-century Australia as the fulcrum of the uneven and combined forces characteristic of world-economic development, specifying it as the conflict between reactionary wool growers oriented to supplying the world market and progressive urban commercial forces seeking to harness rural production to domestic market expansion. (Of course, the agrarian question could arise as an issue of social policy only when Australian settlers obtained self-government in midcentury.)

The resolution of the agrarian question in favor of the progressives led to a shift in the patterns of accumulation and the development of state structures in colonial Australia. This transformation of colonial society not only represented the transition to a modern capitalist nation-state, but also was an integral part of the development of the nineteenth-century world-capitalist economy. Historically, these changes had a singular character, given their reciprocal influence. It is for this reason that we cannot theorize about a capitalist world economy without such historical analysis. The world economy is not a complex of forces *outside of* its constituent states. States in turn are more than just economic actors in the world market. They constitute the social structure of the world market; they mobilize finance; centralize capital; secure forms of labor organization; provide labor, commodity, and capital markets; and so forth.[1] In short, states both constitute and are in turn constituted by the social relations of production and circulation that may be particular to a national economy but simultaneously define its world-historical context.

In the case of colonial Australia, imperial state policy was responsible for the general organization of the settler society until midcentury. With self-government, responsibility devolved upon the individual colonial administrations until the Commonwealth of Australia was created in 1901. These shifts in the structures of political authority were the combined result of social change within

---

[1] This notion has been emphasized to me by Terence K. Hopkins (Department of Sociology, SUNY–Binghamton).

colonial Australia and political developments within the interstate system in which Britain was dominant.

During the time Britain administered Australia as a formal colony, imperial policy determined land use and the deployment of labor. These policies were tailored to British needs, which altered as industrial capitalism transformed the social order. Until the 1830s, Britain needed to dispose of a growing convict population to Australia, and this need adapted to the labor requirements of the colonial wool growers, the exclusive beneficiaries of a discriminatory land-grant policy. Commercial success in the London wool market led this gentry to articulate an ideology expressing their mercantilist relationship with Britain. They proposed a patriarchal colonial society based on bonded labor and supplying wool to metropolitan England. New social policies emerged in Britain, however, as unemployed laborers flooded local parish administrations, far outweighing the dimensions of the convict phenomenon. Henceforth, transferring the laboring poor to the colonies governed imperial policy. Because the settlement colonies were now to receive free laborers, there arose a positive theory toward them, anticipating a liberal development toward self-government.

The attempt to engineer a geographical branch of English agricultural capitalism through systematic colonization was outflanked by the success of colonial wool as a world market commodity. A new form of social conservatism developed in colonial Australia based on squatting by wool growers on an advancing land frontier. Behind this extensive occupation of the hinterland lay commercial credit, advanced by merchants (increasingly metropolitan) interested solely in wool as an object of trade. Squatting was conservative because of its makeshift and exhaustive exploitation of the land, using bonded labor in the age-old shepherding practice. Furthermore, this primitive form of pastoral capital accumulation stemmed from the putting-out relationship within which British merchant capital organized the wool trade. Squatting's dependence on British commercial credit was both its strength as an expanding form of staple production and its weakness in the face of the 1840s commercial crisis. At the same time, in the absence of a functioning colonial labor market, especially on the frontier, squatters depended on the British state's supply of convict labor. When this ended in 1840, pastoral capital's labor costs rose along with its commercial debts (exacerbated by a decline in wool prices).

The crisis of the 1840s highlighted the conservative nature of colonial pastoralism. Political conflict developed around the primary social contradictions of squatting: the issue of bonded labor (which large squatters sought to maintain), the speculative relations with merchant capital within the British mercantile system, and the form of landed property (with squatters demanding preemptive rights to occupied land). The polarization of this conflict into a struggle between urban capital and the squatters posed the agrarian question as the fundamental issue of the colonial political economy. There were three components to this.

1. The conflict resembled the historic struggle between capital and landed property. It concerned the squatting system's barrier to the extension of commerce in, and capitalization of, the landed economy.

2. Given the world-economic context, this question also concerned the impact of the imperial division of labor on the colonial social economy. This had two elements, both revealed by the crisis. On the one hand, there was the question of colonial economic dependence on the world market. On the other was the question of political control of the colonial state because of the pressing issues of land tenure and labor supply (hitherto regulated by the British state).

3. Finally, the conflict embodied the previous struggle of the emancipists against the disproportionate political power of the pastoral oligarchy. By the 1840s the balance of social forces had changed, but the struggle still concerned liberalization of the society. To the leaders of the progressive forces, the urban mercantile class, this goal necessitated subordination of the landed economy to urban capital.

In summary, the agrarian question arose in relation to the wool growers' monopoly of the colonial landed economy, reproduced as it was through an expanding British mercantile system. It concerned the rivalry of two alternative modes of colonial economic development, turning on the question of which social forces would control the colonial state. The trajectory of British hegemony resolved this question because the imperial authorities were committed to a representative form of self-government in colonial Australia. This was so in spite of the significant contribution of colonial wool to the British textile industry by midcentury, which underlay Britain's temporary capitulation in 1847 to the squatters' demands for long-term leasehold rights to their occupied land.

This concession to squatter privilege, which politically emboldened the wealthy squatters, galvanized the antisquatter movement consolidated by the impact of the gold rushes. Gold stimulated colonial commerce and attracted an immigrant constituency for a revitalized urban bourgeoisie. The way was clear to forge liberal constitutions to meet British expectations; that is, Britain relaxed its *formal* control in the event of the consolidation of *substantive* hegemony over the path of colonial development.

Colonial politics centered on the agrarian question insofar as the political success of urban liberals depended on linking the future of independent colonial administrations to a resolution of the land question, and thereby responding electorally to the populist current among unemployed miners and urban workers. The parliamentary dominance of the urban bourgeoisie fostered the land reforms of the early 1860s. Ideologically, the goal of land reform was to open the squatting leaseholds to selection by small farmers, but practically it served the urban bourgeoisie as a political weapon against the economic power of the squatters.

Land legislation submitted selection to an open competitive land market, with no compensating mechanisms such as state financial assistance to the intending small landholder. Selection was only moderately successful, given the squatters' access to financial resources through the strength of the wool trade. Accordingly, threatened squatters secured their holdings by purchasing land. They now required a stable and local labor force, however. The possibility of waged labor for farmers, in addition to land speculation, provided the market environment necessary for successful selectors to accumulate farming capital. Thus, under the stimulus of the land market created by colonial governments, the rural economy was transformed as the fortunes of both pastoral and agricultural capital became linked.

The agent of transformation of the rural economy was urban capital, introduced through the transformation of land into a commodity. There were two aspects to this process.

1. Defensive land purchasing by squatters depended on urban finance, which aided this development with investment loans for water conservation and fencing. Such a relationship with loan

capital – concerned to enhance its commercial profits through increased pastoral profitability – encouraged a transformation of the technical base of wool growing. Pastoral capital accumulation shifted toward a capitalist basis.

2. Crown lands sales generated revenues that were decisive in maintaining colonial government investment in social capital. Railway construction in particular spearheaded the integration of the home market and promoted agricultural settlement.

The policy of creating a land market thus resulted in the politicoeconomic subordination of pastoral capital as the landed economy generally was integrated into the urban-based commercial economy. Wool growing lost its singular dominance of rural production, allowing the development of a home market. As a result of these integrating processes, both economic and political, a unified capitalist state emerged by the century's end. State formation also depended on transformations under way in the late-nineteenth-century world economy.

The reshaping of the world capitalist economy expressed the changing fortunes of British hegemony. As protectionist rivalry threatened the unity of the world market fashioned by Britain, the Empire's significance increased and elevated the political component of British hegemony. Excluded British capital moved to the peripheral zones of the world economy – especially to the Dominions, but to the Empire generally. In colonial Australia, in particular, such capital inflow aided the diversification of primary commodity exports; meat products, butter, grain, fodder, gold, and other minerals joined wool. Additionally, colonial government bonds offered increasing financial security while the challenge to British hegemony grew. British capitalism had a greater neomercantilist framework as it strengthened its imperial ties.

These international processes were rooted in the social dynamic of colonial Australia. In the pastoral industry particularly, local financiers competed successfully with British banking and financial companies now that they had greater access to the London capital market. The same held for urban infrastructure projects. In a real sense, such financial activity was analogous to the role of finance capital in Britain's rival states – capitalizing the productive base and enlarging the infrastructure of emerging national capitalist economies. The Australian colonial governments complemented and encouraged this by consolidating urban capital's dominance through the recomposition of British loan capital into colonial social capital. This whole process expressed the resolution of the agrarian question in favor of the mercantile bourgeoisie.

The social dynamic within colonial Australia, then, was less a product of the interaction between external and internal forces than a working out of world-economic processes within colonial society. At the most elemental level, the struggle between urban and pastoral capital expressed the contradictory unity of British hegemony with its liberal and mercantilist strands. The question of who should control the land wavered between opposing concepts of colonial economic development held by urban mercantile classes (oriented to home-market development) and wool growers (oriented to maintaining the imperial division of labor). The question also raised the issue of political sovereignty, and this depended on the showing of colonial liberalism against the neomercantilism (in domestic and foreign relations) of the wool growers. Success of the former facilitated the transfer of power by Britain as it consolidated its substantive hegemony. Self-government and land reform thus allowed local regulation (and hence transformation) of the primitive form of pastoral capital accumulation that originated in metropolitan mercantile expansion. Henceforth, capitalist social relations held in Australia, even while it retained its primary-producing contribution to the international division of labor.

My analysis has emphasized the world-historical origins of the midcentury agrarian question in Australia. At the same time it has sought to contribute to our conceptualization of a capitalist world economy through historical analysis. This stems from the notion that the world economy is constituted and reconstituted through temporal and spatial processes, thus making it fundamentally a historical relation (see Hopkins 1978). Nevertheless, its essential process – the accumulation of capital on a world scale (involving market and state formation) – has a theoretical foundation in Marx's theory of capital. I have attempted to apply that theory to an analysis of the social relations of commodity production and circulation in an *uneven* world market. This gives an initial understanding of the relations among different forms of capital, so the various colonial interests and social conflicts can be presented in their particular historical context. It has also been necessary to complicate this social matrix with an understanding of the political and ideological relations among states in the nineteenth century because these relations largely structure the processes of capital accumulation. It is for this reason that I began the study with an overview of British hegemony in the nineteenth-century world economy.

This account of my project shows that one can study the processes of the world-capitalist economy through a very specific historical case study like colonial Australia. To put it another way, one cannot understand the formation of modern states adequately without recognizing the world-historical forces that shaped them from inside and out. Accordingly, my focus on the agrarian question is deliberate insofar as it recurred in various forms in other nineteenth- and early-twentieth-century states. The political and military conflicts in the mid-nineteenth-century United States, for example, resembled those in colonial Australia in the same period. Whereas the content and outcome of the respective conflicts were particular to each settler society, the origins of their respective agrarian questions were similar, and the mode of resolution marked a definitive stage in the political history of capitalism in the two states. It was the impact of world-economic processes on local class relations that articulated the particular agrarian question in each society. In each case a powerful landed class, integrated (through the wool and cotton trades) with the world economy and exploiting coerced labor forces on extensive land frontiers, constrained the development of capitalist social relations. Such extensive wool and cotton cultures resulted from intensive capitalist production in English textiles. In these senses, social and political conflicts arising out of claims for the continued monopoly of the frontier landed economy by pastoralist and planter classes alike had world-historical origins.

These origins were not simply because wool and cotton were produced as industrial commodities for British industry. The social organization of these two forms of staple commodity production derived from their origins in the expansion of British state and capital (merchant and landed) into new settlements. Any differences in the social and political organization of the two regions corresponded in large part to their different times of incorporation into world-capitalist development.

The challenge to these forms of primitive capital accumulation and social ideology from politically allied urban classes and farmers concerned their inherent limits to the expansion of the home market. Such conflict was irrepressible precisely because the mercantile origins of pastoral and planter capital no longer suited the emerging requirements of liberal capitalism. What was in question was not simply conservative agrarian social relations, but also the consequences of their reproduction through the structural relations of the world market. To resolve the agrarian question was indeed to resolve a growing contradiction between the interests attached to domestic and world divisions of labor. In each case, political resolution led to a restructuring of exchange relations with the world market as a condition for subsequent industrial capitalist development. This dialectic of local class conflict (and political alliances) and its international dimensions captures the fundamental developmental processes of the world-capitalist economy.

APPENDIXES

APPENDIX 1

SELECTED LAND PURCHASES FROM THE COUNTY REGISTER, 1831–1835

Land purchases

Name	Date	Freehold (acres)	County
John Blaxland	March 1831	7,680	Brisbane
	July 1831	800	Camden
	Jan. 1833	455	Camden
	May 1834	640	Camden
John Blaxland, Jnr.	May 1834	872, 870	Brisbane
	May 1834	4,200, 2,560	Northumberland
Wm. Cox	Oct. 1834	1,920	Bligh
	May 1833	640	Bathurst
Francis Forbes	Dec. 1831	130	Cook
	April 1833	63	Cook
	June 1833	45	Cook
	Oct. 1834	180	Cook
	April 1835	40	Cook
		2,560, 2,560	Durham
R. Jones	April 1834	1,120	Brisbane
	April 1834	1,014	Brisbane
	Oct. 1834	2,560	Brisbane
	Oct. 1834	1,015	Brisbane
Thos. Icely	Feb. 1835	1,396	Bathurst
	Jan. 1835	2,560	Bathurst
Wm. Lawson, Snr.	Jan. 1833	784	Bligh
	Jan. 1833	875	Bligh
	Aug. 1834	640	Bligh
	Oct. 1834	1,113	Bathurst
		717	Phillip

253

Land purchases (cont.)

Name	Date	Freehold (acres)	County
Wm. Lawson	Sep. 1834	5,000	Bligh
	Aug. 1834	2,560	Bligh
	Aug. 1834	2,560	Bligh
	Oct. 1834	1,920	Bligh
	Oct. 1834	120	Bathurst
	Oct. 1834	1,092	Bathurst
	May 1833	40	Cook
	May 1833	52	Cook
	April 1834	100	Cook
		640	Phillip
		2,000	Phillip
		700	Westmoreland
		1,300	Westmoreland
Wm. Macarthur	Oct. 1831	4,000	Argyle
James Macarthur	Oct. 1831	4,000	Argyle
	Dec. 1832	640	
H. H. Macarthur	July 1835	5,000	Argyle

Source: NSW SA 2/1937.

DIFFERENTIATION AMONG SQUATTERS BY LAND POSSESSION AND STOCK, 1844

No. 5 – New England district

Names of occupants	No. of runs	No. of licenses	Estimated extent in sq. mi.	acres	Horses	Cattle	Sheep	Total reduced to sheep	Proportion of sheep per sq. mi.	No. of acres per sheep
Largest occupiers of land and holders of stock										
Mary McIntyre	3	1	443	283,520	9	3,227	—	25,888	58	11
Henry Dangar	2	1	118	76,000	28	1,136	27,739	37,051	314	2
R. R. Mackenzie	2	1	241	154,400	38	1,494	27,300	39,556	164	4
M. H. Marsh	2	1	288	184,320	60	486	13,886	18,254	63	10 1/10
William Boyd	2	1	148	94,720	36	660	4,000	9,568	64	10
C. Coxen	1	1	160	102,400	—	—	1,925	1,925	12	53
A. C. Innes	2	1	66	42,240	9	46	13,848	14,288	216	3
		7	1,464	937,000				146,539		
Smallest occupiers of land and holders of stock										
Messrs. McNab	1	1	24	15,360	7	16	5,107	5,291	220	2 9/10
Brodie & Russell	1	1	42	26,880	10	110	—	960	23	28
Lawson & Alexander	1	1	24	15,360	6	15	2,918	3,086	128	5
Bacon & Gregory	1	1	28	17,520	4	220	—	1,792		
		4	118	75,520				11,129		

Average for £10	Acres	Stock	Sheep to 1 sq. mi.	Acres to a sheep	Acres to an ox
Large holders	133,943	20,933	100	6 2/3	51
Small holders	18,888	2,782	94	6 7/9	52

256

No. 15 – Portland Bay District (Port Phillip)

Names of occupants	No. of runs	No. of licenses	Estimated extent in		Stock depastured				Proportion of sheep per sq. mi.	No. of acres per sheep
			sq. mi.	acres	Horses	Cattle	Sheep	total reduced to sheep		
Largest occupiers of land and holders of stock										
Benjamin Boyd	2	1	94	60,000	12	33	13,358	13,718	146	4⅓
S. G. Henry	2	1	94	60,000	38	700	14,000	19,904	212	3
Neil Black	—	1	78	50,000	33	860	14,498	21,642	278	2⅓
T. E. Boyd & McGill	—	1	47	30,000	5	50	16,000	16,440	350	2 nearly
Bolden Brothers	—	1	42	27,000	10	80	—	720	17	37½
Robert Kerr	—	1	62	40,000	8	50	18,539	19,003	306	2⅖
Edward Henty	—	1	31	20,000	38	700	14,000	19,904	642	1
Clyde Company	—	1	47	30,000	33	512	12,794	17,154	365	1⅖
		8	495	317,000				128,485		
Smallest occupiers of land and holders of stock										
Beatton & Tealy	—	1	3	2,000	—	—	600	600	200	3⅓
Daniel Curdie	—	1	3	2,000	4	1	82	122	40	16
D. & D. McNichol	—	1	3	2,000	3	70	—	584	194	3⅖
Thomas Thomson	—	1	3	2,000	—	2	650	666	222	3 nearly
James Kitson	—	1	6	4,000	—	38	—	304	50	13
M. Nicholson	—	1	—	—	—	3	256	280	—	—
Gerrie & McGregor	—	1	8	5,000	—	—	400	400	50	13
		7	26	17,000				2,956		

Average for £10	Acres	Stock	Sheep to 1 sq. mi.	Acres to a sheep	Acres to an ox
Large holders	39,625	16,060	260	2½	20
Small holders	2,833	422	113[a]	6	24[a]

[a]These figures are not strictly correct because the stock of seven persons is stated but the land of only six.

257

Return of the quantities of land and stock held, respectively, by the four largest and by the four smallest occupiers of land and stock in each of the squatting districts of New South Wales (the district of Bligh alone excepted)

District	No. of acres held by		Quantity of stock[a] held by	
	four largest proprietors	four smallest proprietors	four largest proprietors	four smallest proprietors
Moreton Bay	497,920	71,680	84,336	10,247
Darling Downs	770,560	97,280	73,700	11,060
Clarence River	424,960	26,880	66,036	4,576
McLeay River	360,920	12,800	80,023	4,424
New England	724,640	75,520	120,749	11,129
Liverpool Plains	1,204,480	73,600	145,719	8,164
Wellington	517,440	23,680	75,948	3,038
Lachlan	943,400	1,600	81,300	1,568
Murrumbidgee	474,240	720	67,036	960
Maneroo	363,680	3,200	106,359	2,808
Port Phillip				
Murray	860,000	9,100	104,680	4,286
Gipps' Land	187,000	8,400	77,640	2,248
Western Port	221,000	22,000	52,680	2,389
Portland Bay	210,000	8,000	80,453	1,106
Totals	7,750,640	433,460	1,216,659	68,003

Note: The largest occupiers of land are generally, though not universally, the largest proprietors of stock, and in the same way the smallest occupiers of land are generally, though not universally, the smallest holders of stock.

[a] In this calculation of stock, one horse or one head of cattle is reckoned equal to eight sheep. The word "stock" therefore properly means stock reduced to its equivalent in sheep.

Source: Depasturing Regulations: "Correspondence Relative to Crown Lands," in British Parliamentary Papers, vol. 9: Colonies – Australia, Sessions 1845–46, pp. 438–48 (selections).

APPENDIX 3

STATEMENT SHOWING THE DIFFERENCE BETWEEN CONVICT AND FREE LABOR

———

Rations and slops for one prisoner for twelve months

		£	s.	d.
Rations				
548 lbs. flour, at 20s.		5	9	9
28 lbs. 5% loss on re-weighing				
520 lbs. at 10 lbs. per week (1 lb. extra)				
585 lbs. beef at 3d.		7	6	3
117 lbs. 20% loss on salting, curing, and re-weighing				
468 lbs. at 9 lbs. per week (2 lbs. extra)				
70 lbs. salt and ¼ lb. salt-petre to cure meat		0	3	6
Indulgences				
173 oz. tea – say 11 lbs. at 1s. 6d.		0	16	6
17 oz. 10% loss drying up and re-weighing				
156 oz. at 3 oz. per week				
58 lbs. sugar at 3d.		0	14	6
6 10% loss drying up and re-weighing				
52 lbs. at 1 lb. per week				
129 oz. – say 8 lbs. soap at 4d.		0	2	8
25 oz. 20% loss drying up and re-weighing				
104 oz. at 2 oz. per week				
69 oz. say 4¼ lbs. Tobacco at 2s.		0	8	6
17 oz. 25% loss drying up				
52 oz. at 1 oz. per week				
Slops				
	1 Woollen Jacket	0	10	0
	1 Duck ditto	0	8	0
(1 extra)	4 shirts, at 2s. 6d.	0	10	0
(1 extra)	1 pair duck trowsers, at 4s.	0	8	0
(″)	1 do. Woollen ditto	0	7	0
	4 do. Shoes at 8s.	1	12	0
	1 Hat	0	5	0
	1 Blanket	0	8	0
		19	9	8
640 acres of land purchased at 5s. per acre is £160; £160 at 10% interest p.a. is £16 a year, to procure 6 men; 1 man is therefore		2	13	4
		22	3	0

Rations for one free man for twelve months

	£	s.	d.
Prisoner's Allowance	15	1	8
And 2 lbs. flour, 1 lb. beef, 1 oz. tea, ½ lb. sugar, 2 oz. soap, & 1 oz. tobacco, per week extra, on the same calculation of losses by weight is	3	2	8
	18	4	4
Twenty Guineas Wages:	21	0	0
	39	4	4
Free man draws Slops and extras to the amount of £10 on which you obtain 50% profit	3	6	8
	35	17	8
Deduct expenses of one convict	22	3	0
Expenses of a free man, over & above the convict	£13	14	8

The whole amount of the extra provision, indulgences and slops, allowed the prisoner in this statement is £2 17s. 6d., of which the beef, shirt, & shoes are considered *indispensably* necessary, and tend to procure better attention to the sheep entrusted to them.

The difference in free labour is, therefore, £13 14s. 8d. per man – an object, certainly, at *first* glance, but probably not so much so, in the long run; when it is borne in mind that there are many things wilfully destroyed by the *prisoner*, for which the only compensation you obtain is, to have him punished – and it is also the only redress you have when sheep are carelessly lost; while in both instances, the *free man* would be made to *pay* for *his* negligence, and the knowledge of this ensures their safety. It is therefore to be considered whether *free shepherds*, and *convict hut-keepers*, would not be the cheapest plan of conducting a sheep establishment.

An objection might be made to £2 13 4, the proportion of interest, on purchase of land, in the calculation of the expenses of convict labour; but whatever value might accrue to the land so purchased at an after period, it must be remembered that the primary object was to procure *labour* – & to *labour*, therefore, must the expense go; if I read the land regulations aright, the resale of land forfeits the title of the original purchase to the labour which he acquired thro' the original purchase.

Source: "Disadvantages of a Sheep Station Out of the Boundaries of the Colony of N.S.W. in a North West Direction in 1837," *The Australian Magazine*, Vol. 1, No. II, February 1838, pp. 143–5.

APPENDIX 4

WOOL EXPORTS FROM
NEW SOUTH WALES, 1822–1849

Year	Quantity (lbs.)	Value (£)
1822	172,880	Not known
1823	198,240	Not known
1824	275,560	Not known
1825	411,600	Not known
1826	552,980	48,384
1827	407,116	24,306
1828	834,343	40,851
1829	1,005,333	63,555
1830	899,750	34,907
1831	1,401,284	75,979
1832	1,515,516	73,559
1833	1,734,203	103,692
1834	2,246,943	213,628
1835	3,893,927	299,587
1836	3,693,241	369,324
1837	4,273,715	320,527
1838	5,749,376	405,977
1839	7,213,584	442,504
1840	8,610,755	566,112
1841	8,390,540	517,537
1842	9,428,036	595,175
1843	12,704,899	685,647
1844	13,512,176	645,344
1845	17,861,734	1,009,242
1846	18,479,520	1,019,985
1847	22,379,722	1,272,118
1848	22,969,711	1,240,144
1849	27,963,530	1,238,559

Note: Includes District of Port Phillip.
Source: V&P, NSW, 1840 and 1850; statistical returns.

APPENDIX 5

STATEMENTS CONCERNING PROFITABILITY OF PASTORAL ENTERPRISE, 1842 AND 1844

———

1. EVIDENCE OF M. H. MARSH TO THE SELECT COMMITTEE ON IMMIGRATION, *V&P, NSW*, 1842

I consider that under the best management, and the most favourable circumstances, the wool may be made to pay the annual expenses, in which case the increase is the profit; and the difficulty in answering this question, consists in estimating the value of such increase, in a Colony where the price of sheep, owing to circumstances with which sheep farming has nothing to do, is frightfully fluctuating. The only possible way in which the calculation can be made, is by supposing that the sheep farmer will be able to sell his increase at the same rate that he originally gave for his stock; it is well known that sheep have been sold in this colony within a few years, at from £3 to 3s. each, and although the average price, and perhaps the real intrinsic value is from £1 5s. to £1 10s., let me first for the purpose of this calculation, suppose the price of a mixed quantity of sheep (the way in which they are almost always sold,) to be £1 per head, and let me suppose that the sheep farmer has –

15,000 sheep at £1	£15,000
Fixed capital, including buildings, working oxen, drays, horses, &c., necessary for carrying on an establishment of 15,000 sheep	1,500
Floating capital, being an average of from thirteen to fifteen months advance in wages, on articles, purchases &c., before the wool can be disposed of	2,000
Total	£18,500

Out of 15,000 mixed sheep, about 7,000 will be breeding ewes, and that increase from them, after deducting the decrease amongst the whole 15,000, in consumption of mutton and deaths, may be put at 70 per cent, or in round numbers, 5,000; but one-half of this increase must be wethers, which being a necessary article of consumption, and not the subject of speculation, are not liable to so great a variation in price; reckoning the wethers at 10s., and the ewes at the original price, £1, gives £3,750 as the annual profit on £18,000 – that is to say, the sheep

263

farmer, at the end of the first year, can sell stock to the amount of £3,750, and have the same number left as he originally purchased. It will be suggested that if the average of the sheep is £1, and of the wethers only 10s., the ewes ought to be worth something more than £1; but when it is considered that the sheep farmer, to keep up the character of his original stock, and if possible, to improve them, ought only to sell his oldest and worst ewes, perhaps £1 is very little less than the value. Let me, in the second place, put the price at 10s., which, on 15,000 sheep is £7,500, and with fixed and floating capital as before £11,000, which, with increase as before, and reckoning the wethers at 10s. still, gives £2,500 profit on £11,000. Let me, in the third place, suppose that the original stock are purchased at 5s., that is, 15,000 sheep for £3,250, and with fixed and floating capital as before, £6,750, increase as before 5,000, I will not reckon wethers as worth only 7s. 6d., £1,550 annual profit on an original investment of £6,750. In times of such very great monetary depression as to allow sheep to sink to 10s. and 5s., it is true that the floating and fixed capital required, will not be great as at other times; horses, working oxen, &c., will be cheaper, and the price of labour will be somewhat lessened from the inability of others to employ it in that wasteful and extravagant manner unfortunately too common in this Colony, either in their own personal gratifications, or in wild speculation; but at the same time, most of the great expenses of a sheep establishment, such as taxes, ironmongery, tea, sugar, &c., will not be materially altered. The profit on sheep farming, after deducting 10 per cent interest, is from 10 to 13 per cent, per annum. These calculations are made without any reference to the casualties of the diseases of sheep, so dreadful in their consequences, and which even the best management cannot entirely ward off. Many are only applicable to districts where the sheep farmer can grow his own wheat. The profit I have spoken of can only be obtained by the very best of management; and, I think I am within the mark in stating that it is not obtained in one case out of twenty. It may perhaps be obtained with a very small number of sheep as well as on a large scale, as although, in the latter case the proportion of expenses is less, in the former instance the squatter's own personal labour and exertions will be proportionally more. The calculations are also wholly inapplicable to a sheep farmer who has not ample room on his runs; where he is in the slightest degree hedged in and stinted at his stations, the difference is incalculable, as under such circumstances his flocks cannot be so large, and consequently his expenses will be greater; his sheep cannot be in such good condition, and consequently his wool and increase will be less; and in both instances to a degree of which no one who has not seen the fatal effects of overstocking, can have the slightest conception. I am convinced that the indigenous grasses, with fair treatment, do not deteriorate in quantity and quality, but when a run has once been overstocked, and the grasses pulled up by the roots by the sheep, it is impossible to say how long it may be before the country can recover, as in this climate where once vegetation has been entirely stopped by trampling down, or otherwise, it appears that an almost in-definite time is required before grass will grow there again, when the ground is bare, and open to the drought and the powerful action of the sun's rays.

2. SECOND LETTER TO THE EDITORS OF THE *SYDNEY MORNING HERALD* BY EDWARD T. HAMILTON, ESQ., MAY 2, 1844

And now as to the profits of a grazing establishment...I will take an interval of twelve months, from October 1842 to October 1843. The number of sheep belonging to the estate was the same (about 17,000) at the two periods. The increase was about 5,000; the number sold to the butcher, and paid for, was 3,800; the number of sheep (a few cattle were also slaughtered) consumed for rations was 500; the total decrease, consisting of animals which died from casualty, were destroyed as worthless, or were lost by the shepherds, amounted to 700; the net receipts from the clip of 1842, after payment of freight and all charges in London was 2,700*l.*; the money received from the butcher was 1,120*l.*, making the gross returns during the twelve months, 3,840*l.* As my establishment is a mixed one, comprising horses, sheep and cattle, it is difficult for me to form a very precise estimate of the expenditure incurred exclusively for sheep, but on making as near a calculation as possible, I believe that the whole sum expended, including superintendence, shearing, wool-bagging, commission to the agent for the sale of fat sheep, drovers' wages (which is a very serious charge) and the farm establishment, but exclusive of land-rent, license fee and assessment, would not have exceeded 2,000*l.*, supposing all the men to have been free, and taking the cost of each man at 35*l.* a year, and the average number of flocks throughout the year at 24.

The difference between the receipts and the expenditure during the above period was therefore about 1,800*l.*; and, perhaps, I ought to have stated more explicitly in my former letter, that I used the term "profit," in this sense – the excess of gross return over expenditure. [Note that Hamilton has not included his original investment in sheep in these calculations.]

However unpalatable the assertion may be it is nevertheless true, that mismanagement, chiefly arising from inattention and absence, is one of the real causes, if not the only cause, which makes stock investments apparently unprofitable. It is impossible to exaggerate the evil of absenteeism....
P.S.
Bradley's evidence

Have you ever formed an estimate of the returns of a sheep establishment; can you tell the Committee what net profit you can make out of every thousand sheep you have? – Rather more than 100*l.* on every 1,000...

What would you consider the average profit on every flock in the colony? I think it scarcely amounts to 50*l.* on a 1,000.

To what do you attribute the difference between your own net profit and the general net profit of the colony? – In my own case I attribute it chiefly to my mode of management; there are a great many instances in which merchants and profit men living in Sydney embark in sheep and farming speculations and from their avocations and business being in town, they are unable to give that attention to their concerns up the country which they require, and are obliged to entrust their management to others who do not understand them much better than the owners do themselves. I attribute the success of my establishment to my long experience and close attention to it.

APPENDIX 6

LETTER (DRAFT) TO HENRY DANGAR, SQUATTER, FROM R. CAMPBELL JNR. AND CO., SYDNEY, 1840

Henry Dangar, Esq.

Dear Sir,

In our present extreme distress for money we are anxious to obtain Bills for Discount – and we therefore enclose you a statement of our accounts against you, as regards cash and overdue bills – and we enclose two Bills for your good depositors ... please return to us with as little Delay as possible – Your Wool may probably arrive in time to provide for them. – We have charged you 12% interest on all these transactions which is now the Bank rate on overdue bills and renewals, and which we are obliged to charge you to *save ourselves from loss* ... – We could get the best bills in the colony for discount (if we had money to spare) at 25% Discount and we know that ... *does a great deal at 40%.*

We enclose you the last bill you sent us for renewal and your blank endorsement, check ... as we find it impossible to get a Bill discounted for you except at a tremendous rate – Such is the extreme Distress for money just now, that *good* bills are actually being hawked at Discount of 40% p.a.

You made a good arrangement with us about your wool. We can get any quantity at 1/- per lb. advance or purchase – and good private Bills on London are at a Discount of 5 @ 6%.

Yours faithfully,

R. Campbell Jnr & Co.

Total liabilities to Rob Campbell Jnr. & Co. on 7 November 1840

$£1,674.2.4$

Interest $\underline{70.11.5}$

$£1,744.13.9$

Settled by
Promissory Notes due 10th May 1841
Charged in Campbell's acc. of 22 July
against Wools of Ridgeway, St. Vincent and Beatrice.

Source: M393 *Australian Joint Copying Project misc.*

CORRESPONDENCE: EDWARD CURR TO NIEL BLACK, 1847

---

7 July, 1847
Niel Black, Esq.
My dear Mr. Black,
I did not receive...

I have said it twice, and I need not say, with (just pleasure) and interest, that I am wiser for this reading. I agree with its conclusions, that the minimum price of land is far too high, and that (most) costs arise from labour coming upon us in large and (uncertain) masses ... exceeded by still greater (dearths). This latter cost I always think will be best assisted by borrowing on immigration fund on (ten percent) of the lands, and the instalments of the fund so borrowed would be called for and expanded in immigration in amounts proportional to our average (requirements), and not to the chance sales of any one year.

But I suggest to you to reconsider a very important branch of your argument, namely that "the sale of waste lands is mainly a medium (scale) use of ( ) to abstract the capital of *the Colony*." Now it always appears to me that the sale of waste land *abstracts the Capital of Great Britain*, for when the chain Sales of Land and immigration is set in motion, each producing the other as cause and effect, capitalist immigration always goes hand in hand with it, and if you could analyse the proceedings of the years of prosperity, (so called) you would find that we imported cons. more capital than the absl. amount, large as it was, that we paid for land.

Then I would say as long as we have the room to expand our flocks, never entertain any opportunities that we shall be short of capital to employ any reasonable amount of imported labour. The increase of sheep is capital, just as available to employ labour as money in the bank would be, and the wool of that increased capital can at any moment be either shorn or mortgaged to pay the cost of labour.

Rest assured that immigration would add to cash in hand more than it abstracted.

Then you will say how do you account for the crisis which succeeded the abstraction of capital in 1840 or 1841 to pay for immigration? Numberless other causes were then at work to ... that crisis, and if now you read my answers to the questions of the Land Grievance Committee of 1843 you will find that crisis traced to its causes. Paying for labor certainly assisted in bringing about these results but I suspect we paid the more for luxuries (and not the least was the luxury of speculation) than was paid for land.

I am faithfully yours,
Edward Curr

Source: Niel Black Papers, Inward Correspondence.

APPENDIX 8

MEMO OF ENGLISH CAPITALISTS
ON BEHALF OF SQUATTERS, 1845

———

To the Honourable Lord Stanley, Her Majesty's Secretary of State for the Colonies, etc. . . .

The Memorial of the Merchants, Bankers, Manufacturers, and others, interested in the Colony of New South Wales.

(on the issue of a proposed modification of land-holding regulations in favour of the squatters, the memo continued, noting such modifications:) . . . as of paramount importance to maintain the prosperity of the Colony as well as the Woollen Manufactures of Great Britain, inasmuch as since the production of Fine Wool in these Colonies, the Price of that portion of this important article still requires to be imported from the Continent, has been reduced to about one-third.

THAT your Memorialists, therefore, humbly submit to the consideration of your Lordship, the indispensable necessity of giving security to the large Investments of Capital made by the Licensed Graziers in the production of this most important staple of the Colony; and that Leases for twenty-one years be granted to them of the Stations they occupy, beyond the boundaries of location; and that at the termination of such Leases, if the Government wish to obtain possession of the Stations, that an equitable compensation be awarded for the portion of Capital sunk in Buildings, Fences, Wells, and other improvements, and that on the term-nination of Leases when such Stations will be to be re-let, that the Lessee shall have the right of pre-emption. That the Government reserve to itself the power, at all times, after due notice (subject to the aforesaid equitable compensation) of selling these Grazing Lands so occupied; the occupation to cease immediately after bona fide sale.

THAT there be no compulsory purchase of Waste Lands on the Stations beyond the boundaries of location.

THAT the Crown Land Commissioners in New South Wales be placed under the supervision of the Legislative Council.

THAT the Boundaries of the Stations be not materially lessened, as such a course would be imminently dangerous to the health of the Sheep, and by forcing the approximation of the various flocks of neighbouring

Licensed Graziers to each of the fearfully destructive disease termed "Scab," a disease peculiarly contagious in New South Wales...

THAT your Memorialists would earnestly represent to your Lordship, that confident belief that the only means of securing a progressively increasing Revenue in the Colony of New South Wales, will be by giving full scope and encouragement to the energies of the Colonists, and for the Investment of their Capital; thereby gradually developing the resources of the Colony, and furnishing the Colonists with increased means to consume a larger amount of commodities subject to the Customs Duty, as well as enabling them to make augmented Pastoral Contributions consequent on the increase of Sheep and Cattle...

Source: Despatches, Encl. No. 100 to NSW, 8 August, 1845, p. 693 (A1293).

APPENDIX 9

MEMO FROM LONDON MERCHANTS CONCERNING PASTORAL LABOR SUPPLY, 1847

The following letter, addressed to the Clothiers and Woolen Manufacturers of England and Scotland, on the subject of the Urgent Want of Farm Servants in Australia, has been widely circulated by Messrs. J. T. Simes & Co., Wool Brokers, London, and is in great part borne out by "the Report of the Select Committee on Colonisation from Ireland," of the 21st July, 1847.

GENTLEMEN,

Between your no less ancient than valuable branch of Manufactures and the Australian Settlements, there has now existed a continued relationship of more than 40 years duration and but for the support which the first cultivators of fine wool flocks in that country received in 1803 from your intelligent body, it is very possible that you might not at present be in the receipt of one single pound of fine wool from that quarter...

But if thus, in the short space of forty years, the production of fine wool in Australia has become of vital importance to your interests it is now in danger of as suddenly declining, as it has rapidly arisen. The want of labourers, long felt in Australia as an increasing source of difficulty, has become such, that thousands of sheep perish annually for want of attendants, while tens of thousands are destroyed for the tallow they afford. And unless at the commencement you act in unison with the Australian Colonies and manifest your interest in the welfare of those distant possessions, every account from Sydney and Port Phillip concurs in shewing, how imminent the danger has become, of the chief source of your supply of fine wool being irreparably ruined and destroyed.

In this emergency allow us to suggest that the most legitimate course, that could perhaps be taken, would be to follow the precedent of a former time, and as the Clothiers did in 1803, to address Memorials to the Board of Trade; and also to instruct your Representatives in the new Parliament, to watch over interests, which though remote as to distance, intimately and directly affect the welfare of your trade; and to urge that as long as thousands in the United Kingdom are without sufficiency of food, raiment, and shelter, a free passage may be offered them to Australia, and that the

272

necessary funds may be appropriated by Government for the purpose of transmitting a regular yearly supply of labourers to the Australian Colonies. The relief so afforded to the surplus population of Great Britain would be *final*, and not to mention the less apparent although greatly important advantages of Commerce and Manufactures, the presence of an adequate population in so productive a field would, if regulated according to the demand, increase the local revenues, give value to lands, that are at present of no value, and thus reproduce the funds expended in the passage of those who are now struggling for existence at home.

We are, etc.

Source: Macarthur Papers, vol. 68, p. 165 (A2964).

APPENDIX 10

MEMO REGARDING WIRE FENCING, BY JESSE GREGSON

During this period over which the foregoing reminiscences extend, great changes took place in the pastoral industry of Australia. Queensland north of the Darling Downs and the Burnett was theretofore unstocked and except by a few explorers unknown. In New South Wales cattle began to give place to sheep. Sheep stations hitherto had been small concerns compared with those which have since developed. Few proprietors held more than 50,000 sheep, the majority probably counted no more than 25 or 30,000. As the west of NSW and the west and northwest of Queensland became occupied by stock, larger areas became the rule and were held on leasehold tenure more or less calculated to encourage pioneers. And as numbers were the chief aim little attention was given to improvements in breeding.

In these times sheep were depastured in flocks tended by shepherds by day and guarded by night. In most cases two flocks occupied a "station," the yards were adjacent to each other, the entrance being in opposite ends. They were situated in a position which offered a near hand water supply for the hut, either from a waterhole in a creek or from a well. Constructed mostly of logs laid close and piled on top of each other the fences of the yards afforded harbour for cats and other vermin which disturbed the sheep at night. Very few were of split post and rails. At the older stations the sheep dung formed a mound often 5 to 6 feet high and the approach would be bare of herbage to a distance of a quarter of a mile traversed as it was at morn and night. Beside the yards stood the hut occupied by the two shepherds and the hutkeeper whose duty it was to cook for the shepherds and to see that nothing molested the flock while they were in their yards...

The flocks...numbered from 800 to 2,000 according to the character of the country and the class of the sheep stations were spaced apart, having regard to watering facilities, so as to give 3 or 4 acres to a sheep but the boundaries not being defined it often occurred that a shepherd would encroach on his neighbour's better feed and this led to trouble of course...

Anyhow apart from incidents of this kind, the flocks continued to "reside" at the station as long as the feed enabled them to improve their condition and it was the business of the overseer to judge of this, to detect evidence of falling off assigning it either to carelessness of the shepherd or to failures

274

of the pasture, and to take steps to remedy the fault whatever it was by putting another shepherd in charge or by moving the flock to some other run. Constant were the troubles of the overseer. Sometimes a wing of the flock would separate from the rest and on this being discovered the missing lot had to be found, at other times a shepherd would want to leave the employ – or would be sick and another had to be brought to take his flock. . .

Rations were periodically supplied from the Head station consisting of 8 lbs of flour, 2 lbs sugar, ¼ lb tea and 10 to 12 lbs meat per man for one week. The wages were say £30 per annum for shepherds and £20 for hutkeepers.

The expenses of working a sheep station depended largely on the character of the country. If it was such that the flocks could be large, say from 1,500 to 2,000 in number, the result was as good as could generally be expected but even so the profits could as a general rule ill afford to meet a succession of bad seasons – bad from low prices of wool or stock or from unfair weather. The cost of shearing, of getting the wool to market, of the working staff of the stations, generally ran with a very large proportion of the returns from sales of stock or other produce. This often led to over stocking . . .

All this applies more especially to old established stations in NSW and as stocking proceeded west and north the pioneers found that their difficulties increased rather than diminished. Men were not as easily met with, wages were higher, cost of supplies increased. At one time the cost of carriage between Rockhampton and Springsure was £28 per ton up and £14 per ton for return loading. The result was that in the majority of cases the debt on the station grew apace year by year and many hard working station owners had to see their properties sold by the mortgages and all their labour lost.

In the early sixties some enterprising men in Victoria conceived the idea of enclosing their country and subdividing it by wire fences. The experiment succeeded sufficiently to become the aspiration of pioneers out back and full of objections and drawbacks as the idea seemed at the outset to be the circumstances compelled men to make a trial of it.

Hence arose the present method of depasturing of sheep throughout Australia, a system which revolutionised the pastoral industry – without which it is not too much to say that population could not have existed beyond the older settled districts whose proximity to port obviated so many of the disadvantages experienced further inland.

Victoria being the birthplace of the fencing system men went through from all parts of NSW and Qld to see for themselves what were the results. Needless to say that the circumstances Queensland pioneers had to deal with differed very greatly from those they saw in Victoria. They could not afford the kind of fence adopted in Victoria and with them the question was "What is the cheapest style of fence adopted to be effective with me?"

Some mistakes were inevitable but on the whole the fencing adopted served its purpose and rescued the pastoralists from what had appeared to be unavoidable ruin. Even in conservative NSW the runs were very promptly fenced and the properties being more generally freehold the character of the fencing was justifiably much more substantial than that adopted in Queensland.

Not only in the character of the style of fencing was there much difference in various districts but there was equal diversity in the area of the sub-enclosures. In the older settled districts – when properties are chiefly freehold the paddocks would perhaps have ranged from 2,000 to 5,000 acres at first and at the present day are much smaller. But elsewhere economy had to be more particularly studied and paddocks reach 20 and even 40,000 acres in size.

Watering facilities are in all cases an important factor in this and of late years what are known as subartesian bores have been successfully put down in many parts and have enabled further subdivision to be carried out. It is now generally recognised that paddocks can scarcely be too small and that better use is made of the country while the stock thrive better and are more easily looked after.

It can readily be understood what a vast improvement in the economic returns has been effected by fencing in the runs.

The reduction in the number of employees on a sheep station is probably quite 10% and the stamp of man who is placed in the position of a boundary rider is very different from the shepherds of older times. He is generally a family man and on most stations is provided with a comfortable house and probably keeps a cow and poultry.

His wages are about £45 per annum with rations for himself and his wife. His duty is to supervise so many paddocks to see that the fences are in order, to assist in mustering and generally in work amongst the stock. It requires two or more horses which with saddlery he finds for himself.

The sheep have benefitted by the change of system no less than the employees of the station. Instead of being kept part and parcel of a flock moving in one and the same direction or camping in a dense mass as was formerly the case, every sheep is now an independent individual free to choose its own companions and to feed where and when it likes.... Its bodily condition responds accordingly – the growth of the fleece, no longer impeded and packed by a constant cloud of dust, is more natural and weighs better – the wool fibre is cleaner and stronger – the fleece is not only heavier but is more valuable pound for pound.

Accordingly pastoral occupations are better for employer and employed than they used to be. The employer has no longer to deal with a lot of unreasonable often half..?..caretakers of his stock but is comparatively independent of labour for much of the year and even when shearing or classing entails work it is not essential that it shall be done today or this week but at such times as are convenient.

Subject to vicissitudes of the season the sheep farmer in Australia is today his own master and he finds it profitable to give the attention to breeding and the improvement of his stock which under former conditions was out of the question for many. The quality of the sheep depastured in

Australia has improved wonderfully within the last fifty years. In shepherding days 7 lbs per fleece was a good average weight. Today the average may be as much as from 9 to 12 lbs per merino breeds.

Source: Nisbet Manuscripts: *Pioneering Days in Queensland* (30th October, 1922: Nisbet prefaces this memo: "written by Mr. J.G. at my desire" – but no date of the memo itself) (ML A1533).

REFERENCES

PRIMARY SOURCES

Parliamentary papers

British Parliamentary Papers (1968). Irish University Press (selected volumes).
Report of the Commissioner of Inquiry on the State of Agriculture and Trade in the Colony of New South Wales (J. T. Bigge) (1823). Reprinted in 1966. Adelaide: Libraries Board of South Australia.
Select Documents on British Colonial Policy 1830–1860. K. N. Bell and W. P. Morell, eds. Oxford: Clarendon Press, 1928.
South Australian Parliamentary Documents. South Australian State Archives (select reports, 1860s and 1870s).
Votes and Proceedings, New South Wales, Legislative Council, Sydney (select reports and statistical series, 1830s and 1840s).

Published records and newspapers

Historical Records of Australia, Series I, Vols. I–XXV.
Sydney Morning Herald, 1835–1850.

Records in possession of New South Wales State Archives

Application for Depasturing Licenses, 1836–1837. (4/1117.1)
Census Abstracts, 1836, 1841. (4/1242, 4/1248-8)
County Register, 1822–1853. (2/1937)
Insolvency Cause Papers, 1838–1849. (5/4641,2,3A)
Monthly Returns of Crown Lands Sold, 1837–1840. (X61)
Register of Leases, Crown Lands (NSW), 1831–1842. (2/2235)
Return of Applications to Purchase Particular Portions of Crown Land, 1839–1841. (4/7516)
Returns of Applications for Licenses to Occupy Crown Lands, 1842–1847. (4/7003, 7004)

Returns of Crops and Produce, 1835–1847. (A/7527)
Returns of Mills, Manufactories, etc., 1831–1841, 1842–1850. (4/7267, 7268)

Records in possession of the Genealogical Society of the Church of Jesus Christ of Latter-Day Saints, Salt Lake City, Utah

Abstract of the Returns of Stock and Cultivation at Port Phillip, to Accompany the Census Returns of 1836, in Census Returns of the Province of Victoria for 1836 and 1838. (Microfilm No. 28385)

Private papers in the Mitchell Library, Sydney

Banks Papers. (FM4, 1847–1848)
Brooks, Robert & Co., papers, 1822–1890. (FM4, 2348)
Crooke, Edward, papers, 1835–1870. (B, 1425)
Despatches – Government Correspondence between Colonial Office and Colonial Governors (selections).
Frew papers. (A 738)
Gardner, William (1854). "Production and Resources of the Northern and Western Districts of New South Wales." (CYX A 176)
King Papers. (A 1977)
Levey, Solomon, papers, 1794–1846. (A 5441)
Macarthur Papers. (A2897–3004)
Macqueen, Thomas Potter, letters, 1826–1841. (MSS 215/13)
Marsden Papers. (A 5412; CYA 1992; MSS 719)
Mort Family, letters. (1462/2)
Nisbet Manuscripts. (A 1533)
Riley Papers. (A 107–111)
Segenhoe Estate, papers, 1824–1874. (MSS 215)
Spark, A. B., diary. (A 4869–4870)
Spark, A. B., papers. (MSS 639)
Wentworth Family, papers. (MSS 8/1)
Wilson, W. E. R. "A History of the Australian Agricultural Company." (MSS 1581)

Miscellaneous private papers

Black, Niel, papers. LaTrobe Library, Public Library of Victoria, Melbourne.
Brown, P. L., ed. (1952). *Clyde Company Papers*. London: Oxford University Press.
Campbell & Co., Sydney, Letter to Henry Dangar, 1840. (M393, Australian Joint Copying Project)

Mollison, Alexander, Letters. LaTrobe Library, Public Library of Victoria, Melbourne.

Onslow, S. M., ed. (1914). *Some Early Records of the Macarthurs at Camden.* Sydney: Rigby.

Contemporary Accounts

Atkinson, James (1826). *An Account of the State of Agriculture and Grazing in New South Wales.* Reprinted in 1975. Sydney: Sydney University Press.

Bischoff, James (1828). *The Wool Question Considered.* London: J. Richardson, Royal Exchange.

(1842). *A Comprehensive History of the Woolen and Worsted Manufactures,* 2 vols. Reprinted in 1968. London: Cass.

Blacklock, A. (1841). *Treatise on Sheep.* London.

Bonwick, James (1887). *Romance of the Wool Trade.* London: Griffith, Okeden and Welsh.

Browne, T. A. *My Autobiography* (ML A2132).

Clark, C. M. H., ed. (1971). *Sources of Australian History.* London: Oxford University Press.

Collier, James (1911). *The Pastoral Age in Australasia.* London: Whitcombe & Tombs.

Curr, E. M. (1883). *Recollections of Squatting in Victoria.* Reprinted in 1965. Melbourne: Melbourne University Press.

Hodgson, C. (1846). *Reminiscences of Australia.* London.

James, J. (1857). *History of the Worsted Manufacture in England.* Reprinted in 1968. London: Cass.

McBride, T. F. (1898). *Letters from Victorian Pioneers.* Melbourne: Government Printer.

MacDermott, M. (1842). "On Wool," *Journal of the Agricultural and Horticultural Society of Western Australia*: 41–3.

Mansfield, Ralph (1842, 1847). *Analytical View of the Census of New South Wales for the Year 1841/1846.* Sydney: Kemp & Fairfax.

Mudie, James (1837). *The Felonry of New South Wales.* Reprinted in 1964. Melbourne: Lansdowne Press.

Pritchard, M. F. Lloyd (1968). *The Collected Works of Edward Gibbon Wakefield.* London: Collins.

Southey, Thomas (1848). *The Rise, Progress and Present State of Colonial Wools.* London.

Stanhope, Earl (1828). *A Letter to the Owners and Occupiers of Sheep Farms.* London: James Ridgeway.

Therry, Roger (1863). *Reminiscences of Thirty Years' Residence in New South*

Wales and Victoria. Reprinted in 1974. Sydney: Sydney University Press.

Trimmer, J. K. (1828). *Practical Observations on the Improvement of British Fine Wool and the National Advantages of the Arable System of Sheep Husbandry*. London: James Ridgeway.

SECONDARY SOURCES

Abbott, G. J. (1965). "Staple Theory and Australian Economic Growth, 1788–1820," *Business Archives and History* 5(2):142–54.

(1966). "The Introduction of Railways into New South Wales, 1846–55," *RAHS, J&P* 52(Part 1):33–50.

(1969a). "Governor King's Administration," pp. 162–75 in *Economic Growth of Australia, 1788–1821*, G. J. Abbott and N. B. Nairn, eds. Melbourne: Melbourne University Press.

(1969b). "The Pastoral Industry," pp. 219–44 in *Economic Growth of Australia 1788–1821*, G. J. Abbott and N. B. Nairn, eds. Melbourne: Melbourne University Press.

(1971). *The Pastoral Age: A Re-examination*. Melbourne: Macmillan.

(1972). "Was Labour Scarce in the 1830s?: A Comment," *Australian Economic History Review* XII(2):179–84.

Abbott, G. J., and G. Little (1976). *The Respectable Sydney Merchant, A. B. Spark of Tempe*. Sydney: Sydney University Press.

Anderson, Perry (1965). "Origins of the Present Crisis," pp. 11–52 in *Towards Socialism*, P. Anderson and R. Blackburn, eds. London: Fontana.

(1974). *Lineages of the Absolutist State*. London: New Left Books.

Arrighi, Giovanni (1978a). "Towards a Theory of Capitalist Crisis," *New Left Review* 111:3–24.

(1978b). *The Geometry of Imperialism*. London: New Left Books.

(1982). "A Crisis of Hegemony," pp. 55–108 in *Dynamics of Global Crisis*, Samir Amin, Giovanni Arrighi, Andre Gunder Frank, and Immanuel Wallerstein, eds. New York: Monthly Review Press.

Ashton, T. S. (1972). *An Economic History of England. The Eighteenth Century*. London: Methuen.

Australian Dictionary of Biography, Vol. 1, 1788–1850. A–H (1966). A. G. L. Shaw and C. M. H. Clark, eds. Melbourne: Melbourne University Press.

Australian Dictionary of Biography, Vol. 2, I–Z (1967). A. G. L. Shaw and C. M. H. Clark, eds. Melbourne: Melbourne University Press.

Aydelotte, W. O. (1962). "The Business Interests in the Gentry in the Parliament of 1841–47," Appendix, pp. 290–305 in G. Kitson Clark,

The Making of Victorian England. Cambridge, Mass.: Harvard University Press.

Bagehot, W. (1915). *Lombard Street.* London: Smith, Elder.

Bailey, Frank E. (1940). "The Economics of British Foreign Policy, 1825–50," *Journal of Modern History* XVII(4):449–84.

Bailey, J. D. (1966). *A Hundred Years of Pastoral Banking: A History of the Australian Mercantile and Finance Company, 1863–1963.* Oxford: Clarendon Press.

Baker, D. W. A. (1958). "The Origins of Robertson's Land Acts," *Historical Studies* 8(30):166–82.

(1965). "The Squatting Age in Australia," *Business Archives and History* 5(2):107–22.

Banaji, Jairus (1976). "Kautsky's *The Agrarian Question,*" *Economy and Society* 5(1):3–49.

(1977). "Modes of Production in a Materialist Conception of History," *Capital and Class* 3(Autumn):1–44.

Barker, M. P. (1968). "The Struggle for Survival, 1788–1795." B. Litt. thesis, The University of England, Armidale, New South Wales.

Barnard, Alan (1958). *The Australian Wool Market, 1840–1900.* Melbourne: Melbourne University Press.

(1961). *Visions and Profits. Studies in the Business Career of Thomas Sutcliffe Mort.* Melbourne: Melbourne University Press.

Bartlett, C. J. (1969). "Statecraft Power and Influence," pp. 172–93 in *Britain Pre-eminent. Studies of British World Influence in the Nineteenth Century,* C. J. Bartlett, ed. London: Macmillan.

Bassett, M. (1962). *The Hentys, An Australian Colonial Tapestry.* Melbourne: Melbourne University Press.

Baster, A. S. J. (1929). *The Imperial Banks.* London: P. S. King.

Beever, E. A. (1965). "The Origin of the Wool Industry in New South Wales," *Business Archives and History* 5(2):91–106.

Bell, Roger (1970). "Samuel Marsden – Pioneer Pastoralist," *RAHS, J&P* 56(part 1):48–66.

Bergman, G. F. H. (1964). "Solomon Levey in Sydney: From Convict to Merchant Prince," *RAHS, J&P* 49(part 6):401–22.

Billis, R. V., and A. S. Kenyon (1930). *Pastures New. An Account of the Pastoral Occupation of Port Phillip.* Melbourne: Macmillan.

Birch, Alan (1965). "The Origins of the Colonial Sugar Refining Company 1841–55," *Business Archives and History* 5(1):21–31.

Blackton, C. S. (1955). "The Dawn of Australian National Feeling, 1850–56," *Pacific Historical Review* XXIV:121–38.

Blainey, Geoffrey (1964). "Technology in Australian History," *Business Archives and History* 5(4):117–37.

(1971). *The Tyranny of Distance.* Melbourne: Sun Books.

Block, Fred (1970). "Expanding Capitalism: The British and American Cases," *Berkeley Journal of Sociology* 15:138–65.

Bodelson, C. A. (1970). *Studies in Mid-Victorian Imperialism*. London: Heinemann.

Boehm, E. A. (1971). *Prosperity and Depression in Australia, 1887–1897*. Oxford: Clarendon Press.

Bowle, John (1977). *The Imperial Achievement. The Rise and Transformation of the British Empire*. Harmondsworth: Penguin.

Braden, L. (1968). *Bullockies*. Adelaide: Rigby.

Broeze, F. J. A. (1975). "The Cost of Distance: Shipping and the Early Australian Economy, 1788–1850," *Economic History Review*, Second Series, 28(4):582–97.

Brown, Barratt M. (1970). *After Imperialism*. London: Merlin Press.

(1976). *The Economics of Imperialism*. Harmondsworth: Penguin.

Bucharin, N. (1973). *Imperialism and World Economy*. New York: Modern Reader.

Buckley, Ken (1955 and 1956). "Gipps and the Graziers of New South Wales, 1841–46," *Historical Studies*, Part 1: 6(24):396–412; Part 2: 7(26):178–93.

(1957). "E. G. Wakefield and the Alienation of Crown Land in New South Wales to 1847," *Economic Record* 33(64):80–96.

Burroughs, P. (1965). "Wakefield and the Ripon Land Regulations of 1831," *Historical Studies* 11(44):452–66.

(1967). *Britain and Australia 1831–1855. A Study in Imperial Relations and Crown Land Administration*. Oxford: Clarendon Press.

Butlin, N. G. (1950). " 'Company Ownership' of New South Wales' Pastoral Stations," *Historical Studies* 4(14):89–111.

(1959). "Colonial Socialism in Australia, 1860–1890," pp. 26–78 in *The State and Economic Growth*, H. G. J. Aitken, ed. New York: Social Sciences Research Council.

(1964a). "Growth in a Trading World: The Australian Economy, Heavily Disguised," *Business Archives and History* 4(2):138–58.

(1964b). *Investment in Australian Economic Development, 1861–1900*. Cambridge: Cambridge University Press.

Butlin, S. J. (1947). "Charles Swanston and the Derwent Bank, 1827–50," *Historical Studies* 2(7):161–85.

(1961). *Australia and New Zealand Bank. The Bank of Australasia and the Union Bank of Australia Ltd. 1828–1851*. London: Longmans.

(1963). "British Banking in Australia," *RAHS, J&P* 49(part 2):81–99.

(1968). *Foundations of the Australian Monetary System, 1788–1851*. Sydney: Sydney University Press.

Buxton, G. L. (1967). *The Riverina, 1861–1891*. Melbourne: Melbourne University Press.

Cain, P. J., and A. G. Hopkins (1980). "The Political Economy of British Expansion Overseas, 1850–1914," *Economic History Review*, Second Series, XXXIII:463–90.

Caincross, A. K. (1953). *Home and Foreign Investment, 1870–1913. Studies in Capital Accumulation.* Cambridge: Cambridge University Press.

Cameron, Rondo (1953). "The *Credit Mobilier* and the Economic Development of Europe," *Journal of Political Economy* LXI(6):461–88.

(1967). "England 1750–1844," pp. 15–59 in *Banking in the Early Stages of Industrialization*, R. Cameron et al., eds. New York: Oxford University Press.

Campbell, J. F. (1923). "The First Decade of the Australian Agricultural Company, 1824–1834," *RAHS, J&P* 9(part 3):113–60.

(1968). "Squatting on Crown Lands in New South Wales," edited and annotated by B. T. Dowd. *RAHS*, in association with Angas & Robertson, Sydney.

Carrothers, W. A. (1966). *Emigration from the British Isles.* London: Cass.

Cecco, Marcello de (1974). *Money and Empire. The International Gold Standard, 1890–1914.* New Jersey: Rowman & Littlefield.

Cell, John W. (1970). *British Colonial Administration in the Mid-Nineteenth Century: The Policy-Making Process.* New Haven and London: Yale University Press.

Chapman, S. D. (1977). "The International Houses: The Continental Contribution to British Commerce, 1800–1860," *Journal of European Economic History* VI:5–48.

Checkland, S. G. (1964). *The Rise of Industrial Society in England, 1815–1885.* New York: St. Martin's Press.

Clapham, J. H. (1945). *The Bank of England*, vol. II. New York: Macmillan.

(1959). *An Economic History of Modern Britain. The Early Railway Age, 1820–1850.* Cambridge: Cambridge University Press.

(1966). *Economic Development of France and Germany, 1815–1914.* Cambridge: Cambridge University Press.

(1967). *The Woolen and Worsted Industries.* London: Methuen.

(1971). "*Zollverein* Negotiations 1828–65," pp. 465–79 in *Cambridge History of British Foreign Policy 1783–1919. II: 1815–1866*, Sir A. W. Ward and G. P. Gooch, eds. Westport, Conn.: Greenwood Press.

Clark, C. M. H. (1963). *A Short History of Australia.* New York: Mentor.

Cochrane, Peter (1980). *Industrialization and Dependence. Australia's Road to Economic Development.* St. Lucia: University of Queensland Press.

Coghlan, T. A. (1969). *Labour and Industry in Australia*, 4 vols. Melbourne: Macmillan.

Connell, R. W., and T. H. Irving (1980). *Class Structure in Australian History.* Melbourne: Longman Cheshire.

(1982). "A Reply to Reviews," *Intervention* 16:31–36.

Conze, Werner (1969). "The Effects of Nineteenth-Century Liberal Agrarian Reforms on Social Structure in Central Europe," pp. 53–81 in *Essays in European Economic History 1789–1914*, F. Crouzet, W. H. Chaloner, and W. M. Stern, eds. London: Edward Arnold.

Cotter, R. (1976). "The Golden Decade," pp. 113–34 in *Essays in Economic History of Australia*, J. Griffin, ed. Sydney: Jacaranda Press.

Cowles, Virginia (1975). *The Rothschilds. A Family of Fortune*. London: Futura.

Crawford, R. M. (1952). *Australia*. London: Hutchinson's University Library.

Crouzet, Francois (1964). "Wars, Blockade, and Economic Change in Europe, 1792–1815," *Journal of Economic History* XXIV:567–90.

(1980). "Toward an Export Economy: British Exports during 'The Industrial Revolution,'" *Explorations in Economic History* 17:48–93.

Denholm, David (1972). "Some Aspects of Squatting in New South Wales and Queensland, 1847–64." Ph.D. dissertation, Australian National University.

Dovring, Folke (1966). "The Transformation of European Agriculture," pp. 604–72 in *Cambridge Economic History of Europe*, VI, part II, H. J. Habakkuk and M. Postan, eds. Cambridge: Cambridge University Press.

Dow, G. M. (1974). *Samuel Terry. The Botany Bay Rothschild*. Sydney: Sydney University Press.

Droz, Jacques (1967). *Europe Between Revolutions 1815–1848*. New York: Harper & Row.

Dunn, Michael (1975). "Early Australia: Wage Labour or Slave Society?" pp. 33–46 in *Essays in the Political Economy of Australian Capitalism*, vol. 1, E. L. Wheelwright and Ken Buckley, eds. Sydney: ANZ Book Co.

Dunsdorfs, E. (1970). *The Australian Wheat-Growing Industry, 1788–1948*. Melbourne: Melbourne University Press.

Dyster, B. (1965). "Support for the Squatters, 1844," *RAHS, J&P* 51(part 1):41–59.

(1967). "Prosperity, Prostration, Prudence: Business and Investment 1833–1851," pp. 51–76 in *Wealth and Progress. Studies in Australian Business History*, A. Birch and D. S. MacMillan, eds. Sydney: Angas and Robertson.

(1968). "The Role of Sydney and the Role of Its Citizens, 1841–1851." M.A. thesis, University of Sydney.

(1978). "The Discrete Interest of the Bourgeoisie, before the Age of Gold," pp. 1–11 in *Nineteenth-Century Sydney*, Max Kelly, ed. Sydney: Sydney University Press.

Ebbels, N., ed. (1960). *The Australian Labor Movement 1850–1907*. Sydney: Australasian Book Society.

Eddy, J. J. (1969). *Britain and the Australian Colonies 1818–1831*. Oxford: Clarendon Press.

Ellis, M. H. (1942). "Some Aspects of the Bigge Commission of Inquiry into the Affairs of New South Wales, 1819–21," *RAHS, J&P* 27(part 2):93–125.

Feis, Herbert (1965). *Europe, the World's Banker, 1870–1914*. New York: Norton.

Fielden, K. (1969). "The Rise and Fall of Free Trade," pp. 76–100 in *Britain Pre-eminent. Studies of British World Influence in the Nineteenth Century*, C. J. Bartlett, ed. London: Macmillan.

Fitzpatrick, B. C. (1946). *The Australian People 1788–1945*. Melbourne: Melbourne University Press.

  (1947). "The Big Man's Frontier and Australian Farming," *Agricultural History* 21(1):8–12.

  (1968). *The Australian Labour Movement*. Melbourne: Macmillan.

  (1969). *The British Empire in Australia. An Economic History, 1834–1939*. Melbourne: Melbourne University Press.

  (1971). *British Imperialism and Australia, 1783–1833*. Sydney: Sydney University Press.

Fletcher, B. H. (1964). "The Development of Small-Scale Farming in New South Wales under Governor Hunter," *RAHS, J&P* 50(part 1):1–31.

  (1969). "Agriculture," pp. 191–218 in *Economic Growth of Australia 1788–1821*, G. J. Abbott and N. B. Nairn, eds. Melbourne: Melbourne University Press.

  (1973). "Government Farming and Grazing in New South Wales, 1788–1810," *RAHS, J&P* V(59, part 3):182–98.

  (1976a). *Colonial Australia Before 1850*. Melbourne: Nelson.

  (1976b). *Landed Enterprise and Penal Society*. Sydney: Sydney University Press.

Fogarty, J. P. (1968). "The New South Wales Pastoral Industry in the 1820s," *Australian Economic History Review* 8:110–22.

Forsyth, W. D. (1970). *Governor Arthur's Convict System*. Sydney: Sydney University Press.

Foster, John (1974). *Class Struggles and the Industrial Revolution*. London: Methuen.

Friedmann, Harriet (1978a). "Simple Commodity Production and Wage Labour in the American Plains," *The Journal of Peasant Studies* 6(1):71–100.

  (1978b). "World Market, State and Family Farm: Social Bases of Household Production in an Era of Wage Labor," *Comparative Studies of Society and History* 20(4):545–86.

Fry, K. L. (1973). "Boiling Down in the 1840's: A Grimy Means to a Solvent End," *Labor History* 25:1–18.

Gallagher, John, and Ronald Robinson (1953). "The Imperialism of Free Trade," *Economic History Review* VI(1):1–15.

Garrett, R. (1976). "Capitalist Development in the American South: A Study of Primitive Accumulation and Uneven Development." Ph.D. dissertation, New School for Social Research, New York.

Gayer, A. D., W. W. Rostow, and A. J. Schwartz (1953). *The Growth and Fluctuation of the British Economy 1790–1850*, 2 vols. Oxford: Clarendon Press.

Genovese, E. D. (1961). *The Political Economy of Slavery*. New York: Vintage.

(1971). *The World the Slaveholders Made*. New York: Vintage.

(1976). *Roll Jordan Roll. The World the Slaves Made*. New York: Vintage.

Gilbert, Felix, ed. (1975). *The Historical Essays of Otto Hintze*. New York: Oxford University Press.

Gilpin, Robert (1975). *U.S. Power and the Multinational Corporation. The Political Economy of Foreign Direct Investment*. New York: Basic Books.

Glynn, Sean (1975). *Urbanisation in Australian History, 1788–1900*. Melbourne: Nelson (Australia).

Gollan, Robin (1966). *Radical and Working Class Politics: A Study of Eastern Australia, 1850–1910*. Melbourne: Melbourne University Press.

Goodwin, Craufurd D. W. (1974). *The Image of Australia. British Perception of the Australian Economy from the Eighteenth Century to the Twentieth Century*. Durham, N.C.: Duke University Press.

Grigg, D. B. (1974). *The Agricultural Systems of the World*. Cambridge: Cambridge University Press.

Habakkuk, H. J. (1975). "Free Trade and Commercial Expansion, 1853–1870," pp. 751–805 in *Cambridge History of the British Empire*, vol. II, J. Holland Rose, A. P. Newton, and E. A. Benians, eds. Cambridge: Cambridge University Press.

Hainsworth, D. R., ed. (1968). *Builders and Adventurers. The Traders and the Emergence of the Colony, 1788–1821*. Melbourne: Cassell (Australia).

(1972). *The Sydney Traders*. Melbourne: Cassell (Australia).

Hall, A. R. (1963). *The London Capital Market and Australia, 1870-1970*. Canberra: ANU Press.

Handlin, Oscar and Mary (1950). "Origins of the Southern Labor System," *William and Mary Quarterly* VII(2):199–222.

Harris, Alexander (1964). *Settlers and Convicts*. Melbourne: Melbourne University Press.

Hartwell, R. M. (1954a). *The Economic Development of Van Dieman's Land, 1820–1850*. Melbourne: Melbourne University Press.

(1954b). "Colonial Money and Banking during the Industrial Revolution," *Economic Record* XXX:73–84.

(1956). "Australia's First Trade Cycle," *RAHS, J&P* 42(part 2):51–67.

Hartz, Louis (1964). *The Founding of New Societies*. New York: Harcourt Brace Jovanovich.

Hawgood, J. A. (1960). "Liberalism and Constitutional Developments," pp. 185–212 in *New Cambridge Modern History. X. The Zenith of European Power 1830–70*, J. P. T. Bury, ed. Cambridge: Cambridge University Press.

Hayes, C. J. H. (1941). *A Generation of Materialism 1871–1900*. New York: Harper & Row.

Hayes, Paul (1975). *The Nineteenth Century 1814–1880*. New York: St. Martin's Press.

Heaton, Herbert (1929–1930). "Benjamin Gott and the Anglo-American Cloth Trade," *Journal of Economic and Business History* II:146–62.

(1931). "Benjamin Gott and the Industrial Revolution in Yorkshire," *Economic History Review* III:45–66.

(1948). *Economic History of Europe*. London: Harper & Row.

Hechter, Michael (1981). "Karl Polanyi's Social Theory: A Critique," *Politics and Society* 10(4):399–429.

Hidy, Ralph (1941). "The Organisation and Functions of Anglo-American Merchant Bankers, 1815–1860," *Journal of Economic History*, Supplement I:53–66.

Hilton, B. (1977). *Corn, Cash, Commerce, The Economic Policies of the Tory Governments 1815–1830*. London: Oxford University Press.

Hirst, J. B. (1973). *Adelaide and the Country, 1870–1917: Their Social and Political Relationship*. Melbourne: Melbourne University Press.

(1983). *Convict Society and Its Enemies*. Sydney: Allen & Unwin.

Hobsbawm, E. J. (1962). *The Age of Revolution 1789–1848*. New York: Mentor.

(1969). *Industry and Empire*. Harmondsworth: Penguin.

(1975). *The Age of Capital*. New York: Scribner.

Hobsbawm, E. J., and George Rude (1968). *Captain Swing*. New York: Pantheon.

Hobson, C. K. (1968). *The Export of Capital*. London: Constable.

Hoffman, R. J. S. (1933). *Great Britain and the German Trade Rivalry*. Philadelphia: University of Pennsylvania Press.

Holder, R. F. (1970). *Bank of New South Wales. A History*, 2 vols. Sydney: Angas & Robertson.

Hopkins, Terence K. (1978). "World-System Analysis: Methodological Issues," pp. 199–217 in *Social Change in the Capitalist World Economy*, Barbara Hockey Kaplan, ed. Beverly Hills: Sage.

Hughes, Helen (1964). *The Australian Iron and Steel Industry 1848–1962*. Melbourne: Melbourne University Press.

Hutchinson, Lester, ed. (1969). Karl Marx, *The Story of the Life of Lord Palmerston*. New York: International Publishers.

Hynes, W. G. (1976). "British Mercantile Attitudes Towards Imperial Expansion," *The Historical Journal* 19(4):969–79.

Iliasu, A. A. (1971). "The Cobden-Chevalier Commercial Treaty of 1860," *The Historical Journal* XIV(1):67–98.

Imlah, A. H. (1950). "The Terms of Trade of the United Kingdom, 1798–1913," *Journal of Economic History* X(2):170–94.

(1958). *Economic Elements in the 'Pax Britannica.' Studies in British Foreign Trade in the Nineteenth Century.* Cambridge, Mass.: Harvard University Press.

Innis, H. A., ed. (1956). *Essays in Canadian Economic History.* Toronto: University of Toronto Press.

Irving, T. H. (1963). "Some Aspects of the Study of Radical Politics in New South Wales before 1856," *Labor History* 5: 18–25.

(1964). "The Idea of Responsible Government in New South Wales before 1856," *Historical Studies* 11(42):192–205.

(1967). "The Development of Liberal Politics in New South Wales, 1843–1856." Ph.D. dissertation, University of Sydney.

(1976). "1850–70," pp. 124–64 in *A New History of Australia*, F. Crowley, ed. Melbourne: Heinemann.

Jackson, R. V. (1977). *Australian Economic Development in the Nineteenth Century.* Canberra: ANU Press.

Jeans, D. N. (1966). "Crown Land Sales and the Accommodation of the Small Settler in New South Wales, 1825–42," *Historical Studies* 12(46):205–12.

(1972). *An Historical Geography of New South Wales to 1901.* Sydney: Reed Education.

Jenks, Leland H. (1973). *The Migration of British Capital to 1875.* New York: Harper & Row.

Jervis, James (1942). "Alexander Berry, the Laird of Shoalhaven," *RAHS, J&P* 27(part 1).

Joyce, Alfred (1969). *A Homestead History.* Melbourne: Oxford University Press.

Karr, Clarence (1974). "Mythology vs. Reality: The Success of Free Selection in New South Wales," *RAHS, J&P* 60(part 3):199–206.

(1975). "Origins of the New South Wales Farmers' Union Movement," *RAHS, J&P* 61(3):199–206.

Kay, Geoffrey (1975). *Development and Underdevelopment: A Marxist Analysis.* London: Macmillan.

Kenyon, A. S. (1926). "The Port Phillip Boom and Its Results," *RAHS, J&P* 12:202–23.

Ker, Jill (1960). "Merchants and Merinos," *RAHS, J&P* 46(part 4):206–23.

(1961). "The Macarthur Family and the Pastoral Industry," *RAHS, J&P* 47(part 3):131–55.

(1956, 1962). "The Wool Industry in New South Wales, 1803–1830," *Business Archives and History* I: 1(9):28–49; II: 2(1):18–54.

Keynes, J. M. (1971). *The Economic Consequences of the Peace*. New York: Harper & Row.

Kiddle, Margaret (1967). *Men of Yesterday*. Melbourne: Melbourne University Press.

Kiernan, V. G. (1969). *The Lords of Human Kind*. Boston: Little, Brown & Co.

Kindleberger, C.P. (1975). "The Rise of Free Trade in Western Europe, 1820–1875," *Journal of Economic History* XXXV:20–55.

King, H. (1971). *Richard Bourke*. London: Oxford University Press.

King, W. T. C. (1972). *History of the London Discount Market*. London: Cass.

Knaplund, Paul (1968). "Colonial Problems and Colonial Policy, 1815–1837," *The Cambridge History of the British Empire*, II, J. Holland Rose, A. P. Newton, and E. A. Benians, eds. Cambridge: Cambridge University Press.

Knorr, K. E. (1963). *British Colonial Theories 1570–1850*. Toronto: University of Toronto Press.

Knowles, L. C. A. (1924). *The Economic Development of the British Overseas Empire*. London: Routledge.

Kolson, H. (1961). "Company Formation in N.S.W.: 1828–1851," *Bulletin of Business Archives Council of Australia* 1(6):11–21.

Kondratieff, N. D. (1955). "The Long Waves in Economic Life," *The Review of Economic Statistics* XVII(6):105–15.

Lamb, P. N. (1967). "Crown Land Policy and Government Finance in New South Wales, 1850–1900," *Australian Economic History Review* 7:38–68.

Lambi, I. N. (1963). *Free Trade and Protection in Germany 1868–1879*. Wiesbaden: Steiner.

LaNauze, J. A. (1948). "Australian Tariffs and Imperial Control," *Economic Record* XXIV:1–17.

    (1955). "Merchants in Action: The Australian Tariffs of 1852," *Economic Record* XXXI:77–89.

    (1967). "The Gold Rushes and Australian Politics," *Australian Journal of Politics and History* XIII(1):90–94.

Land, Aubrey (1965). "Economic Base and Social Structure: The Northern Chesapeake in the Eighteenth Century," *Journal of Economic History* XXV(4):639–54.

Landes, David S. (1969). *Bankers and Pashas*. New York: Harper & Row.

    (1972). *The Unbound Prometheus. Technical Change 1750 to the Present*. Cambridge: Cambridge University Press.

Lansbury, Coral (1979). *Arcady in Australia. The Evocation of Australia in Nineteenth-Century English Literature*. Melbourne: Melbourne University Press.

Lazonick, William (1974). "Karl Marx and Enclosures in England," *Union of Radical Political Economists Review* 6(2):1–59.

Lenin, V. I. (1961). *Collected Works*, vol. 5. Moscow: Foreign Languages Publishing House.

   (1972). *The Development of Capitalism in Russia: Collected Works*, vol. 3. Moscow: Progress Publishers.

LeRoy, P. E. (1961). "Samuel Terry," *RAHS, J&P* 47(part 5):281–92.

Levine, D. P. (1961). "Marx on Technical Change." Unpublished manuscript.

Lichtheim, G. (1971). *Imperialism*. London: Lane.

Linge, G. J. R. (1975). "The Forging of an Industrial Nation: Manufacturing in Australia 1788–1913," pp. 150–81 in *Australian Space Australian Time. Geographical Perspectives*, J. M. Powell and M. Williams, eds. Melbourne: Oxford University Press.

Lipson, E. (1953). *A Short History of Wool and Its Manufacture*. Cambridge, Mass.: Harvard University Press.

Louis, Wm. Roger, ed. (1976). *Imperialism. The Robinson and Gallagher Controversy*. New York: New Viewpoints.

Loveday, Peter (1956). " 'Democracy' in New South Wales. The Constitution Committee of 1853," *RAHS, J&P* 42(4):187–200.

Luxemburg, Rosa (1963). *The Accumulation of Capital*. London: Routledge & Kegan Paul.

Lythe, S. G. E. (1969). "Britain, the Financial Capital of the World," pp. 31–53 in *Britain Pre-eminent. Studies of British World Influence in the Nineteenth Century*, C. J. Bartlett, ed. London: Macmillan.

McCarty, J. W. (1964). "The Staple Approach to Australian Economic History," *Business Archives and History* 4(1):1–22.

   (1973). "Australia as a Region of Recent Settlement in the Nineteenth Century," *Australian Economic History Review* 13(2):148–67.

   (1977). "A General Approach to Australian Economic Development 1845–1895." Department of Economics monograph, Monash University.

McDonagh, Oliver (1962). "The Anti-Imperialism of Free Trade," *Economic History Review*, Second Series XIV:489–501.

Macdonald, L. R. (1975). "Merchants against Industry: An Idea and Its Origins," *The Canadian Historical Review* 56(3):263–81.

MacGillivray, Leith G. (1982). "Land and Settlement in the South East of South Australia, 1840–1940." Ph.D. dissertation, The University of Adelaide, Adelaide.

Mackay, A. L. Gordon (1931). *The Australian Banking and Credit System*. London: P. S. King.

McLean, David (1976). "Finance and 'Informal Empire' before the First World War," *Economic History Review*, Second Series XXIX:291–305.

McMichael, Philip (1977). "The Concept of Primitive Accumulation: Lenin's Contribution," *Journal of Contemporary Asia* 7(4):497–512.

MacMillan, D. S. (1960). *The Debtor's War. Scottish Capitalists and the Economic Crisis in Australia, 1841–1846.* Melbourne: Cheshire.

(1967). *Scotland and Australia 1788–1850.* Oxford: Clarendon Press.

McNaughton, I. D. (1977). "Colonial Liberalism, 1851–92," pp. 98–144 in *Australia. A Social and Political History*, Gordon Greenwood, ed. Sydney: Angas and Robertson.

McQueen, Humphrey (1970). *A New Britannia.* Harmondsworth: Penguin.

Madgwick, R. B. (1969). *Immigration into Eastern Australia 1788–1851.* Sydney: Sydney University Press.

Main, J. M. (1957). "Making Constitutions in New South Wales and Victoria, 1853–1854," *Historical Studies* 28:369–86.

Mandel, Ernest (1971). *Marxist Economic Theory.* London: Merlin Press.

(1976). *Late Capitalism.* London: New Left Books.

Mandle, J. R. (1972). "The Plantation Economy: An Essay in Definition," *Science and Society* XXXVI:49–62.

Mann J. de L. (1971). *The Cloth Industry in the West of England from 1640 to 1880.* Oxford: Clarendon Press.

Manning, H. T. (1965). "Who Ran the British Empire 1830–1850?" *Journal of British Studies* V(1):88–121.

Marshall, Ann (1966). "The 'Environment,' and Australian Wool Production: One Hundred and Fifty Years," pp. 120–37 in *Frontiers and Men*, J. Andrews, ed. Melbourne: Cheshire.

Marshall, Peter (1964). "The First and Second British Empires: A Question of Demarcation," *History* XLIX:13–23.

Martin, A. W. (1956–7). "The Legislative Assembly of New South Wales, 1856–1900," *Australian Journal of Politics and History* 2:46–67.

(1973). "Australia and the Hartz 'Fragment Thesis,'" *Australian Economic History Review* XIII(2):131–47.

Marx, Karl (1965–67). *Capital*, 3 vols. Moscow: Progress Publishers.

(1968). *Theories of Surplus Value*, part II. Moscow: Progress Publishers.

(1973). *Grundrisse.* New York: Vintage.

Marx, Karl, and F. Engels (1968). *The German Ideology.* Moscow: Progress Publishers.

Mathias, Peter (1969). *The First Industrial Nation.* New York: Scribner.

Matthews, R. C. O. (1954). *A Study in Trade-Cycle History.* Cambridge: Cambridge University Press.

Meinig, D. W. (1976). *On the Margins of the Good Earth. The South Australian Wheat Frontier, 1869–1884.* Adelaide: Rigby.

Melbourne, A. C. V. (1963). *Early Constitutional Development in Australia*, R. B. Joyce, ed. St. Lucia: University of Queensland Press.

Mellor, G. R. (1961). *British Imperial Trusteeship 1783–1850.* London: Faber & Faber.

Mills, J. E. (1942). "The Composition of the Victorian Parliament 1856–1881," *Historical Studies* II(5):25–39.
Mills, R. C. (1974). *The Colonisation of Australia 1829–42*. Sydney: Sydney University Press.
Milward, A. S., and S. B. Saul (1973). *The Economic Development of Continental Europe 1780–1870*. London: Allen & Unwin.
Moore, Barrington, Jr. (1968). *Social Origins of Dictatorship and Democracy*. Boston: Beacon.
Moraze, Charles (1968). *The Triumph of the Middle Classes*. New York: Anchor.
Morrell, W. P. (1966). *British Colonial Policy in the Age of Peel and Russell*. London: Cass.
Morrissey, Sylvia (1976). "The Pastoral Economy, 1821–1850," pp. 51–112 in *Essays in Economic History of Australia*, J. Griffin, ed. Sydney: Jacaranda Press.
Mukherjee, Ramkrishna (1974). *The Rise and Fall of the East India Company*. New York and London: Monthly Review Press.
Musson, A. E. (1972). "The 'Manchester School' and Exportation of Machinery," *Business History* XIV:17–50.
North, D. C. (1966). *The Economic Growth of the United States*. New York: Norton.
Orlove, Benjamin S. (1977). *Alpacas, Sheep and Men: The Wool Export Economy and Regional Society in Southern Peru*. New York: Academic Press.
Owen, Roger (1972). "Egypt and Europe: From French Expedition to British Occupation," pp. 195–209 in *Studies in the Theory of Imperialism*, Roger Owen and Bob Sutcliffe, eds. London: Longman.
Pares, Richard (1937). "The Economic Factors in the History of the Empire," *Economic History Review* VII:119–44.
Parsons, T. G. (1972). "Does the Bigge Report Follow from the Evidence?" *Historical Studies* 15(58):268–75.
Patterson, G. D. (1968). *The Tariff in the Australian Colonies 1856–1900*. Melbourne: Cheshire.
Peel, Lynette J. (1974). *Rural Industry in the Port Phillip Region 1835–1880*. Melbourne: Melbourne University Press.
Pentland, H. C. (1950). "The Role of Capital in Canadian Economic Development before 1875," *The Canadian Journal of Economics and Political Science* XVI(4):457–72.
Perry, T. M. (1963). *Australia's First Frontier. The Spread of Settlement in New South Wales 1788–1829*. Melbourne: Melbourne University Press.
Philipp, J. (1960). "Wakefield Influence and New South Wales 1830–32," *Historical Studies* IX(34):178–84.
Phillips, Anne (1977). "The Concept of 'Development,' " *Review of African Political Economy* 8:7–20.

Pike, Douglas (1967). *Paradise of Dissent: South Australia, 1829–1857*. Melbourne: Melbourne University Press.

Platt, D. C. M. (1968a). "The Imperialism of Free Trade: Reservations," *Economic History Review*, Second Series XXI:296–306.

(1968b). *Finance, Trade and Politics in British Foreign Policy 1815–1914*. Oxford: Clarendon Press.

(1972). *Latin America and the British Trade 1806–1914*. London: Adam and Charles Block.

(1980). "British Portfolio Investment Overseas before 1870: Some Doubts," *Economic History Review*, Second Series XXXIII:1–16.

Polanyi, Karl (1957). *The Great Transformation*. Boston: Beacon.

Pollard, Sidney (1974). *European Economic Integration 1815–1970*. London: Harcourt Brace Jovanovich.

Powell, E. T. (1966). *The Evolution of the Money Market 1885–1915*. New York: A. M. Kelley.

Powell, J. M. (1970). *The Public Lands of Australia Felix. Settlement and Land Appraisal in Victoria 1834–91 with Special Reference to the Western Plains*. Melbourne: Oxford University Press.

Ratcliffe, Barrie M. (1975). "The Origins of the Anglo-French Commercial Treaty of 1860: A Reassessment," pp. 125–51 in *Great Britain and Her World 1750–1914. Essays in Honour of W. O. Henderson*, Barrie M. Ratcliffe, ed. Manchester: Manchester University Press.

Read, D. (1967). *Cobden and Bright. A Victorian Political Relationship*. London: Arnold.

Reeves, W. Pember (1969). *State Experiments in Australia and New Zealand*. Melbourne: Macmillan.

Reynolds, Henry (1982). *The Other Side of the Frontier*. Harmondsworth: Penguin.

Rimmer, W. G. (1969). "The Economic Growth of Van Dieman's Land 1803–21," pp. 327–51 in *Economic Growth of Australia 1788–1821*, G. J. Abbott and N. B. Nairn, eds. Melbourne: Melbourne University Press.

Ritchie, John (1967). "The Colonial Office, New South Wales and the Bigge Reports, 1815–1822," *Historical Journal* (ANU Historical Society) 4:29–37.

(1970). *Punishment and Profit*. Melbourne: Heinemann.

(1974). "John Thomas Bigge and His Reports on New South Wales," *RAHS, J&P* 60(part 1):12–27.

(1976). "Towards Ending an Unclean Thing: The Molesworth Committee and the Abolition of Transportation, 1837–40," *Historical Studies* 17(67):144–64.

Robbins, Lionel (1958). *Robert Torrens and the Evolution of Classical Economics*. London: Macmillan.

Roberts, S. H. (1931). "The Australian Wool-Trade in the Forties," *RAHS, J&P* 17(part 6):337–68.

   (1968). *History of Australian Land Settlement 1788–1920.* New York: Johnson Reprint Corporation.

   (1970). *The Squatting Age in Australia 1835–1847.* Melbourne: Melbourne University Press.

Robertson, J. R. (1964). "Equipping a Pastoral Property: Warrah, 1861–1875," *Business Archives and History* 4(1):223–43.

Robinson, E. A. G. (1954). "The Changing Structure of the British Economy," *The Economic Journal* LXIV(255):443–61.

Robinson, F., and B. York (1977). *The Black Resistance. An Introduction to the History of the Aborigines' Struggle against British Colonialism.* Camberwell, Victoria: Widescope.

Robinson, K. W. (1969). "Land," pp. 74–104 in *Economic Growth of Australia, 1788–1821*, G. J. Abbott and N. B. Nairn, eds. Melbourne: Melbourne University Press.

Robson, L. L. (1965). *The Convict Settlers of Australia.* Melbourne: Melbourne University Press.

Roe, Michael (1965). *Quest for Authority in Eastern Australia 1835–1851.* Melbourne: Melbourne University Press.

   (1976). "1830–1850," pp. 82–123 in *A New History of Australia*, F. Crowley, ed. Melbourne: Heinemann.

Rosenberg, Hans (1943). "Political and Social Consequences of the Great Depression of 1873–1896 in Central Europe," *Economic History Review* 8:58–73.

Rostow, W. W. (1961). *British Economy of the Nineteenth Century.* Oxford: Clarendon Press.

Rowley, C. D. (1974). *The Destruction of Aboriginal Society.* Ringwood, Victoria: Penguin.

Rowley, K. (1972). "Pastoral Capitalism: Australia's Pre-Industrial Development," *Intervention* 1:9–26.

Rubenstein, W. D. (1977a). "The Victorian Middle Classes: Wealth, Occupation and Geography," *Economic History Review*, Second Series XXX:602–23.

   (1977b). "Wealth, Elites and Class Structure in Britain," *Past and Present* 76:99–126.

Rubinson, Richard (1978). "Political Transformation in Germany and the United States," pp. 39–74 in *Social Change in the Capitalist World Economy*, Barbara Hockey Kaplan, ed. Beverly Hills: Sage.

Rude, George (1978). *Protest and Punishment.* Oxford: Clarendon Press.

Ruggiero, G. de (1959). *The History of European Liberalism.* Boston: Beacon.

Saul, S. B. (1960). *Studies in British Overseas Trade 1870–1914.* Liverpool: Liverpool University Press.

Saville, John (1961). "Some Retarding Factors in the British Economy before 1914," *Yorkshire Bulletin of Economic and Social Research* XII:51–60.

(1969). "Primitive Accumulation and Early Industrialisation in Britain," pp. 247–71 in *Socialist Register 1969*, Ralph Miliband and John Saville, eds. London: Merlin.

Scammell, W. M. (1968). *The London Discount Market*. London: Elek Books.

Schumpeter, J. (1939). *Business Cycles*, I. New York: McGraw-Hill.

Schurmann, Franz (1974). *The Logic of World Power*. New York: Pantheon.

Schuyler, R. L. (1945). *The Fall of the Old Colonial System*. London: Oxford University Press.

Semmel, Bernard (1970). *The Rise of Free Trade Imperialism. Classical Political Economy and the Empire of Free Trade and Imperialism 1750–1850*. Cambridge: Cambridge University Press.

Shann, E. O. G. (1930). *An Economic History of Australia*. Cambridge: Cambridge University Press.

Shaw, A. G. L. (1966). *Convicts and Colonies*. London: Faber & Faber.

(1969). "Labour," pp. 105–18 in *Economic Growth in Australia, 1788–1821*, G. J. Abbott and N. B. Nairn, eds. Melbourne: Melbourne University Press.

, ed. (1970). *Great Britain and the Colonies, 1815–65*. London: Methuen.

(1976). "1788–1810," pp. 1–44 in *A New History of Australia*, F. Crowley, ed. Melbourne: Heinemann.

Sherington, Geoffrey (1980). *Australia's Immigrants 1788–1978*. Sydney: Allen & Unwin.

Simon, Matthew (1968). "The Pattern of New British Portfolio Foreign Investment, 1865–1914," pp. 15–44 in *The Export of Capital from Britain 1870–1914*, A. R. Hall, ed. London: Methuen.

Sinclair, W. A. (1971). "Was Labour Scarce in the 1830s?" *Australian Economic History Review* XI(2):115–32.

(1972). "Was Labour Scarce in the 1830s?: A Reply," *Australian Economic History Review* XII(2):185–8.

(1976). *The Process of Economic Development of Australia*. Melbourne: Cheshire.

Skocpol, Theda (1977). *States and Social Revolutions*. New York: Cambridge University Press.

Smith, Abbott (1947). *Colonists in Bondage*. Chapel Hill: University of North Carolina Press.

Southgate, Donald (1969). "Imperial Britain," pp. 152–71 in *Britain Preeminent. Studies of British World Influence in the Nineteenth Century*, C. J. Bartlett, ed. London: Macmillan.

Steven, Margaret (1965). *Merchant Campbell 1769–1846. A Study of Colonial Trade*. London: Oxford University Press.

(1969a). "Enterprise," pp. 119–35 in *Economic Growth of Australia, 1788–1821*, G. J. Abbott and N. B. Nairn, eds. Melbourne: Melbourne University Press.

(1969b). "The Changing Pattern of Commerce," pp. 176–87 in *Economic Growth of Australia 1788–1821*, G. J. Abbott and N. B. Nairn, eds. Melbourne: Melbourne University Press.

Stokes, Eric (1975). "Uneconomic Imperialism," *The Historical Journal* XVIII(2):409–16.

Takahashi, K. (1978). "A Contribution to the Discussion," pp. 68–97 in *The Transition from Feudalism to Capitalism*, Rodney Hilton, ed. London: New Left Books.

Teeple, Gary (1972). "Land, Labour, and Capital in pre-Confederation Canada," pp. 43–66 in *Capitalism and the National Question in Canada*, Gary Teeple, ed. Toronto: University of Toronto Press.

Thompson, E. (1968). *The Making of the English Working Class*. Harmondsworth: Penguin.

Thompson, F. M. L. (1963). *English Landed Society in the Nineteenth Century*. London: Routledge & Kegan Paul.

Tomich, Dale (1976). "Prelude to Emancipation: Sugar and Slavery in Martinique: 1830–1848." Ph.D. dissertation, University of Wisconsin.

Wadham, S., R. K. Wilson, and Joyce Wood (1957). *Land Utilization in Australia*. Melbourne: Melbourne University Press.

Walker, R. B. (1957). "Squatter and Selector in New England, 1802–1895," *Historical Studies* 8(29):66–79.

Wallerstein, Immanuel (1974a). *The Modern World System. Capitalist Agriculture and the Origins of the European World-Economy in the Sixteenth-Century*. New York: Academic Press.

(1974b). "The Rise and Future Demise of the World Capitalist System: Concepts for Comparative Analysis," *Comparative Studies in Society and History* 16(4):387–415.

(1980). *The Modern World System II. Mercantilism and the Consolidation of the European World Economy, 1600–1750*. New York: Academic Press.

Walsh, G. P. (1963a). "The Geography of Manufacturing in Sydney, 1788–1851," *Business Archives and History* 3(7):20–52.

(1963b). "The Geography of Manufacturing in Sydney, 1788–1851," *Business Archives and History* V(3):20–52.

(1969). "Manufacturing," pp. 245–66 in *Economic Growth of Australia 1788–1821*, G. J. Abbott and N. B. Nairn, eds. Melbourne: Melbourne University Press.

Ward, J. M. (1948). *British Policy in the South Pacific*. Sydney: Australasian Publishing Co.

(1976). *Colonial Self-Government. The British Experience 1759–1856*. Toronto: University of Toronto Press.

Ward, Russel (1970). *The Australian Legend*. London and Melbourne: Oxford University Press.

Waterson, D. B. (1968). *Squatter, Selector, and Storekeeper. A History of the Darling Downs, 1839–93*. Sydney: Sydney University Press.

Watkins, M. (1963). "A Staple Theory of Economic Growth," *Canadian Journal of Economics and Political Science* XXIX(2):141–58.

Watson, D. R. (1969). "The British Parliamentary System and the Growth of Constitutional Government in Western Europe," pp. 101–27 in *Britain Pre-eminent. Studies of British World Influence in the Nineteenth Century*, C. J. Bartlett, ed. London: Macmillan.

Weber, Max (1958). *The Protestant Ethic and the Spirit of Capitalism*. New York: Scribner.

(1976). "The Protestant Sects and the Spirit of Capitalism," pp. 302–22 in *From Max Weber: Essays in Sociology*, H. H. Gerth and C. Wright Mills, eds. New York: Oxford University Press.

Webster, Sir Charles (1957). *The Foreign Policy of Palmerston 1830–41*, I. London: G. Bell.

Wehler, Hans-Ulrich (1970). "Bismarck's Imperialism 1862–1890," *Past and Present* 48:119–55.

Williams, M. (1975). "More and Smaller Is Better: Australian Rural Settlement 1788–1914," pp. 61–103 in *Australian Space Australian Time*, J. M. Powell and M. Williams, eds. Melbourne: Oxford University Press.

Winch, D. (1965). *Classical Political Economy and Colonies*. Cambridge, Mass.: Harvard University Press.

Woodruff, William (1967). *Impact of Western Man. A Study of Europe's Role in the World Economy 1850–1960*. New York: St. Martin's Press.

Yarwood, A. T. (1977). *Samuel Marsden*. Melbourne: Melbourne University Press.

INDEX